CU00751851

THE BOOK OF LAMENTATIONS

In this commentary, Joshua A. Berman considers Lamentations as a literary work that creates meaning for a community in the wake of tragedy through its repudiation of Zion theology. Drawing from studies in collective trauma, his volume is the first study of Lamentations that systematically accounts for the constructed character of the narrator, a pastoral mentor who engages in a series of dialogues with a second constructed character, daughter Zion, who embodies the traumatized community of survivors. In each chapter, the pastoral mentor speaks to a different religious typology and a different sub-community of post-destruction Judeans, working with daughter Zion to reconsider her errant positions and charting for her a positive way forward to reconnecting with the LORD. Providing a systematic approach to the careful structure of each of its chapters, Berman illuminates how biblical writers offered support to their communities in a way that is still relevant and appealing to a therapy-conscious contemporary society.

Joshua A. Berman is a professor in the Department of Bible at Bar-Ilan University in Israel. He is the author of *Created Equal: How the Bible Broke with Ancient Political Thought* (Oxford University Press, 2008), which was a National Jewish Book Award Finalist in Scholarship, and *Inconsistency in the Torah: Ancient Literary Convention and the Limits of Source Criticism* (Oxford University Press, 2017).

NEW CAMBRIDGE BIBLE COMMENTARY

GENERAL EDITOR: Ben Witherington III

HEBREW BIBLE/OLD TESTAMENT EDITOR: Bill T. Arnold

EDITORIAL BOARD
Bill T. Arnold, *Asbury Theological Seminary*
James D. G. Dunn, *University of Durham*
Michael V. Fox, *University of Wisconsin-Madison*
Robert P. Gordon, *University of Cambridge*
Judith M. Gundry, *Yale University*
Ben Witherington III, *Asbury Theological Seminary*

The New Cambridge Bible Commentary (NCBC) aims to elucidate the Hebrew and Christian Scriptures for a wide range of intellectually curious individuals. While building on the work and reputation of the Cambridge Bible Commentary popular in the 1960s and 1970s, the NCBC takes advantage of many of the rewards provided by scholarly research over the last four decades. Volumes utilize recent gains in rhetorical criticism, social scientific study of the Scriptures, narrative criticism, and other developing disciplines to exploit the growing advances in biblical studies. Accessible jargon-free commentary, an annotated "Suggested Readings" list, and the entire New Revised Standard Version Updated Edition (NRSVUE) text under discussion are the hallmarks of all volumes in the series.

PUBLISHED VOLUMES IN THE SERIES
Hosea, Joel, and Amos, Graham Hamborg
1 Peter, Ruth Anne Reese
Ephesians, David A. deSilva
Philippians, Michael F. Bird and Nijay K. Gupta
Acts, Craig S. Keener
The Gospel of Luke, Amy-Jill Levine and Ben Witherington III
Galatians, Craig S. Keener
Mark, Darrell Bock
Psalms, Walter Brueggemann and William H. Bellinger, Jr.
Matthew, Craig A. Evans
Genesis, Bill T. Arnold
The Gospel of John, Jerome H. Neyrey
Exodus, Carol Meyers
1–2 Corinthians, Craig S. Keener
James and Jude, William F. Brosend II
Judges and Ruth, Victor H. Matthews
Revelation, Ben Witherington III

The Book of Lamentations

Joshua A. Berman

Bar-Ilan University

Shaftesbury Road, Cambridge CB2 8EA, United Kingdom

One Liberty Plaza, 20th Floor, New York, NY 10006, USA

477 Williamstown Road, Port Melbourne, VIC 3207, Australia

314–321, 3rd Floor, Plot 3, Splendor Forum, Jasola District Centre, New Delhi – 110025, India

103 Penang Road, #05–06/07, Visioncrest Commercial, Singapore 238467

Cambridge University Press is part of Cambridge University Press & Assessment, a department of the University of Cambridge.

We share the University's mission to contribute to society through the pursuit of education, learning and research at the highest international levels of excellence.

www.cambridge.org
Information on this title: www.cambridge.org/9781108424417

DOI: 10.1017/9781108334921

© Joshua A. Berman 2023

This publication is in copyright. Subject to statutory exception and to the provisions of relevant collective licensing agreements, no reproduction of any part may take place without the written permission of Cambridge University Press & Assessment.

First published 2023

A catalogue record for this publication is available from the British Library.

Library of Congress Cataloging-in-Publication Data
NAMES: Berman, Joshua A., 1964– author.
TITLE: The Book of Lamentations / Joshua A. Berman, Bar-Ilan University.
DESCRIPTION: Cambridge, United Kingdom ; New York , NY, USA:
Cambridge University Press, 2023. | Series: New Cambridge Bible commentary |
Includes bibliographical references and index.
IDENTIFIERS: LCCN 2022027015 | ISBN 9781108424417 (hardback) |
ISBN 9781108334921 (ebook)
SUBJECTS: LCSH: Bible. Lamentations – Commentaries.
CLASSIFICATION: LCC BS1535.53 .B475 2023 | DDC 224/.3–dc23/eng/20220830
LC record available at https://lccn.loc.gov/2022027015

ISBN 978-1-108-42441-7 Hardback
ISBN 978-1-108-44014-1 Paperback

Cambridge University Press & Assessment has no responsibility for the persistence or accuracy of URLs for external or third-party internet websites referred to in this publication and does not guarantee that any content on such websites is, or will remain, accurate or appropriate.

עַל אֵלֶּה אֲנִי בוֹכִיָּה

In memory of my great-grandmother Chaya-Esther Udovitch

Her daughter Menucha, son-in-law
Yosef, and their three children

Her son Tanchun, and daughter-in-law
Gita and their five children

who perished on the Ukrainian steppe at the hands of
the Nazis and their collaborators, Sept. 14–16, 1941

Contents

List of Supplements		*page* xi
Preface		xiii
Suggested Readings		xv
List of Abbreviations		xix
INTRODUCTION		1
	What Is Lamentations?	1
	Is There a Structure in This Text?	7
	The Voices of Lamentations	9
	The Narrator as Pastoral Mentor	12
	Jeremiah as the Implied Author of Lamentations	15
	Collective Trauma Theory and the Poetics of Lamentations	17
	A Polemic against Zion Theology	19
	The Unity of Lamentations	20
1	PLOTTING A PATH FOR ZION'S SPIRITUAL REHABILITATION	25
	Introduction	28
	The Pastoral Mentor's Theological Platform (vv. 1–9b)	32
	The Nine Stages of Bat-Zion's Spiritual Rehabilitation (vv. 9c–22)	36
	Bat-Zion's Naïve Appeal to the LORD (9c)	36
	Bat-Zion Calls Again to the LORD, Despite His Silence (11c)	38
	Bat-Zion Acknowledges, Yet Criticizes the LORD's Role in Her Affliction (12–13)	38
	Bat-Zion Acknowledges Her Guilt, But Deems the Punishment Disproportionate (14–15b)	41
	Bat-Zion Yearns for Closeness with the LORD (16)	41
	Bat-Zion Validates the LORD's Judgment (18)	43
	Bat-Zion Concedes the Futility of Turning to Other Nations (19)	45
	Bat-Zion Expresses Her Spiritual Distress (20)	45
	Bat-Zion Calls to Avenge Her Suffering (21–22)	46
	Conclusion	47

2   DISPELLING DELUSIONS I: THE LORD AND HIS LOVE FOR ZION   50

Introduction   53
The Pastoral Mentor Reveals the LORD's Wrathful Nature (vv. 1–12) 58
    The Pastoral Mentor's Introduction (1)   59
    The LORD's Destruction of His People Judah (2–5)   60
    The LORD's Destruction of His City and Temple (6–10)   62
The Pastoral Mentor Breaks Down in Empathy (vv. 11–12)   67
The Pastoral Mentor Appeals to Bat-Zion (vv. 13–19)   69
    The Conventional Reading: A Call to Pray to the LORD (13–17)   69
    A New Proposal: A Call to Reject the False Prophets (13–17)   72
    The Pastoral Mentor Urges Bat-Zion to Express Vexation
    to the LORD (18–19)   78
Bat-Zion's Charge Sheet against the LORD (vv. 20–22)   82
Conclusion   85

3   REDIRECTING ZION'S ANGER: THE *GEBER* AS MODEL   87

Introduction   90
The Pastoral Mentor's Personal Vexation with
the LORD (vv. 1–20)   95
The Pastoral Mentor Reconsiders His Predicament (vv. 21–39)   101
The Community Dismisses the Call of the Pastoral
Mentor (vv. 40–47)   106
The Pastoral Mentor Recalibrates and Composes a Lament
for Bat-Zion (vv. 48–66)   112
Conclusion   120

4   DISPELLING DELUSIONS II: ZION AND HER SOCIAL STRUCTURES   122

Introduction   124
A Critique of the Zion Theology Social Order (vv. 1–16)   128
The Community Reconsiders Its Political Theology (vv. 17–20)   138
The Promise of Salvation in the Wake of Confession (vv. 21–22)   142
Conclusion: The King's Prayer of Psalm 144 as Backdrop
to Lamentations 4   148

5   PURGING PRAYER OF ZION THEOLOGY   153

Introduction   154
In the Absence of Fathers (vv. 2–7)   160
The Experience of Humiliation (vv. 8–16)   165
Loss of Connection, Appeal for Connection (vv. 17–22)   167
Conclusion   174

Index of Scriptural Passages   176

Supplements

A Closer Look: *Bat-Ṣiyyon* – "Daughter Zion" or "Daughter
   of Zion"?   *page* 34
A Closer Look: Mesopotamian Laments and
   the Book of Lamentations   64
A Closer Look: The Order of the Hebrew Alphabet   71
Bridging the Horizons: Lamentations in the Christian Tradition   143
A Closer Look: Acrostic Structure and the Book of Lamentations   150
Bridging the Horizons: Lamentations in the Jewish Tradition   159

Preface

To have the opportunity to share my interpretation of Lamentations within the framework of a major commentary series has been a dream of mine for more than two decades. I can hardly think of a forum that better fulfills my aspirations for this work than the New Cambridge Bible Commentary series and salute its commitment to biblical scholarship informed by rhetorical criticism, social scientific study of the scriptures, and narrative criticism and to bringing the fruits of this scholarship to a general audience. My heartfelt thanks therefore are expressed to the series general editor, Bill T. Arnold, for extending me an invitation to write this commentary. My thanks, also, to Beatrice Rehl and Kaye Barbaro at Cambridge University Press for their efforts in the production of this volume. Much of the material in my commentary to chapter 1 of Lamentations initially appeared in my study, "The Drama of Spiritual Rehabilitation in Lamentations 1," *JBL* 140:3 (2021): 557–78, and my thanks to the journal for permission to reprint the material here.

***

While at work on this commentary, in the summer of 2019, my son and I ventured to Romanivka, a ghost town two hundred kilometers east of Odessa in the vast expanse of the southern Ukrainian plains. Here deserted homes line the town's only thoroughfare. These were the homes of the roughly one thousand Jews who lived in the town prior to the Second World War. The largest structure in the town is the hulking shell of its main synagogue, built to accommodate several hundred worshippers on two floors. We met Vladimir, a 93-year-old Ukrainian who recalled the names of the Jewish boys he played with as a teenager and several Yiddish phrases he had learned from them. Vladimir pointed us to the site of the mass grave where he had witnessed the execution of Romanivka's Jews, one of whom had been my great-grandmother, Chaya-Esther Udovitch, who lived in the town in the final years of her life. Bubbe Esther was Bat-Zion; she endured starvation, the suffering of her children, later murdered, and here, at the mass grave of the Jews of Romanivka, a violent end.

What astonished me most, though, in our visit to Romanivka was the Russian inscription on the monument above the grave: "Here lie 1000 peaceful Soviet citizens who perished during the occupation." There was no mention that these "peaceful Soviet citizens" happen to have all been Jews and that was why they were murdered. From my work on Lamentations, I knew that when lives are cut short by collective tragedy, their memory has an afterlife in which there is jockeying for the making of meaning – how their deaths are used, by whom and for what purpose. Here, the meaning was clear: the murder of Romanivka's Jews would now serve in the strengthening of a pan-Soviet identity.

From Romanivka we journeyed some sixty kilometers to an equally small farming hamlet, Bobrovy Kut, where my grandfather was born and raised. In the fields surrounding the town there is a giant well some twelve feet in diameter, now covered by concrete slabs. At the bottom of the well lie some nine hundred Jewish residents of Bobrovy Kut, among them Esther's youngest son, Tanchun, and his family. We met an elderly woman named Maryam, who sobbed and recalled that at the age of six she had been pulled out of the line at the well at the last moment because while her father was Jewish, her mother was Ukrainian. And here, too, we encountered a monument above the well lamenting the "peaceful Soviet citizens" who had perished in the occupation.

However, the greatest erasure of identity we witnessed was in the last stop on our journey, in Kherson, a city on the Black Sea, where Esther's daughter, Menucha and family had lived. They were among its twelve thousand Jewish residents who were executed at a trench in a vast expanse of steppe on the outskirts of the city. But there is no current memory in Kherson of where this site is, though the best guess is that it lies beneath what is now a large field of solar panels. I was astonished that the earth could swallow up twelve thousand souls and that no one today can tell you where that happened.

To my grandfather's mother, brother, sister, nephews, and nieces, I dedicate this volume and within its binding fulfill the words of the prophet (Isa 56:5 NKJV): "To them I will give in my house and within my walls a place and a name ... an everlasting name that shall not be cut off."

Suggested Readings

COMMENTARIES

The following are the major commentaries on Lamentations cited in this volume:

Assis, Elie. *Lamentations: From Despair to Prayer* Sheffield: Sheffield Phoenix Press, 2022.

Bergant, Dianne. *Lamentations.* AOTC. Nashville: Abingdon Press, 2003.

Berges, Ulrich. *Klagelieder.* HThkAT. Freiburg: Verlag Herder, 2012.

Berlin, Adele. *Lamentations.* OTL. Louisville: Westminster John Knox Press, 2002.

Boecker, Hans Jochen. *Klagelieder.* ZBK 21. Zürich: Theologischer Verlag, 1985.

Dobbs-Allsopp. F.W. *Lamentations.* IBC. Westminster: John Knox Press, 2002.

Gordis, Robert. *The Song of Songs and Lamentations: a Study, Modern Translation and Commentary.* Rev. and augm. Ed. New York: Ktav, 1974.

Hillers, Delbert. *Lamentations.* 2nd Revised Ed. AB 7A. New Haven: Yale University Press, 2007.

House, Paul R. and Duane Garrett. *Song of Songs and Lamentations.* WBC 23B. Grand Rapids: Zondervan, 2016.

Huey, F.B. *Jeremiah, Lamentations: An Exegetical and Theological Exposition of Holy Scripture.* NAC 16. Nashville: Broadman & Holman Publishers, 1993.

Kaiser, Otto. 'Klagelieder.' Pages 93–198 in Hans-Peter Mueller, Otto Kaiser and James A. Loader, *Das Hohelied, Klagelieder, Das Buch Ester.* Fourth fully revised edition. Göttingen: Vandenhoeck & Ruprecht, 1992.

Klein, Jacob. *Lamentations* [Hebrew]. Miqra Le-Yisrael. Jerusalem: Magnes, 2017.

Kraus, Hans-Joachim. *Klagelieder (Threni).* BKAT 20. Neukirchen-Vluyn: Neukirchener Verlag, 1956.

Parry, Robin. *Lamentations*. Grand Rapids: Eerdmans, 2010.

Provan, Iain. *Lamentations*. NCB. Grand Rapids: Eerdmans, 1991.

Renkema, Johan. *Lamentations*. HCOT. Leuven: Peeters, 1998.

Salters, R.B. *Lamentations*. ICC. London: T&T Clark, 2011.

Weiser, Artur. "Klagelieder." Pages 295–370 in Helmer Ringgren, Artur Weiser, and Walther Zimmerli, *Sprüche, Prediger, Das Hohe Lied, Klagelieder, Das Buch Esther*. Gottingen: Vandenhoeck & Ruprecht, 1962.

Wiesmann, Herman. *Die Klagelieder*. Frankfurt: Philosophisch-theologische Hochschule Sankt Georgen, 1954.

MONOGRAPH STUDIES

Many of the works cited below effectively comment on large parts of Lamentations, yet without the format of a running commentary. Other works explore major themes central to the book of Lamentations.

Albertz, Rainer. *Israel in Exile: The History and Literature of the Sixth Century B.C.E*. SBL 3. Leiden: Brill, 2004.

Albrektson, Bertil, *Studies in the Text and Theology of the Book of Lamentations with a Critical Edition of the Peshitta Text*. STL 21. Lund: CWK Gleerup, 1963.

Barstad, Hans. *The Myth of the Empty Land: A Study in the History and Archaeology of Judah during the "Exilic" Period*. Oslo: Scandinavian University Press, 1996.

Berrigan, Daniel. *Lamentations: From New York to Kabul and Beyond*. Lanham, MD: Rowman & Littlefield, 2003.

Bier, Miriam J. *"Perhaps there is Hope": Reading Lamentations as a Polyphony of Pain, Penitence, and Protest*. London: T&T Clark, 2016.

Blumenthal, David R. *Facing the Abusing God: A Theology of Protest*. Louisville: Westminster John Knox Press, 1993.

Boase, Elizabeth. *The Fulfilment of Doom? The Dialogic Interaction between the Book of Lamentations and the Pre-Exilic/Early Exilic Prophetic Literature*. London: T&T Clark, 2006.

Dobbs-Allsopp, F.W. *Weep, O Daughter of Zion: A Study of the City-Lament Genre in the Hebrew Bible, BibOr 44*. Rome: Pontificio Istituto Biblico, 1993.

Ferris, Paul W. *The Genre of Communal Lament in the Bible and the Ancient Near East*. SBLDS 127. Atlanta: Scholars Press, 1993.

Gottwald, Norman K. *Studies in the Book of Lamentations*. SBT 14. London: SCM Press, 1962.

Kaiser Jr., Walter C. *Grief and Pain in the Plan of God: Christian Assurance and the Message of Lamentations*. Fearn: Christian Focus Publications, 2004.

Lee, Nancy. *The Singers of Lamentations: Cities under Siege, from Ur to Jerusalem to Sarajevo*. BibInt 60. Leiden: Brill, 2002.

Linafelt, Tod. *Surviving Lamentations: Catastrophe, Lament, and Protest in the Afterlife of a Biblical Book*. Chicago: University of Chicago Press, 2000.

Middlemas, Jill. *The Troubles of Templeless Judah*. Oxford: Oxford University Press, 2005.

Middlemas, Jill. *Lamentations: An Introduction and Study Guide*. London: T&T Clark, 2021.

Morrow, William S. *Protest Against God: The Eclipse of a Biblical Tradition*. Sheffield: Sheffield Phoenix Press, 2007.

Pham, Thi Xuan Huong. *Mourning in the Ancient Near East and the Hebrew Bible*. Sheffield: Sheffield Academic Press, 2000.

Rom-Shiloni, Dalit. *Voices from the Ruins: Theodicy and the Fall of Jerusalem in the Hebrew Bible*. Grand Rapids: Eerdmans, 2021.

Thomas, Heath. *Poetry and Theology in the Book of Lamentations: The Aesthetics of an Open Text*. Sheffield: Sheffield Phoenix Press, 2013.

FEMINIST STUDIES

The figure of Bat-Zion is one of the most evocative woman figures in the Hebrew Bible and recent decades have produced a wealth of insights on Lamentations from a feminist perspective:

Brenner, Athalya and Fokkelien van Dijk-Hemmes. *On Gendering Texts: Female and Male Voices in the Hebrew Bible*. Leiden: Brill, 1993.

Day, Peggy. "The Personification of Cities as Female in the Hebrew Bible: The Thesis of Aloysius Fitzgerald, F.S.C." Pages 283–302 in volume II of *Reading from This Place*. Edited by Fernando F. Segovia and Mary Ann Tolbert. Minneapolis: Fortress Press, 1995.

Dobbs-Allsopp, F.W. and Tod Linafelt. "The Rape of Zion in Thr 1,10." *ZAW* 113:1 (2001): 77–81.

Guest, Deryn. "Hiding Behind the Naked Women in Lamentations: Recriminative Response." *BibInt* 7:4 (1999): 413–48.

Linafelt, Tod. "Zion's cause: The Presentation of Pain in the Book of Lamentations." Pages 267–79 in *Strange Fire: Reading the Bible after the Holocaust*. Edited by Tod Linafelt. New York: New York University Press, 2000.

Maier, Christl M. *Daughter Zion, Mother Zion: Gender, Space, and the Sacred in Ancient Israel.* Minneapolis: Fortress Press, 2008.

Mandolfo, Carleen. *Daughter Zion Talks Back to the Prophets: a Dialogic Theology of the Book of Lamentations.* SemeiaSt 58. Leiden: Brill, 2007.

O'Connor, Kathleen H. *Lamentations & the Tears of the World.* Maryknoll: Orbis, 2004.

Seidman, Naomi. "Burning the Book of Lamentations." Pages 278–88 in *Out of the Garden: Women Writers on the Bible.* Edited by Christina and Celina Spiegel. New York: Fawcett Columbine, 1995.

Abbreviations

AB	Anchor Bible
ABL	Harper, Robert F., ed. *Assyrian and Babylonian Letters Belonging to the Kouyunjik Collections of the British Museum.* 14 vols. Chicago: University of Chicago Press, 1892–1914
AIL	Ancient Israel and Its Literature
ALFIHR	The Arnold and Leona Finkler Institute of Holocaust Research
ANET	Pritchard, James B., ed. *Ancient Near Eastern Texts Relating to the Old Testament.* 3rd ed. Princeton: Princeton University Press, 1969
ANETS	Ancient Near Eastern Texts and Studies
AOTC	Abingdon Old Testament Commentaries
ASOR	American Schools of Oriental Research
BASOR	*Bulletin of the American Schools of Oriental Research*
Bib	*Biblica*
BibInt	*Biblical Interpretation*
BibInt	Biblical Interpretation Series
BibOr	Biblica et Orientalia
BKAT	Biblischer Kommentar, Altes Testament
BSac	*Bibliotheca Sacra*
BZAW	Beihefte zur Zeitschrift für die alttestamentliche Wissenschaft
CAD	Gelb, Ignace J., et al. *The Assyrian Dictionary of the Oriental Institute of the University of Chicago.* 21 vols. Chicago: The Oriental Institute of the University of Chicago, 1956–2010
CBQ	*Catholic Biblical Quarterly*
COS	Hallo, William W., and K. Lawson Younger, Jr., eds. *The Context of Scripture.* 4 vols. Leiden: Brill, 1997–2016
EJSS	Eshkolot – Jewish Studies Series
Enc	*Encounter*

ET	English Translation
ETCSL	*Electronic Text Corpus of Sumerian Literature* (etcsl.orinst. ox.ac.uk)
FOTL	Forms of the Old Testament Literature
GKC	Kautzsch, Emil, ed., Cowley, Arthur E., trans. *Gesenius' Hebrew Grammar.* 2nd ed. Oxford: Oxford University Press, 1910
HAR	*Hebrew Annual Review*
HAT	Handbuch zum Alten Testament
HBC	Mays, James L. et al., eds. *Harper's Bible Commentary.* San Francisco: Harper & Row, 1988
HBT	*Horizons in Biblical Theology*
HCOT	Historical Commentary on the Old Testament
HThKAT	Herders Theologischer Kommentar zum Alten Testament
IBC	Interpretation: A Bible Commentary for Teaching and Preaching
ICC	International Critical Commentary
JAJSup	Journal of Ancient Judaism Supplements
JANES	*Journal of the Ancient Near Eastern Society*
JBL	*Journal of Biblical Literature*
JR	*Journal of Religion*
JSJSup	Supplements to the Journal for the Study of Judaism
JSOT	*Journal for the Study of the Old Testament*
JSOTSup	Journal for the Study of the Old Testament Supplement Series
KAT	Kommentar zum Alten Testament
KJV	King James Version
KRI	Kitchen, K. A. *Ramesside Inscriptions, Historical and Biographical.* 8 vols. Oxford: Blackwell, 1969–1990
LHBOTS	The Library of Hebrew Bible/Old Testament Studies
MC	Mesopotamian Civilizations
Midr.	Midrash
MJ	*Modern Judaism*
MT	Masoretic Text
NAB	New American Bible
NAC	New American Commentary
NCB	New Century Bible Commentary
NCV	New Century Version
NIB	Keck, Leander E., ed. *The New Interpreter's Bible.* 12 vols. Nashville: Abingdon, 1994–2004
NIBCOT	New International Bible Commentary on the Old Testament

NJPS	*Tanakh: The Holy Scriptures: The new JPS Translation according to the Traditional Hebrew Text*
NKJV	New King James Version
NPNF	Schaff, Philip, and Henry Wace, eds. *A Select Library of Nicene and Post-Nicene Fathers of the Christian Church*. 28 vols. in 2 series. 1886–1889
NRSVue	New Revised Standard Version Updated Edition
OTL	Old Testament Library
RB	*Revue biblique*
SBL	Society of Biblical Literature
SBLDS	Society of Biblical Literature Dissertation Series
SBLMS	Society of Biblical Literature Monograph Series
SBT	Studies in Biblical Theology
SemeiaSt	Semeia Studies
SJOT	*Scandinavian Journal of the Old Testament*
SLTHS	Siphrut: Literature and Theology of the Hebrew Scriptures
STL	Studia Theologica Lundensia
TAD	Porten, Bezalel, and Ada Yardeni, eds. and trans. *Textbook of Aramaic Documents from Ancient Egypt: Newly Copied, Edited and Translated into Hebrew and English by Bezalel Porten and Ada Yardeni*. 4 vols. Jerusalem: The Hebrew University, Department of the History of the Jewish People, 1986–1999
TOTC	Tyndale Old Testament Commentaries
TTS	Trierer Theologische Studien
VT	*Vetus Testamentum*
WBBCS	Wiley Blackwell Bible Commentaries Series
WBC	Word Biblical Commentary
YJS	Yale Judaica Series
ZAW	*Zeitschrift für die alttestamentliche Wissenschaft*
ZBK	Zürcher Bibelkommentare

Introduction

WHAT IS LAMENTATIONS?

The fall of Jerusalem in 586 BCE was an event of the most cataclysmic proportions. For the people of Judah, it meant the loss of their temple – their primary mode of worship of the LORD. But it also entailed loss of political independence, economic devastation, loss of control over their ancestral lands, an upending of social structures, and the exile of their leadership. It challenged ideas that were at the bedrock of Israelite theology such as the election of Israel and called into question the continued viability of the notion of a covenant between Israel and the LORD. All of these facets of collective trauma are reflected in the book of Lamentations.

But what is Lamentations? Who is its audience, and what is its purpose? Scholars have put forward an astonishing array of approaches to these most fundamental questions, typically by prioritizing one part of the book over others.

Classically, many expositors understood Lamentations as addressed to the survivors of the catastrophe and that its purpose was didactic: to bring the people to recognize the ways of divine justice, to confess their misdeeds, and to bring them to pray toward the LORD for their salvation.[1] These scholars point to the many passages in Lamentations that align theologically with Deuteronomic thought and the prophetic literature. The LORD has full control of history; sin is the root cause of destruction. All five poems in the book agree that the downfall of Jerusalem is a punishment for her sins (1:5; 2:14; 3:42; 4:6; 5:16). There are ample literary correspondences between the covenant curses threatened in Deut 28 and the reality detailed in Lamentations.[2]

---

[1]   Gottwald, *Studies in the Book*; Albrektson, *Studies in the Text*.
[2]   For parallels between Deuteronomy and Lamentations, see Klein, *Lamentations*, 47–49. He identifies eighteen parallel phrases between Lamentations and Deuteronomy 28 and six between Lamentations and the Song of Moses in Deuteronomy 32.

Lamentations makes references to the "Day of YHWH" trope (Lam 1:21; 2:1; 22) found in many prophetic books and employs prophetic tropes such as the goblet of punishment (Lam 4:21).[3] These scholars typically see Chapter 3 as the focal point of the book, with its message of hope, but also its explicit calls to identify suffering with sin, on the personal and collective levels.

Another school that has grown in numbers since the mid-twentieth century pushes back against this classic understanding and maintains that Lamentations has no lesson to teach the survivors. Indeed, the audience of Lamentations is the traumatized community itself. But rather than sermonizing to the community, the book serves the survivors as an expression of what they endured. Here the impulse toward meaning-making is upended, as the meaning of the laments is to be found in their very expression. The healing process following collective trauma requires the community not to repress their grief and shock but to face it. Lamentations allows communal pain to be reexperienced and perhaps healed.[4] These scholars point to the many elements of the genre of lament found in the book.[5] These include the formerly great attributes of the victim versus their fallen state, the pain of the lamenter at the joy of the enemy, and the request for divine vengeance. Indeed, the very name we attach to this work, "Lamentations" – which first appears in the Septuagint – suggests as much. It is true that sin is invoked as the cause of the downfall in every chapter of the book. However, for these expositors, Israel's sinfulness is not the dominant note struck in Lamentations; her suffering is.

At the same time, it is puzzling that a work ostensibly written as a lament should include so many passages critical of the victim. Biblical laments, such as David's lament for Saul and Jonathan (2 Sam 1:17–27) never include critique of the lamented individual, even when they are deserving of critique. Mesopotamian laments for the cities of Ur, likewise, express no critique of the fallen city.[6]

---

[3] Throughout this work, I have generally employed the epitaph "the Lord" in place of the tetragrammaton. I retain the transliteration "YHWH" when referring to an accepted term in the scholarship (as in the present case), and when transliterating verses within the body of the commentary.

[4] Hillers, *Lamentations*, 5; Kathleen O'Connor, "Lamentations," in *Introduction to Prophetic Literature, Isaiah, Jeremiah, Baruch, Letter of Jeremiah, Lamentations, Ezekiel*, NIB 6 (Nashville: Abingdon, 2001), 1013; Klein, *Lamentations*, 22; Knut M. Heim, "The Personification of Jerusalem," in *Zion, City of Our God*, ed. Gordon J. Wenham and Richard S. Hess (Grand Rapids: Eerdmans, 1999), 130.

[5] Berlin, *Lamentations*; Linafelt, *Surviving Lamentations*; Claus Westermann, *Lamentations: Issues and Interpretation*, trans. Charles Muenchow (Minneapolis: Fortress, 1994); Michael S. Moore, "Human Suffering in Lamentations," *RB* 90 (1983): 534–55.

[6] See "A Closer Look: Mesopotamian Laments," pp. 64–66.

A variation of this approach holds that the book is indeed one of lament, but that its primary audience is not the reeling Judeans of the sixth century BCE. Rather, the book is written for posterity. By this reading, Lamentations is a memorialization of the grief and trauma of the destruction of Jerusalem, preserving the memory of that event for future generations.[7] For Iain Provan, "We are further being invited to learn from their experience to participate in their attempt to relate their experience to the reality of God. The book reminds us in a forceful way of the challenge of suffering to faith, and invites us to feel and to ponder its significance."[8] There is no doubt that the reception history of the book bears this out, as Lamentations has assumed a prominent place in the liturgy for Jews on the anniversary of the destruction of the temple on the Ninth of Ab. But the reception of the book by later readers must be kept distinct from the question of the original purpose of its composition. Lamentations assumes its readers possess a great familiarity with the background events that led to the destruction. No individuals, not even the Babylonians themselves, are mentioned by name throughout. Only the most oblique references are made to former treaty partners. A work written for posterity – for those who live at a time and place far removed from sixth century Judah – would be better served by providing at least the bare-bones context, for such an ostensibly distanced reading and listening audience.

For others, by contrast, the audience of Lamentations is none other than the LORD himself. By this view, the lamenting that takes place in this work is not merely cathartic – expression for expression's sake. Rather, Lamentations was composed and recited in order to confront the LORD with the affliction that he has caused, with the intent of softening his heart and provoking a salvific response from him.[9] These expositors point to the prayers found within Lamentations (Lam 1:9, 11, 21–22; 2:20–22; 3:56–66) and especially its climax in Chapter 5, where either the narrator or perhaps the community offers an impassioned prayer to the LORD to consider the community's deprivation and to restore the covenantal relationship between the LORD and Israel.[10] Yet, here, too, the characterization of the book as a whole seems to rest on a selective emphasis of evidence. While

---

[7] Berlin, *Lamentations*, 15–17; Dobbs-Allsopp, *Lamentations*, 103.
[8] Provan, *Lamentations*, 24.
[9] Berlin, *Lamentations*, 9; Salters, *Lamentations*, 28.
[10] Elie Assis sees prayer as the central theme of the book, and that the author seeks to draw the Jerusalem community from a state of despair to a state of prayer. See Assis, *Lamentations*.

appeal to the LORD is an important part of Lamentations, the text before us seems to engage other concerns as well, unlike, say, Psalms 74 and 79, which are devoted entirely to appealing to the LORD for salvation in the wake of the temple's destruction.

Others, still, take the notion of the LORD as the audience of Lamentations even further and maintain that the purpose of the book is not to appeal for salvation. Rather, the book stages a resistance to divine acts executed in the name of divine justice.[11] Its champion is Bat-Zion who is hurt and hurting but able to rise in the midst of suffering to confront her God.[12] For these scholars, Lamentations implicitly asks whether in fact Zion's suffering exceeds what is warranted. For these readers, the focus of the book is directed toward the question of who should be blamed for Israel's pain, rather than how the relationship shall be restored between the LORD and Israel. To be sure, these expositors recognize that Lamentations never abandons sin. They insist, however, that the thrust of the progression of the poems displaces it and reduces its importance relative to Bat-Zion's anger and accusation against God. These approaches point to the fact that the book ends on a note of doubt as to whether the LORD can or will hear Israel's pain and prayers, and not on a note of hope or expectation that he will. These readers challenge the claim that the center of Lamentations is in Chapter 3, with the *geber*'s call for repentance.[13] Todd Linafelt has gone so far as to critique these long-held positions from a hermeneutic of suspicion. If expositors have championed Chapter 3 as the center of Lamentations, it is because of an inherent male bias toward the male figure of Chapter 3 and a distinctly Christian bias toward the suffering man of that chapter, based on a perceived similarity to the figure of Jesus.[14] Scholars like Linafelt argue

---

[11]   Dobbs-Allsopp, *Lamentations*; Lee, *The Singers of Lamentations*; Linafelt, *Surviving Lamentations*; O'Connor, *Tears of the World*; Middlemas, *Lamentations*; Blumenthal, *Facing the Abusing God*; Hillers *Lamentations*; Edward L. Greenstein, "The Wrath at God in the Book of Lamentations," in *The Problem of Evil and Its Symbols in Jewish and Christian Tradition*, ed. Henning Graf Reventlow and Yair Hoffman (London: T&T Clark International, 2004).

[12]   The epitaph for the remnant community, *Bat-Ṣiyyon*, is typically rendered either as "Daughter Zion" or "Daughter of Zion." However, these bear very different meanings and it is likely that the author intended both. See "A Closer Look: Bat-Ṣiyyon – 'Daughter Zion' or 'Daughter of Zion'," pp. 34–36, where I explain the nuances of each and my choice to neutrally transliterate the term 'Bat-Zion.'

[13]   The male poet who narrates Chapter 3 in the first person self-identifies in 3:1 as *ha-geber*, literally "the man", with specific connotations of one who walks in the ways of the LORD. Characterizations of the *geber* abound in the scholarly literature. See discussion on pp. 91–94.

[14]   Linafelt, *Surviving Lamentations*, 5.

that we ought to shift our focus to the figure of Bat-Zion and her pain in Chapters 1 and 2, giving pride of place in Lamentations to confrontation over capitulation.[15]

This line of reading, however, has been critiqued.[16] Not only is sin identified as the cause of the destruction in all five of the poems, but also by all of its characters, including Bat-Zion herself (1:18). And, in fact, the passages that overtly decry and assail God's actions amount to but several verses in the whole work (1:12–15; 2:20–22; 3:43) and the trope seems entirely missing from Chapters 4 and 5. That said, these scholars have drawn proper attention to an important element of Lamentation's tapestry that has gone underappreciated in other readings of the book.

Thus, paradoxically, Lamentations critiques Israel as sinful and deserving of harsh punishment but also critiques God as cruel. It is no wonder that Johan Renkema concludes that the theology of Lamentations is "a theology ending in a question mark."[17] The book is a mélange of seemingly incompatible genres; part prayer, part hortatory sermonizing, part lament, and part polemic against the LORD. On the employ of genres in biblical literature, Carol Newsom writes, "Texts may participate in more than one genre … The point is not simply to identify a genre in which a text participates, but to analyze that participation in terms of the rhetorical strategies of the text."[18] Nowhere is this challenge greater than in Lamentations.

Faced with this disparity of genres and viewpoints, scholars increasingly have become suspicious of the attempt to monologize the text, identifying within it a primary theme of theodic or of anti-theodic interpretation. With greater frequency, expositors in the early decades of the twenty-first century have sought in Lamentations, "intersecting perspectival discourses in which no single speaker, no particular viewpoint silences the others."[19] By this view, Lamentations is predicated upon shifting voices whose testimonies volley in disquieting tension and conflict.[20] By these readings, to

---

[15] See Mandolfo, *Daughter Zion Talks Back*; Seidman, "Burning the Book"; Guest, "Hiding Behind."

[16] See House, *Lamentations*, 322–23; Thomas, *Poetry and Theology*, 34–39; Tremper Longman III, *Jeremiah, Lamentations*, NIBCOT (Peabody, MA: Hendrickson Publishers, 2008), 339.

[17] Renkema, *Lamentations*, 579.

[18] Carol A. Newsom, *The Book of Job: A Contest of Moral Imaginations* (New York: Oxford University Press, 2003), 12.

[19] O'Connor, "Lamentations," 1022.

[20] See in this vein, Bier, *"Perhaps There Is Hope"*; Provan, *Lamentations*; Dobbs-Allsopp, *Lamentations*; Thomas, *Poetry and Theology*; Boase, *The Fulfillment of Doom?*; O'Connor, *Tears of the World*, 14; Alan Cooper, "The Message of Lamentations," *JANES* 28 (2001): 1–18.

assume that there is one major theological thrust in the book is to superim-
pose *apriori* assumptions.

These views, seeing Lamentations as a book of debate about the meaning of the fall of Jerusalem, are a great advance in our understanding of the
book. The approach is appealing not only because it solves the exegetical
conundrum of juxtaposed conflicting viewpoints but also because it accords
with what we know about the variety of viewpoints held in Jerusalem before
and after the fall of the city from the books of Jeremiah and Ezekiel. From a
rhetorical perspective, these two books stand distinct in prophetic literature
in that they ubiquitously cite other voices – either statements attributed to
individuals who are identified by name, title, or social circle or popular sayings attributed simply to the people. Dalit Rom Shiloni has identified forty-
eight such quotations in Ezekiel 1–39 and 136 in Jeremiah. These voices
typically represent a deliberate and articulated opposition to the positions
expressed by the prophetic protagonists of those books.[21]

The fall of Jerusalem, as reported in the book of Jeremiah, did nothing to
quell debate about the theological meaning of what had happened. Despite
the fact that Jeremiah's prophecies concerning the temple's fall and the city's
conquest had now come to fruition, the people express no acceptance of his
interpretation of events. The assassination of the Babylonian-installed governor of Judah, Gedaliah, by loyalists to the Davidic throne (41:1–3) demonstrates that the belief in the immutable election of the Davidic line was still
strong in some quarters. Others continued to relate to the temple mount as
a site of pilgrimage and cultic worship (41:4–5). Large contingents of survivors continue to question whether Jeremiah communicates and represents
the LORD's will (43:2). Against Jeremiah's counsel, his opponents argue for
syncretistic worship of multiple deities in Egypt, implicitly critiquing the
power of the LORD, and a lack of belief in his promise to sustain a remnant
in Jerusalem (44:15–20).

The notion that collective catastrophe engenders a shattering of theological paradigms and results in competing theological stances in its wake is
well born out in contemporary times as well. In his study, *Faith and Doubt
of Holocaust Survivors*, Reeve Robert Brenner interviewed more than 700
survivors and asked more than a hundred questions concerning their religious beliefs and practices prior, during, and after the war.[22] Even among
those who were religious before the war and remained so afterward, his

[21]   Rom-Shiloni, *Voices from the Ruins*, 80–81.
[22]   Reeve Robert Brenner, *Faith and Doubt of Holocaust Survivors* (New York: Free Press, 1980).

study reveals a surprising diversity of religious stances. What Brenner uncovers in Israel's most recent national calamity, Lamentations uncovers within its first.

Yet, while there is great merit in identifying multiple viewpoints within Lamentations, the approach can be critiqued from two standpoints.

Scholars who adopt this position maintain that all viewpoints in Lamentations need to be regarded as equally valid in the eyes of its author or authors. As Miriam Bier has written, "the critical mistake to avoid is prematurely equating the Poet's point of view – the point of view of the text – with any one constructed point of view within the work." Yet, as some scholars have noted, these approaches – all products of late-twentieth and early twenty-first-century writers – align well with postmodern notions of truth.[23] This however, raises the specter that there is anachronism in reading such contemporary notions back into the minds and intentions of Israelite authors living in the sixth century BCE. Of all the views presented in Lamentations, are none the author's own? If each of the protagonists in the book – the narrator, Bat-Zion, the *geber*, the community – expresses deep and heartfelt convictions, why is the author, by ostensibly presenting all these views on equal footing, a theological fence-straddler? The book of Job, which also presents multiple viewpoints about issues of theodicy, ultimately endorses the position of Job over that of his companions. The book of Ecclesiastes offers multiple versions of the good life, but concludes by endorsing a life of piety.[24]

IS THERE A STRUCTURE IN THIS TEXT?

However, these more recent approaches highlighting the multiplicity of viewpoints within Lamentations carry a more serious drawback. They leave the book – both as a whole and with regard to each of its chapters – entirely bereft of a structure.[25] As Frederick Dobbs-Allsopp has written, "the poems never really go anywhere either individually or as a collection ... the poetry

---

[23] Boase, *The Fulfilment of Doom?*, 17; Dobbs-Allsopp, *Lamentations*, 24.
[24] I take the epilogue of Ecclesiastes to be integral to the book and not a later addition. See Stuart Weeks, "'Fear God and Keep His Commandments': Could Qohelet Have Said This?," in *Wisdom and Torah*, JSJSup 163 (Leiden: Brill, 2013), 101–18.
[25] Several studies have attempted to identify various structuring mechanisms to the whole of Lamentations such as chiasmus, and concatenation, although by and large these have not fared well when subject to rigorous examination. See Bo Johnson, "Form and Message in Lamentations," *ZAW* 97:1 (1985): 58–73; Carl Wilhelm Eduard Nägelsbach, "Die Klagelieder" in *Der Prophet Jeremia, Die Klagelieder*, Theologisch-homiletisches

seems to be transitional or processual in nature, always moving but never getting anywhere."[26] For Jill Middlemas, throughout Lamentations, "the jumble of images bubble up to the surface in random order."[27] Concerning Chapter 1, Robert Salters has gone so far as to write, "the verses are not in any particular order. Indeed, one could place vv. 12–19 in almost any order without serious loss of effect."[28] Heath Thomas rightly observes, "no research at present observes how the *whole* of Lamentations presents its theology in concert synthetically."[29]

Remarkably, not a single expositor of this school of multiple voices maintains that there must indeed be a structure but that it eludes us. Rather, finding neither consistent theology nor clear structure in the poem, scholars have made a virtue of necessity, offering poetic rationales for this seeming randomness. Many scholars celebrate the multivocality and polyvalence of the text. For Charles Miller, there is no order, nor conclusion, for the conflict "remains unresolved and unresolvable."[30] Robert Salters seeks literary virtue in the fractured nature of the poem. For Salters, the disjointed nature of the speeches contributes to a dramatic effect of disoriented speakers, reeling in the aftermath of the destruction.[31]

These approaches level an enormous exegetical weight on this explanation of intentional randomness. Consider the exegetical implications of this through the following illustrative examples. The most optimistic note in the entire book is at the close of Chapter 4, where the narrator prophesizes that Bat-Zion will experience no more exile and that Edom will be requited for her misdeeds. But why does this appear at the point that it does? Why is this not, for example, the closing note of the entire book? What is it about the rhetorical aims of Chapter 4 – and only Chapter 4 – that mandates that this note appears where it does? Can it be that there is really no reason for this, other than the random placement of ideas and images? Or, consider the shift

Bibelwerk 15 (Bielefeld: Velhagen und Klasing, 1868); William Shea, "The Qinah Structure of the Book of Lamentations," *Bib* 60 (1979), 103–7; Johan Renkema, *The Literary Structure of Lamentations (I–IV)*, JSOTSup 74 (Sheffield: JSOT, 1988), 294–396; Elie Assis, "The Unity of the Book of Lamentations," *CBQ* 71 (2009): 306–29. See review of the issue in Thomas, *Poetry and Theology*, 25–34.

26   Dobbs-Allsopp, *Lamentations*, 27; see similarly, Boase, *The Fulfillment of Doom?*, 1.
27   Middlemas, *Lamentations*, 10.
28   Robert B. Salters, "Structure and Implication in Lamentations 1?," *SJOT* 14 (2000): 299.
29   Thomas, *Poetry and Theology*, 8.
30   Charles William Miller, "Reading Voices: Personification, Dialogism, and the Reader of Lamentations 1," *BibInt* 9 (2001): 407.
31   Salters, "Structure and Implication," 300; cf. Klein, *Lamentations*, 6.

of voices in Chapter 1. Across the first nine verses of the chapter, only the narrator speaks. From there on, the voice of Bat-Zion predominates, with occasional interruptions by the narrator. Why is the discourse structured in this way? Why do we not hear Bat-Zion across the first nine verses? What is achieved by the narrator's interruptions in vv. 15 and 17? Or, consider this: In Chapter 2, we find that in vv. 12–19, the narrator directly addresses Bat-Zion in second person. This happens nowhere else, with the exception of 4:21. But why is direct address included here in the middle of Chapter 2 and virtually nowhere else? This approach is all the more surprising given that the author(s) of Lamentations has gone to such lengths to carefully craft acrostic compositions in Chapters 1–4.[32] It seems unlikely that the author would expend great attention to the form of his work, while lacking any plan for the order of the poem's content. To ascribe all of this – and much more – to a poetic of randomness found nowhere else in the Hebrew Bible requires an enormous interpretive leap of faith. It is the purpose of the present commentary to focus on precisely these issues. This commentary places a premium on understanding how themes are developed in a systematic fashion within each chapter. It puts pride of place on understanding the rhetorical aims and design of each chapter and how the chapters cohere into a whole.[33]

.

THE VOICES OF LAMENTATIONS

The departure point for understanding the systematic fashion in which Lamentations conveys its theology is through appreciating its employ of a distinct poetic device. Discussions of the poetics of Lamentations routinely address the structural features of acrostic, repetition, and meter – poetic devices found widely throughout the Hebrew Bible. But what makes the poetics of Lamentations distinct is the ubiquitous presence of shifting voices found throughout its first four chapters. Understanding the interrelationship of these voices is the key to understanding the design and aims of the book as a whole.

---

[32]   The author's penchant for order and structure is further borne out by the elaborate and tight chiastic structures witnessed in Lamentations 1 and 2. See my study, Joshua Berman, "Criteria for Establishing Chiastic Structure: Lamentations 1 and 2 as Test Cases," *Maarav* 21 (2014): 51–69.

[33]   Philological and grammatical issues will, of course, be dealt with, but not at length if previous commentaries have already addressed them adequately. For commentaries that address these issues thoroughly, see particularly Renkema, *Lamentations*; Westermann, *Lamentations*; Salters, *Lamentations*; Klein, *Lamentations*.

William Lanahan's 1974 study ushered in the recognition by scholars that Lamentations works around a series of characters that are in dialogue, and this is an aspect of the book that has been recognized by all who have written on Lamentations ever since.[34] Scholars differ on how many voices Lamentations employs, though all agree that the voices heard most often are those of the narrator, who employs a third-person discourse concerning Jerusalem, and of Bat-Zion, who speaks of Jerusalem in first-person discourse.[35] There is broad consensus that the author has constructed these characters to express different moods and viewpoints.

It is remarkable, therefore, that one finds in this scholarship no developed profile of either of these characters. There is good reason for this; both the narrator and Bat-Zion, respectively, enunciate widely varying points of view. The narrator can be stern on the one hand, as seen in 1:5, "Her foes have become the masters; her enemies prosper because the LORD has made her suffer for the multitude of her transgressions."[36] And on the other hand, the narrator can be deeply empathetic, as found in 2:11–13, "My eyes are spent with weeping; my stomach churns; my bile is poured out on the ground because of the destruction of my people, because infants and babes faint in the streets of the city ... What can I say for you, to what compare you, O daughter Jerusalem? To what can I liken you, that I may comfort you, O virgin daughter Zion? For vast as the sea is your ruin; who can heal you?" Contemporary assessments of the stance of the narrator in Lamentations label him as distanced emotionally from the events themselves.[37] For Frederick Dobbs-Allsopp, he is "impartial."[38] For Delbert Hillers, he is

---

[34]   William F. Lanahan, "The Speaking Voice in the Book of Lamentations," *JBL* 93 (1974): 41–49; See also Barbara Bakke Kaiser, "Poet as 'Female Impersonator': The Image of Daughter Zion as Speaker in Biblical Poems of Suffering," *JR* 67 (1987): 164–82. The most highly developed analysis of the speakers is Heim, "The Personification of Jerusalem," 129–69.

[35]   Wiesmann, *Die Klagelieder*, 132, 167, 209, 241–42, 271, identifies six in total: Zion, narrator, the people, Jeremiah, and two choirs. Lanahan, "The Speaking Voice," 41–49, sees five: a reporter, Zion, a defeated soldier, a bourgeois (ch. 4), and the community as a whole (ch. 5). For Provan (7), there are three: narrator, Zion, and the people of Zion.

[36]   Unless otherwise noted, all translations follow the NSRVue.

[37]   There are no linguistic markers in Lamentations 1 that mandate an understanding of the narrator as male. However, it stretches credulity to assume that the author intended to create an androgynous figure, and expositors have generally assumed this to be a male voice. Feminist readings of Lamentations have profitably interpreted the narrator as male, establishing an apposition between the male narrator and Daughter Zion. See Seidman, "Burning the Book," 278–88; Guest, "Hiding Behind," 413–48; Linafelt, "Zion's Cause," 267–90; O'Connor, *Tears of the World*, 110.

[38]   Dobbs-Allsopp, *Weep, O Daughter*, 33.

"external" to the events described.[39] Iain Provan says the narrator is "uninvolved."[40] His role, for Adele Berlin, is, "the voice of an observer."[41] William Lanahan terms the narrator of Lamentations "a reporter."[42] While there is, indeed, a descriptive aspect to the narrator's discourse, Miriam Bier is correct that he is, at the same time, fully involved in Bat-Zion's plight, as we noted in his direct address to her in 2:11–13.[43] To that we may add that at several other points, his descriptions are suffused with sympathy for Bat-Zion, such as when he describes the tears on her face (1:2). He even interjects personally addressing either her or the LORD concerning the extent to which she has been violated by the enemy (1:10).

A full profile of Bat-Zion reveals equal complexity. At once she is repentant, as in 1:18, "The LORD is in the right, for I have rebelled against his word." And yet in Chapter 2, she is defiant (2:20–21): "Look, O LORD, and consider! To whom have you done this? Should women eat their offspring, the children they have borne? … my young women and my young men have fallen by the sword; in the day of your anger you have killed them, slaughtering without mercy."

This use of characters in poetic discourse is unparalleled in the Hebrew Bible. We may compare the use of constructed characters here fruitfully with the use of constructed characters in the book of Job. There as well, we find multiple characters enunciating multiple viewpoints. But there, each of the characters – Job on the one hand and his companions on the other – accords to consistent profiles throughout the book. The situation in Lamentations, however, is more akin to what we discover in the Song of Songs. Here, the constructed figures of the man and the woman engage in running dialogue. It is difficult, however, to establish in a consistent fashion the positions that they adopt and whether there is clear movement across the book.[44] In Lamentations, the primary characters – the narrator and Bat-Zion – lack clear definition to an even greater extent. Toward what end did the author of Lamentations create characters with distinct labels, yet who do not seem to possess distinct opinions?

---

[39] Hillers, *Lamentations*, 79.
[40] Provan, *Lamentations*, 34.
[41] Berlin, *Lamentations*, 48.
[42] Lanahan, "The Speaking Voice," 41–49.
[43] Bier, "*Perhaps There Is Hope*," 41–43.
[44] For a survey of opinions, see Gordon H. Johnston, "The Enigmatic Genre and Structure of the Song of Songs: Part I," *BSac* 166 (2009): 36–52, and Gordon H. Johnston, "The Enigmatic Genre and Structure of the Song of Songs: Part II," *BSac* 166 (2009):163–80.

Moreover, to present complex viewpoints that stand in tension does not require the employ of multiple voices. In many of the Psalms one finds divergent viewpoints, but all said in the same voice. Thus, we find in Psalm 27 absolute trust in the LORD (v. 1) and also doubt (v. 9); in Psalm 89, we find celebration of the LORD's election and sustaining of the Davidic line (vv. 1–38) and accusation and consternation concerning the LORD's abandonment of the Davidic line (vv. 39–53). In Ecclesiastes, one and the same voice offers multiple accounts of the makeup of the good life. The special challenge of Lamentations, then, is to adduce a reading strategy that accounts for all of its complexity. Why, as noted earlier, does Lamentations employ conflicting genres of lament, protest, prayer, and rebuke? Why are characters constructed that are difficult to profile in a comprehensive and systematic way?

THE NARRATOR AS PASTORAL MENTOR

In exegesis of Lamentations through the 1980s, it was commonplace for scholars to assign the narrator the position of the objective view, thus establishing a hierarchy between his voice and that of Bat-Zion.[45] As we noted earlier, more recent commentators generally place the voices on equal footing and maintain that both speakers are authoritative representatives of the author in the competing claims they make about sin and suffering. For these expositors there is no dominant or privileged voice in the work and the poem gives credence to both speakers.[46] Scholars who hold that the narrator's voice has pride of place, as well as those who hold that all the voices of Lamentations have equal standing, tend to state their positions axiomatically, rather than arguing for the validity of their positions on the basis of evidence.

In this commentary, I will read the voice of the narrator as representative of the voice of the author and maintain that he responds to the other voices in the book as he engages their claims. I ground this contention on the basis of the use of multiple unmarked voices we find elsewhere in biblical poetry.

---

[45]   Hillers, *Lamentations*, 79; Barbara Kaiser, "Reconsidering Parallelism: A Study of the Structure of Lamentations 1, 2, and 4" (PhD dissertation, University of Chicago, 1983), 187; Renate Brandscheidt, *Gotteszorn und Menschenleid: Die Gerichtsklage des leidenden Gerechten in Klgl 3*, TTS 41 (Trier: Paulinus-Verlag, 1983), 99; Lanahan, "The Speaking Voice," 41.

[46]   Bier, *"Perhaps There Is Hope,"* 71; Miller, "Reading Voices," 393; Dobbs-Allsopp, *Lamentations*, 61.

Here I draw narratological inspiration from Carleen Mandolfo's identification of the didactic voice in her study of Psalms. She notes that in a number of psalms we hear a constructed human voice that is distinct from that of the supplicant. This second voice of interjected didactic comments is characterized by a shift to third-person discourse.[47] This voice speaks of God and for God, rather than to him, and is thus didactic, rather than prayerful. The function of the didactic voice for Mandolfo is pastoral – it offers reassurance and gives direction.[48] For an illustration of this, consider Ps 7:9–10 [ET 8–9]. The bulk of Psalm 7, an individual lament, is framed as the supplicant's second-person discourse directed at the LORD. The strophes set off here in italics are the didactic voice, third-person discourse that interrupts the supplicant's own voice:

> [8] *YHWH arbitrates between the peoples*
> Judge me, YHWH, according to my innocence,
> And according to my integrity within me.
> [9] Let the wickedness of the evil ones cease
> And establish the just.
> *The one who tests the thoughts and emotions is a just God.*[49]

Building on Mandolfo's work, Nancy Lee has drawn our attention to how this play of voices is present in Jeremiah.[50] Here we see instances where Jerusalem speaks in her own voice through unmarked and unintroduced direct discourse,[51] followed by the supportive words of the prophet in response. In Jer 8:18, Jerusalem speaks about her own suffering, and in 8:21–23, the prophet responds – likewise with unmarked and unintroduced direct discourse – with his own words of empathy.[52] Similarly, in Jer 10:19–20, Jerusalem speaks about losing her children, which is followed in vv. 21 by the words of Jeremiah blaming the kings for the loss of the children:

---

[47] Carleen Mandolfo, "Finding Their Voices: Sanctioned Subversion in Psalms of Lament," *HBT* 24:2 (2002): 27–52.

[48] Carleen Mandolfo, "Dialogic Form Criticism: An Intertextual Reading of Lamentations and Psalms of Lament," in *Bakhtin and Genre Theory in Biblical Studies*, ed. Roland Boer (Leiden: Brill, 2008), 85.

[49] As translated in Mandolfo, "Dialogic Form Criticism," 74–75.

[50] Lee, *The Singers of Lamentations*, 42.

[51] See Marjo C. A. Korpel, "Who Is Speaking in Jeremiah 4:19–22? The Contribution of Unit Delimitation to an Old Problem," *VT* 59 (2009): 88, who notes that in ancient Semitic texts, this kind of unintroduced direct oration is by no means rare.

[52] See discussion in Lee, *The Singers of Lamentations*, 63.

¹⁹ Woe is me because of my hurt!
  My wound is severe.
But I said, "Truly this is my punishment,
  and I must bear it."
²⁰ My tent is destroyed,
  and all my cords are broken;
my children have gone from me,
  and they are no more;
there is no one to spread my tent again
  and to set up my curtains.
²¹ *For the shepherds are stupid,*
  and do not inquire of the LORD;
therefore they have not prospered,
  and all their flock is scattered.

It is well established that Lamentations is indebted to Jeremiah and Psalms for much of its language.⁵³ By understanding the voice of the narrator in Lamentations as a didactic voice, I extend this debt to Jeremiah and Psalms to the area of poetics as well.

As a further illustration, I note the exchange between Bat-Zion and the prophet in Jer 4:19–21 and 4:30–31. Here we can see the employ of a hierarchy of unmarked voices as well as a second rhetorical device which, as we shall see, is employed throughout the exchanges of the narrator and Bat-Zion in the book of Lamentations. It concerns the proclivity of the speakers to appropriate each other's words:

Bat-Zion: Jer 4:19–21	Jeremiah: Jer 4:30–31
¹⁹ My innards! My innards!	³⁰ And you who are doomed **to be ravaged**
How I writhe!	(*šādûd*)
Oh, the walls of my heart!	What do you accomplish by wearing
My (*lî*) heartmoans within me	crimson,
I cannot be silent;	By decking yourself in jewels of gold,
For **my soul hears** (*napšî šāmaʿat*) the	By enlarging your eyes with kohl?
sound (*qôl*) of horns,	You beautify yourself in vain:
Alarms of war	Lovers despise you,
	They seek your life!

⁵³   For a synoptic table of linguistic parallels between Lamentations and Jeremiah see House, *Lamentations*, 286 and Klein, *Lamentations*, 49. These parallels are discussed at length in Lee, *The Singers of Lamentations*, 75–162. For a synoptic table of parallels between Lamentations and Psalms, see Klein, *Lamentations*, 51–54.

[20] Disaster overtakes disaster For all the land **has been ravaged** (*šudədâ*) Suddenly my tents **have been ravaged** (*šudədû*) In a moment, my tent cloths. [21] How long must I see standards And hear (*'ešmə'â*) the sounds (*qôl*) of horns?[54]	[31] **I hear a sound** (*qôl šāma'tî*) as of one in travail Anguish as of a woman bearing her first child The **sound** (*qôl*) of Bat-Zion Panting, stretching out her hand: Alas for *me (lî)*! My soul (*napšî*) is faint Before the killers.

In vv. 30–31, the prophet responds empathically to Bat-Zion's plight in vv. 19–21. Specifically, the prophet responds to the words of Bat-Zion by echoing and invoking them. This literary dynamic of constructing a collective character, Bat-Zion, in dialogue with the prophet speaking in his own voice is unique within prophetic literature to the book of Jeremiah. This is what we encounter in Lamentations 1–4, where Bat-Zion and the narrator respond to each other by invoking each other's words. Thus, within the books of Lamentations and Jeremiah, we see that the two works portray a pastoral, guiding figure that moves between strophes of critique and strophes of sympathy. Moreover, both books feature dialogue between the voice of Bat-Zion and the voice of this pastoral figure. Several scholars have suggested that Lamentations, with its different speakers, was meant to be performed, or, I would add, at least read as dialogue.[55] We may think of Lamentations as a "reading drama" as some scholars propose reading the various voices present in Isaiah 40–55.[56]

JEREMIAH AS THE IMPLIED AUTHOR OF LAMENTATIONS

Understanding the stance of the didactic voice of the narrator – the voice I am calling the pastoral mentor – is bound up with the question of the book's authorship, and specifically the question of its relation to the prophet Jeremiah.

---

[54] Translations are based on the NRSVue. In isolated instances, I have adjusted the translation to hew more closely to the original Hebrew.

[55] Salters, "Structure and Implication," 296; Wilhelm Rudolph, *Das Buch Ruth, Das Hohe Lied, Die Klagelieder*, KAT 17.1–3 (Gütersloh: Mohn, 1962), 209.
Joseph M. Henderson, "Who Weeps in Jeremiah VIII 23 (IX 1)? Identifying Dramatic Speakers in the Poetry of Jeremiah," *VT* 52 (2002): 192.

[56] Annemarieke van der Woude, "'Hearing Voices While Reading': Isaiah 40–55 as a Drama," in *One Text, a Thousand Methods: Studies in Memory of Sjef van Tilborg*, ed. Patrick Chatelion Counet and Ulrich Berges, BibInt 71 (Boston: Brill, 2005), 166–73; Lena-Sofia Tiemeyer, "Isaiah 40–55: A Judahite Reading Drama," in *Daughter Zion: Her Portrait, Her Response*, ed. Mark J. Boda, Carol J. Dempsey, and LeAnn Snow Flesher, AIL 13 (Atlanta: SBL, 2012), 55–75.

The two books share much in common. Some see references to events in the life of Jeremiah in the account of the *geber* (Lam 3:14, 53–56 cf. Jer 20:7; 38:6–8). Both books attribute the downfall of Jerusalem to sin, while also displaying an outpouring of grief for the city (cf. Jer 14–15). Additionally, the books share many distinct phrases such as "eyes flow down with tears" (Lam 1:16; 2:11; 3:48–49; cf. Jer 9:1, 18; 13:17; 14:17); "terror on every side" (Lam 2:22; cf. Jer 6:25).[57] Both books assail the priests and false prophets as agents responsible for the downfall (Lam 2:14, 4:13; cf. Jer 2:7–8; 5:31; 14:13; 23:11–40; 27:1–28:17); both critique the appeal to weak and unreliable allies (Lam 1:2, 19; 4:17; cf. Jer 2:18, 36; 30:14, 37:5–10), and both share the expectation that Jerusalem's foes will share her bitter fate.

Despite this, the proposition that Jeremiah is the author of Lamentations has very few proponents in contemporary scholarship. Scholars note viewpoints expressed in Lamentations that stand counter to the thought of Jeremiah. Many expositors point to Chapter 4, in particular. Here we find a favorable view of establishing a treaty with Egypt, whereas Jeremiah railed against precisely this (Jer 2:18; 37:5–10). Lamentations seems to herald King Zedekiah (4:20), whereas Jeremiah castigated him (Jer 37:17). In Lam 2:20–22, intensely angry accusations are laid against the LORD as a murderer, which seem out of step with Jeremiah for whom the LORD's anger is justified through the prophetic theology of sin.

However, when expositors cite such passages as proof positive that the author of Jeremiah and the author of Lamentations could not have been the same person, they do so on the basis of an implicit assumption: that all voices in Lamentations represent the author's point of view. However, counter to these claims, it should be noted well: None of the statements in Lamentations that counter the words of the prophet in Jeremiah are made by the *narrator*, the didactic voice of the pastoral mentor. All of these statements are made by the *community* – either in the plural voice or through the agency of Bat-Zion. To determine the congruence (or lack thereof) between the worldview of Lamentations and that of Jeremiah, it is insufficient to weigh and measure the statements of "Lamentations" versus those of Jeremiah. The voices of Lamentations exist in a hierarchy, and the opinions of the implied author are those voiced through the pastoral mentor.

At the same time, there are other reasons to suspect that Lamentations was written by someone other than Jeremiah. Lamentations seems to invoke the book of Ezekiel at several junctures, which would suggest a date

---

[57]   Salters, *Lamentations*, 6; Klein, *Lamentations*, 7.

of authorship in the latter half of the sixth century, somewhat late for the prophet Jeremiah himself.[58] Most significantly, the developments within Judah reported in 5:9 and 5:18 would not have been witnessed by the prophet who was among the émigrés to Egypt after the fall of Jerusalem. If Jeremiah did, in fact, return to Jerusalem, his eponymous book is silent on the matter.

Thus, on the one hand, the phrasing of Lamentations and its employ of unmarked, unintroduced discourse between a narrator and Bat-Zion suggest an affiliation with Jeremiah. Moreover, many theological stances in Lamentations accord with those in Jeremiah, and those that do not are never enunciated by the narrator, who is the representative voice of the author. Yet, on the other hand, some attestations concerning conditions in Judah are incongruous with the presence of the prophet in Egypt. This tension has spawned an intermediate position concerning the book's authorship and its relationship to Jeremiah: The author of Lamentations is a disciple of Jeremiah or a member of a Jeremiah school, situated in Judah.[59] While the actual author of the book could well have been such an individual, the constructed, didactic voice of the pastoral mentor may be construed as that of Jeremiah. That is, within the world of Lamentations, Jeremiah is a poetic persona, the implied author.[60] Like Jeremiah, the narrator – the pastoral mentor – is himself a member of the traumatized community and thus commiserates with Bat-Zion. And like Jeremiah, as we shall see, he moves between expressions of sympathy and even empathy on the one hand, but on the other hand, can level criticism. This explains the heavy indebtedness of Lamentations to the book of Jeremiah, in its language, poetics, and its theology.

COLLECTIVE TRAUMA THEORY AND THE POETICS OF LAMENTATIONS

But toward what end has the author of Lamentations constructed two primary characters, standing in hierarchic relationship – the didactic voice of the pastoral mentor and Bat-Zion? My reading of these two constructed

---

[58] For a synoptic table of linguistic parallels between Lamentations and Ezekiel, see Klein, *Lamentations* 49–50.

[59] In modern scholarship, this approach was introduced by Max Löhr, "Threni III. und die jeremianische Autorschaft des Buches der Klagelieder," *ZAW* 24 (1904): xiii–xv, who says the book stems from a "Jeremiah school" member. The notion that Jeremiah's scribe, Baruch ben Neriah was the author of Lamentations is already found in the medieval midrash, The *Alphabet of Ben Sira*. See Norman Bronznick, "The Alphabet of Ben Sira," in *Rabbinic Fantasies: Imaginative Narratives from Classical Hebrew Literature*, ed. David Stern and Mark J. Mirsky, *YJS* 29 (New Haven, CT: Yale University Press, 1998), 177.

[60] See Lee, *The Singers of Lamentations*, 3 and discussion in Berlin, *Lamentations*, 54.

figures is animated by observations concerning the sociology of collective trauma.[61] As Irene Smith Landsman notes, trauma calls into question the basic assumptions that inform our experience of ourselves, the world, and the human condition, and often engenders a crisis of meaning at the deepest level.[62] The crisis of meaning concerns, among other things: concepts of justice, control, sense of trust, and the nature and character of the divine. In the midst of trauma, no coherence is likely to be found. According to Jeffrey Alexander and Elizabeth Breese, into this void step culture creators who create scripts of meaning for the traumatized community.[63] Through symbolic actions and the composition of literature, collective trauma is socially mediated.[64] For a decimated community, the new metanarrative around a shared story begins the process of reconstructing meaning.

Consider the shaping of the meaning of the Holocaust for Jews who came to the United States following the Second World War. When these Jews first reached the shores of the United States from the horrors of wartime Europe, they kept a low profile, focusing on building new lives and fitting in. Those around them did not want to hear their stories and encouraged them to Americanize. It was the publication in English of Elie Wiesel's *Night* in 1960 that ushered in a newfound conscience for survivors about the nobility of bearing witness and the importance of sharing their wartime experiences.[65]

Another watershed moment came in 1978, when the television miniseries *Holocaust* was broadly viewed by millions of Americans. Interest grew in the historical plight of an oppressed group of people. Initially, those that had endured the Holocaust were referred to with any number of designations: *refugees, displaced persons, liberated prisoners, immigrants, greenhorns,* or the Yiddish version, *greene.* These various labels all bore connotations of passivity and victimhood. Now able to share their collective story in prime time, Jews could highlight and share their trauma. The process allowed Jews

---

[61]   I am indebted in this section for the references to collective trauma theory to Elizabeth Boase, "Fragmented Voices: Collective Identity and Traumatization in the Book of Lamentations," in *The Bible through the Lens of Trauma*, eds. Elizabeth Boase and Christopher G. Frechette, SemeiaSt 86 (Atlanta: SBL Press, 2016), 49–66.

[62]   Irene Smith Landsman, "Crises of Meaning in Trauma and Loss," in *Loss of the Assumptive World: A Theory of Traumatic Loss*, ed. Jeffrey Kauffman (New York: Brunner-Routledge, 2002), 13.

[63]   Jeffrey C. Alexander and Elizabeth Butler Breese, "Introduction: On Social Suffering and Its Cultural Construction," in *Narrating Trauma: On the Impact of Collective Suffering*, ed. Ron Eyerman, Jeffrey C. Alexander, and Elizabeth Butler Breese (Boulder, CO: Paradigm Publishers, 2013), xxvii.

[64]   Jeffrey C. Alexander, *Trauma: A Social Theory* (Cambridge: Polity, 2012), 6.

[65]   Elie Wiesel, *Night*, trans. Stella Rodway (New York: Hill and Wang, 1960).

to take back their power and strength, and the new way of thinking about such Jews was not as immigrants, but as *survivors*, a term that connotes resilience, perseverance, and even ingenuity, and which was rarely used beforehand.[66]

These examples strongly bear out the observation of Jeffrey Alexander and Elizabeth Breese who write, "Instituting a dominant trauma narrative is a singular social accomplishment. It stabilizes not only collective memory but also contemporary sense of social reality, pointing the way forward in a confident way."[67] Elizabeth Boase has astutely noted that although the expressive function of Lamentations has long been recognized, its constructive role of shaping collective identification is seldom recognized. In this commentary, I read the book's literary forms, metaphors, personifications, and multiple voices not only as expressions of pain and anguish, but also as vehicles to draw sixth-century Judeans toward a common metanarrative that explains their plight.[68]

A POLEMIC AGAINST ZION THEOLOGY

As many scholars have concluded, the poems of Lamentations were composed in the middle of the sixth century in Judah.[69] In this study, I maintain that the book of Lamentations is written for a sixth-century Judean audience with sixth-century Judean concerns: the overwhelming totality of the destruction, despair, and spiritual dislocation without a clear road map of what lies ahead. Put differently, the poem is written not merely about Bat-Zion, but indeed, for Bat-Zion herself – the survivors of the destruction. In this regard, I am in agreement with Knut Heim, who writes that Lamentations is akin to "a public dialogue that reflects a community's grasping for meanings as the world around it collapses."[70]

The author of Lamentations seeks to create a script of meaning for his community. As was the role of so many of the classical prophets of Israel, the author of Lamentations offers a metanarrative to his listening and

---

[66]   Diane L. Wolf, "What's in a Name? The Genealogy of Holocaust Identities," *Genealogy* 1:4 (2017): art. 19, pp. 1–12, https://tinyurl.com/5n74tjph.
[67]   Alexander and Breese, "Social Suffering," xxx.
[68]   Boase, "Fragmented Voices," 63.
[69]   On the dating of Lamentations, see Berlin, *Lamentations*, 33–36; Klein, *Lamentations*, 6–9. Of particular influence in this discussion has been F. W. Dobbs-Allsopp, "Linguistic Evidence for the Date of Lamentations," *JANES* 26 (1998): 1–36.
[70]   Heim, "The Personification of Jerusalem," 168.

reading audience that challenges them to reinterpret the events that have
befallen them, and thereby reconstruct meaning for a decimated community. It stabilizes collective memory and obliquely and implicitly points the
way forward. At the center of the dialogues between the pastoral mentor
and Bat-Zion lie competing claims about the legitimacy of Zion theology –
the belief in the immutable election of the Davidic monarchy, the people of
Zion, Jerusalem, and the temple.[71] Lamentations throughout questions and
contextualizes these traditions. As we noted earlier, although Jeremiah had
repeatedly prophesied the fall of the city and the temple, once his prophecies
had come to fruition, no recognition accrued to him for it. Zion theology
still thrived. At only a single juncture do the residents of Judah approach
the prophet for advice, asking where they should take up residence following their dislocation (Jer 42:1–3). The prophet consults with the LORD and
returns them the answer that they are to remain in Jerusalem, and that all
will be well with them if they do. By contrast, should they seek shelter at a
distance from the Babylonians, under the protective aegis of Egypt, they will
perish (Jer 42:7–22). His audience hears his words and immediately sets off
for Egypt. The lessons learned by the people in the wake of the destruction
of the city and the temple are summed up in Jer 44:10: "They have shown no
contrition or fear to this day." This continued, determined rejection of the
prophetic theology of sin then is the backdrop to the book of Lamentations.

THE UNITY OF LAMENTATIONS

A key issue for any exposition of Lamentations concerns the fundamental
question: Is Lamentations one work, or five? This question is sometimes
mistaken for the question of authorship, but they are not one and the
same. Scholars are split on whether Lamentations is written by a single
author or by many; hard and fast evidence is hard to come by on this for
Lamentations as for any of the biblical books.[72] However, more crucial for
the exposition of the book is the question of its unity. Even if the book was

---

[71]   Studies that see in Lamentations a refutation of Zion theology include Albrektson,
       Studies in the Text, 230; Johnson, "Form and Message," 59–60; and Magne Sæbø, "Who
       is 'the Man' in Lamentations 3.1?," in *On the Way to Canon: Creative Tradition History in
       the Old Testament*, JSOTSup 191 (Sheffield: Sheffield Academic, 1998), 294–306.
[72]   Scholars who argue for a single author include Salters, *Lamentations*, 98; Otto Plöger,
       "Die Klagelieder," in *Die fünf Megilloth: Ruth, das Hohelied, Esther von Ernst Würthwein,
       Der Prediger von Kurt Galling, Die Klagelieder von Otto Plöger*, HAT 18 (Tübingen: Mohr
       Siebeck, 1969), 129–30; R. K. Harrison, *Jeremiah and Lamentations: An Introduction and*

written by more than one hand, it may have been redacted in a manner and its chapters placed in an order to convey meaning.[73] Those that maintain the disunity of the five poems (and implicitly maintain multiple authorship) point to the divergent theological perspectives, say, between the theodic tone of Chapter 3 versus the anti-theodic disposition of Chapter 2. On linguistic grounds, they note that while Chapters 1–4 feature acrostic structure, the order of the alphabet in Chapter 1 places the letter *ʿayin* before the letter *peh*, the order familiar to us today, whereas in Chapters 2–4, those letters appear in reverse order.

However, many others point to signs of unity between the five poems. All five chapters are 22 verses long, with the exception of Chapter 3, which is triple that number in length. Chapters 1–4 are all acrostics. Chapters 1–4 all employ multiple voices, a rhetorical feature, as pointed out earlier, found only scantly in Jeremiah within prophetic literature, and practically nowhere else at all. In Lamentations 1–4, the use of this poetic device is widespread. However, the strongest clue that these poems stand in unity is the resemblance of their linguistic detail. The subject matter of the five poems is actually broad. Some passages focus on the destruction of the temple; others on the effects of starvation; Chapter 5 seems to take place during the Babylonian occupation, sometime after the initial conquest of the city itself. Chapter 3 makes no overt reference to the destruction at all (although there are allusions to it in vv. 40–47), and most of the chapter focuses on the individual travails of the *geber*. Nonetheless, the five poems share an uncommonly wide range of terms and phrases.[74] This calls for an interpretation of the book in holistic fashion.

***

With these methodological positions in place, I now state my thesis about the function, theology, and coherence of Lamentations. The book addresses a sixth-century Judean audience in crisis and is *constructive* and

---

Commentary, TOTC 21 (London: Tyndale, 1973), 198; Assis, *Lamentations*, 46. Scholars who argue for multiple authorship include Gordis, *Lamentations*, 125–27; Westermann, *Lamentations*, 121–22; Norman Gottwald, "Lamentations," HBC (San Francisco: Harper & Row, 1988), 541–42.

[73] See Renkema, *Lamentations*, 52–54; Thomas, *Poetry and Theology*, 47; Hillers, *Lamentations*, 14; Provan, *Lamentations*, 29. See also, David Marcus, "Non-Recurring Doublets in the Book of Lamentations," *HAR* 10 (1986): 177–95.

[74] For synoptic tables of the language and phrases shared by the poems, see Klein, *Lamentations*, 43–46; Assis, *Lamentations*, 18–31; and Thomas, *Poetry and Theology*, 164–65, 205–6, 238–40.

didactic in nature. It is a culture script designed to take issue with the persistent belief in Zion theology, even following the fall of Jerusalem and the destruction of the temple. In each of the first four chapters, the pastoral mentor engages Bat-Zion in discussion. As we noted earlier, the books of Jeremiah and Ezekiel reveal to us that this was a period of great theological foment, as evidenced by the ubiquitous presence of cited theological stances uttered by the prophet's antagonists. In terms of the beliefs of the times, "the people" cannot be treated as a monolithic entity, any more than in contemporary times were religious Jews monolithic in their beliefs about God during the Holocaust and in its immediate aftermath. I maintain that within Lamentations, the uneven presentation of the narrator, and particularly of Bat-Zion, reflects the fact that in each poem, the author is addressing a different audience – a different subset within the survivor community. By my reading, the constructed character Bat-Zion is not a single consistent character across these four chapters. Rather, in each, Bat-Zion represents a distinct religious typology found within the community. The pastoral mentor engages each of these, adjusting his tone and content accordingly. This interpretive matrix allows us to make sense of the varying use of genre, the shifting points of view and sometimes inconsistent positions expounded by Bat-Zion from one chapter to the next. The key in each chapter is to tease out the religious typology that Bat-Zion embodies and to understand how the pastoral mentor offers her guidance. Here, the cited positions of Jeremiah's antagonists and the positions enunciated within the post-destruction Psalms play a crucial role. In each chapter, I will demonstrate that one of these dissenting positions is, respectively, the religious worldview of Bat-Zion within that chapter. Within each chapter, the pastoral mentor engages Bat-Zion about her positions and seeks to offer comfort and yet also chart a way forward for her to better make meaning of the events that have befallen her.

In Chapter 1, "Plotting a Path for Zion's Spiritual Rehabilitation," Bat-Zion is aware of the theological notion that her sins can have repercussions for her. But the unprecedented enormity of the destruction has shaken the foundations of her theological moorings. The pastoral mentor guides her through nine stages of theological growth, bringing her to a full understanding of her own complicity in the destruction and to a restored connection with the LORD.

In Chapter 2, "Dispelling Delusions I: The LORD and His Love for Zion," the pastoral narrator confronts a second religious typology: the entrenched belief in Zion theology – the LORD could not have wrought all this, because the LORD loves his elect people Israel and his elect city Jerusalem and the seat of his presence – the temple. However, the pastoral mentor knows that the hard truth will be highly disillusioning for Bat-Zion and leave her extremely bitter toward the LORD, if she continues to engage him at all. He works with her to bring her to understand that the LORD is not as she had conceived him and to create a space for her to express her anger and disillusionment.

Chapter 3, "Redirecting Zion's Anger: The *Geber* as Model," picks up where Chapter 2 leaves off. Here, the pastoral mentor – the *geber* – offers his personal experience of bitterness toward the LORD as a model for how Bat-Zion should negotiate and resolve her own anger.

In Chapter 4, "Dispelling Delusions II: Zion and Her Social Structures," the pastoral mentor takes on the entrenched social structure engendered by Zion theology. Jerusalem high society revolved around the person of the Davidic king. Status accrued to those who ministered to him – priests, false prophets, and elites. Here, the pastoral mentor rips the mask off these to reveal their impotence and to lead Bat-Zion to reconsider a series of political truths that had guided those that held to Zion theology before the fall.

Finally, in Chapter 5, "Purging Prayer of Zion Theology", the pastoral mentor utters a didactic prayer – a prayer designed to instill hope in the hearts of his audience. Yet at the same time, the pastoral mentor stays clear of any mention of the LORD's special relationship with Israel. Within the world of Zion theology, the LORD's love for Israel, Jerusalem, and the Temple was unconditional, and thus represented a corruption of the dynamics of covenant as laid out in Deuteronomy and in the prophetic literature. His prayer stands in stark contrast to similar prayers that we find in Psalms 74 and 79, which may have well been composed by those who ascribed to precisely the theology the pastoral mentor seeks to dispel.

While I have tried here to ground my reading strategy for Lamentations, the identification of the religious typology that is the focus respectively of each chapter is difficult to "prove" by reference to a single statement within the composition. At the beginning of each chapter, I offer an introduction where I propose a characterization of the religious typology taken up in that chapter. Ultimately, though, the proof of the pudding is in the eating. In this case, that means that the validity of my interpretation can only be measured at the end of each chapter by the degree to which it accounts for the various twists and turns taken in the dialogue between the narrator and

Bat-Zion. It is my hope and prayer that this interpretive matrix will allow us to see that within Lamentations, it is far from true that we have a "jumble of images that bubble up to the surface in random order,"[75] and that we will be able to appreciate the deliberate and systematic way in which its author crafted a script of meaning for the traumatized community of sixth-century Judah.

[75]   As cited earlier; Middlemas, *Lamentations*, 10.

1 Plotting a Path for Zion's Spiritual Rehabilitation

¹ How lonely sits the city
    that once was full of people!
How like a widow she has become,
    she that was great among the nations!
She that was a princess among the provinces
    has become subject to forced labor.

² She weeps bitterly in the night,
    with tears on her cheeks;
among all her lovers,
    she has no one to comfort her;
all her friends have dealt treacherously with her;
    they have become her enemies.

³ Judah has gone into exile with suffering
    and hard servitude;
she lives now among the nations;
    she finds no resting place;
her pursuers have all overtaken her
    in the midst of her distress.

⁴ The roads to Zion mourn,
    for no one comes to the festivals;
all her gates are desolate;
    her priests groan;
her young girls grieve,[a]
    and her lot is bitter.

⁵ Her foes have become the masters;
    her enemies prosper

[a]   1.4 Meaning of Heb uncertain

because the LORD has made her suffer
    for the multitude of her transgressions;
her children have gone away,
    captives before the foe.

⁶ From daughter Zion has departed
    all her majesty.
Her princes have become like stags
    that find no pasture;
they fled without strength
    before the pursuer.

⁷ Jerusalem remembers*ᵇ* all the
    precious things that were hers in days of old.
When her people fell into the hand of the enemy
    and there was no one to help her,
the enemy looked on; they mocked
    over her downfall.

⁸ Jerusalem sinned grievously,
    so she has become a filthy thing;
all who honored her despise her,
    for they have seen her nakedness;
she herself groans
    and turns her face away.

⁹ Her uncleanness was in her skirts;
    she took no thought of her future;
her downfall was appalling,
    with none to comfort her.
Look, O LORD, look at my affliction,
    for the enemy has triumphed!

¹⁰ Enemies have stretched out their hands
    over all her precious things;
she has even seen the nations
    invade her sanctuary,
those whom you forbade
    to enter your congregation.

¹¹ All her people groan
    as they search for bread;

ᵇ   1.7 Q ms: MT adds *in the days of her affliction and wandering*

they trade their treasures for food
  to revive their lives.
Look, O Lord, and see
  how worthless I have become.

¹² Is it nothing to you,^c all you who pass by?
  Look and see
if there is any sorrow like my sorrow,
  which was brought upon me,
which the Lord inflicted
  on the day of his fierce anger.

¹³ From on high he sent fire;
  it went deep into my bones;
he spread a net for my feet;
  he turned me back;
he has left me stunned,
  faint all day long.

¹⁴ My transgressions were bound^d into a yoke;
  by his hand they were fastened together;
they weigh on my neck,
  sapping my strength;
the Lord handed me over
  to those whom I cannot withstand.

¹⁵ The Lord has rejected
  all my warriors in the midst of me;
he proclaimed a time against me
  to crush my young men;
the Lord has trodden as in a winepress
  the virgin daughter Judah.

¹⁶ For these things I weep;
  my eyes^e flow with tears;
for a comforter is far from me,
  one to revive my courage;
my children are desolate,
  for the enemy has prevailed.

¹⁷ Zion stretches out her hands,
  but there is no one to comfort her;

---

^c   1.12 Meaning of Heb uncertain
^d   1.14 Meaning of Heb uncertain
^e   1.16 Heb *my eye, my eye*

the Lord has commanded against Jacob
　　that his neighbors should become his foes;
Jerusalem has become
　　a filthy thing among them.

[18] The Lord is in the right,
　　for I have rebelled against his word;
but hear, all you peoples,
　　and behold my suffering;
my young women and young men
　　have gone into captivity.

[19] I called to my lovers,
　　but they deceived me;
my priests and elders
　　perished in the city
while seeking food
　　to revive their lives.

[20] Look, O Lord, at how distressed I am;
　　my stomach churns;
my heart is wrung within me
　　because I have been very rebellious.
In the street the sword bereaves;
　　in the house it is like death.

[21] They heard how I was groaning,
　　with no one to comfort me.
All my enemies heard of my trouble;
　　they are glad that you have done it.
Bring on the day that you have announced,
　　and let them be as I am.

[22] Let all their evil doing come before you,
　　and deal with them
as you have dealt with me
　　because of all my transgressions;
for my groans are many,
　　and my heart is faint.

INTRODUCTION

Scholars have long struggled to discern within Lamentations 1 a discernible order or progression in its ideas and messages. There is consensus that the poem features two speakers: the narrator whose voice alone is heard in vv. 1–9b and Bat-Zion, whose voice is dominant, although hardly exclusive, in vv.9c–22. But scholars have struggled to discern distinct and contrasting theological agendas within these two speakers: Each of them voices both theodic and anti-theodic messages. The absence of a clear theological agenda for either speaker is matched by a sense that the poem lacks any progressive structure.

We can resolve these issues, however, by construing the relationship between the speakers in the fashion that I laid out in the introduction. The poem addresses a sixth-century Judean audience in crisis and is *constructive* and *didactic* in nature. The author seeks to create a script of meaning for his community. As was the role of so many of the classical prophets of Israel, the author offers a metanarrative to his listening and reading audience that challenges them to reinterpret the events that have befallen them, and thereby reconstruct meaning for a decimated community. It stabilizes collective memory and obliquely and implicitly points the way forward.

A cursory reading of Lamentations 1 reveals that it mentions sin more often than any other of the book's five poems (Lam 1:5, 8, 9, 14, 18, 20, 22). But the chapter's aim is not merely to preach to Bat-Zion that she has sinned. Rather, our author, through the agency of the narrator, the pastoral mentor, seeks to respond to and guide a specific religious typology.

This typology is vividly identified via reference to a religious response to collective trauma during modern times. During the years 1939–42, Rabbi Kolonymus Kalman Shapira, the Piaseczno Rebbe, wrote down the sermons he gave in the Warsaw Ghetto in a collection that has survived under the title *Sermons from the Years of Rage*.[1] Throughout the sermons from the earlier years of the collection, Rabbi Shapira held fast to the rabbinic principle that when the people of Israel suffer, it is a sign of punishment from the Almighty. Yet in the closing portions of the collection, particularly once the liquidation of the ghetto began in July 1942 and its Jews were deported to the Treblinka death camp, Rabbi Shapira abandoned this paradigm. No degree of sin could hold Israel responsible for this degree of wrath and suffering.

---

[1]   The sermons are published in a critical edition and in a facsimile edition and transcription by Daniel Reiser, *Rabbi Kalonymus Kalman Shapira – Sermons from the Years of Rage: The Sermons of the Piaseczno Rebbe from the Warsaw Ghetto, 1939–1942 (Daniel Reiser edition) [Hebrew]*, ed. Amos Geula, 2 vols. (Jerusalem: World Union of Jewish Studies, 2017). For a study of his theological perspectives, see James A. Diamond, "The Warsaw Ghetto Rebbe: Diverting God's Gaze from a Utopian End to an Anguished Now," *MJ* 30 (2010): 299–331.

A similar impetus is seen in the laments composed by rabbinic figures at war's end. These laments typically decry the suffering of the victims of the Holocaust, and plea to the Almighty for salvation. Yet, in these compositions, written by figures who affirm the basic paradigm of sin and punishment the notion that the Holocaust may have been a divine response to sinful behavior is only obliquely mentioned, if at all.[2] This silence speaks volumes to the discomfort within these religious writers with the notion of a God capable of such wrath. It also speaks to a second truth: In the wake of the Holocaust, no one who had survived would have had the gumption to cast guilt and aspersion on those who had not by suggesting that the Holocaust was a response to sinful behavior. Thus, the theological notion that the Holocaust was a divine response to Israel's sins problematized these survivors' conception of the Almighty as well as their conception of their martyred brethren.

While modern and obviously culturally different from the biblical corpus, these examples are worth considering. They demonstrate that even those who ascribe to notions of divine punishment for Israel's sins, struggle with the concept when the suffering of those ostensibly enduring punishment reaches massive and unprecedented levels.

This would appear to be the theological mindset of the members of the community that the prophet cites in Jer 16:10. When Jeremiah tells them of the utter obliteration that awaits them, the people respond, "Why has the LORD pronounced all this great evil against us? What is our iniquity? What is the sin that we have committed against the LORD our God?" These are a people who are familiar with the notion that the covenant with the LORD is far from unconditional; sin has consequences, and they understand that the LORD can be expected to punish Israel when she is unfaithful (cf. Jer 2:23, 35, 5:19). But the annihilation that the prophet had foretold in the prior verses, and indeed in many passages throughout the book of Jeremiah, was of a degree that was without precedent. In the wake of the fall of the city, the issue for this segment of the community is not that the LORD punishes Israel for her sins. It is that the suffering engendered by the destruction seemed to them entirely disproportional to any offense they could have perpetrated.

The author of Lamentations 1 knows that to preach to the decimated community about its sinful ways and to expect their instantaneous transformation

---

[2]   See generally, Judith T. Baumel, *"Kol-Bikhiot" (A Voice of Lament): The Holocaust and Prayer* [Hebrew], ALFIHR 3 (Ramat Gan, Israel: Bar-Ilan University Press, 1992).

is wishful thinking. The author understands that to bring the community to an awareness and acceptance of its agency in the downfall, it must engage a process in which they migrate from their bewilderment, anger and dissolution to a place of acceptance of the LORD's judgment. But this cannot happen in a single step; all rehabilitation is a process. The author creates a metanarrative of meaning through the exchange of two stand-ins. The first is the voice of the culture creating author, the figure of the pastoral mentor. The pastoral mentor is himself a member of the traumatized community and thus commiserates with Bat-Zion. At the same time, he is a representative of a theology that bears strong affinity to that of Jeremiah, and it is that perspective that he wishes to instill within her. As we shall see, he moves between expressions of sympathy and even empathy on the one hand, but on the other hand, can level criticism. The stand-in for the traumatized community is the figure of Bat-Zion. The interaction between the pastoral mentor and Bat-Zion in this poem is a map of that developmental process.

Critical to my reading strategy is the realization that Bat-Zion is a construct, a model of what the author believes they *ought* to say and feel. Sociologists Jeffrey Alexander and Elizabeth Breese note that in response to collective trauma, culture creators will adduce trauma scripts. "These scripts are not descriptions of what is; they are arguments for must have been, and, at least implicitly what should be. The truth of cultural scripts emerges not from their descriptive accuracy, but from the power of their enactment." In like fashion, the Bat-Zion that we encounter in our poem is an *idealized* Bat-Zion, created by the poet for didactic purposes.

By my reading, the key to understanding Lamentations 1 is to track the change, the theological conversion that the constructed figure of Bat-Zion undergoes from her first utterance in v. 9c, progressively through her last pronouncements in v. 22. Her first utterance at 9c, I will argue, is only a first step, and is fraught with theological error. The author seeks to show the community an image of Bat-Zion as she works through pain and disillusionment, and through nine progressive stages comes to a full and proper realization of the nature of her relation with the LORD and with the invading nations. What we have before us is not, as is so often suggested in the literature, two monologues, one by him and one by her.[3] Rather, the pastoral mentor speaks in order to get Bat-Zion to reflect and respond.

---

[3] Berlin, *Lamentations*, 48; Charles William Miller, "Reading Voices: Personification, Dialogism, and the Reader of Lamentations 1," *BibInt* 9 (2001): 394; Bier, "*Perhaps There Is Hope*," 71.

As we shall see, Bat-Zion is a master at echoing and reusing terms and phrases that appear earlier in their shared discourse. In the earlier part of her development, she repurposes language initially uttered by the pastoral mentor in order to polemicize against him. As she evolves further in her development, she reuses his words in ways that mirror his semantic intentions, thus aligning her view with his. In the final stages of her development, Bat-Zion reuses terms and phrases from her own earlier polemical discourse, now recontextualizing them to serve as affirmations of the pastoral mentor's theology. This reading strategy lays bare a highly structured, linear progression of thought and ideas, particularly in the exchange of voices heard in vv. 9c–22.

THE PASTORAL MENTOR'S THEOLOGICAL PLATFORM (VV. 1–9b)

Over the first nine verses the poet appeals to his audience of Judean survivors through the agency of the pastoral mentor. The interjection of Bat-Zion at 9c suggests that the pastoral mentor's soliloquy of vv. 1–9b is said in her presence. In these verses he aims to accomplish two goals. The first is to establish credit and trust with Bat-Zion by striking a consistently sympathetic posture. By establishing credit with her that he deeply understands her pain and her perspective, he will create a space for her to hear his insights on how she has arrived at this nadir. In the first four verses he raises no critique of her at all. His depiction of her plight demonstrates to her that he appreciates the depth of her suffering and its various manifestations, in terms of abandonment, loss, disorientation and pain. In the opening verse he validates her theological perspective by casting her as a widow – that is, her sense that the LORD has seemingly abandoned her. In v. 2, he offers the comfort of simply affirming what she is experiencing by stating it aloud. His is a presence and a voice that notices her tears and that understands her sense of betrayal by the nations that have turned on her. Above all, he affirms her vulnerability and loneliness: "she has no one to comfort her." Her loneliness is accentuated in vv. 3–4. Not only is she bereft of support – either divine or political, as per vv. 1–2 – but she is bereft of her young, who have been driven off to exile (v. 3), with the result (v. 4) that the approaches to the city are now desolate.

In vv. 5–9, the pastoral mentor modulates between critique and sympathy and, even his references to her sinful past in vv. 5, 8, and 9 are not specified in detail. Moreover, as the pastoral mentor records the results of these sins, he does so without sharp notes of rebuke and reprimand. Rather his tones display an understanding of the depth of her pain as a result of the punishments she has brought upon herself. Consider v. 5b, where the reference to her sins is enveloped by exclamations about the upper hand given to her enemies at the beginning of the verse, and the evocative image of her infant children being marched into exile at its close. Similarly in v. 8, mention of her unspecified sin is followed with a detailed account of her experience of debasement and her futile attempts to escape her emotional tormenters. All of this is designed so that Bat-Zion in the poem – and the traumatized Judean community with her – can feel assured that the pastoral mentor senses their pain and shares in it.

But no less, we should also read the pastoral mentor's soliloquy as a presentation of a series of theological propositions with which he wishes to engage Bat-Zion, to clarify and establish the meaning of what has befallen them. Jeffrey Alexander notes that in remapping meaning for a traumatized community, culture creators must attribute responsibility and resolve the identity of the perpetrator, the "antagonist."[4] This, as it turns out, is the crux of the matter Bat-Zion must reconsider. As we shall see, clarifying and understanding the true antagonist and properly attributing responsibility are the points with which Bat-Zion will wrestle as she moves through the stages of her spiritual rehabilitation in the second half of the poem. The pastoral mentor wishes her to consider four points:

1. Her suffering at the hands of her enemies is not due to their strength. Rather, her sin evokes the LORD's wrath, and he, in turn, enlists the nations to punish her. Verse 5 stresses this point, by breaking from the causal order of this process, and starting with the result: "Her foes have become the masters; her enemies prosper because the LORD has made her suffer for the multitude of her transgressions." As per the cited voice in Jer 16:10, it was unimaginable for some that the LORD could devastate his people, no matter what their actions. But this is the truth to which they must own up.
2. Her victimization does not stem from the LORD's absence; in fact, the LORD is fully present and guiding events.
3. As a vulnerable political entity, Bat-Zion seeks support. But this support can only truly come from the LORD, not from surrounding powers (v.2).

4　Jeffrey C. Alexander, "Toward a Theory of Cultural Trauma," in *Cultural Trauma and Collective Identity*, ed. Jeffrey C. Alexander (Berkeley: University of California Press, 2004), 15.

4. Most significantly, the prophet challenges Bat-Zion to note what issues are primary in her own mind and what issues she suppresses. This is achieved through the double use of the word *zākərâ*, and the question of what she remembers (*zākərâ*) and what she doesn't remember (*lōʾ zākərâ*). The prophet states that she "remembers" during her suffering, "all the precious things that were hers in days of old" (v. 7). By contrast, she couldn't prospectively remember (*lōʾ zākərâ*) what would be in store for her on account of her adulterous activities (v. 9). Put differently, the semantic field invoked reflects his view that Bat-Zion is more acutely aware of her suffering than she is of its true cause – her own behavior.

A CLOSER LOOK: *BAT-ṢIYYON* – "DAUGHTER ZION" OR "DAUGHTER OF ZION"?

Expressions of the form *bat-X*, similar to epithets, occur twenty times in Lamentations. While the term *bat-ṣiyyon* is used already by Micah and Isaiah, its use peaks in the sixth-century texts of Lamentations and Jeremiah. For long, scholars have debated the syntactic and semantic meaning of the term, marshalling a wide array of arguments from the study of biblical metaphor, comparison to parallel forms in cognate literature and from the perspective of Hebrew grammar.

Since the 1960s, the dominant view has been to understand the phrase *bat-ṣiyyon* as an appositional genitive. Therefore, the phrase should be translated not in accord with the regular understanding of the genitive form, as "daughter of Zion," but as "daughter Zion." The formulaic expression does not metaphorically imagine that Zion *has* a daughter, but rather that Zion *is* a daughter.[5] By this reading, construct phrases in biblical Hebrew should be considered lexemes in their own right. In the major study in this vein, the nomen regens, *bat*, is the metaphor and the nomen rectum, *ṣiyyon*, is the reference to which the metaphor is applied.

---

[5] See William Franklin Stinespring, "No Daughter of Zion: A Study of the Appositional Genitive in Hebrew Grammar," *Enc* 26 (1965): 133–41. This interpretation has been advanced in a full-length study in Magnar Kartveit, *Rejoice, Dear Zion! Hebrew Construct Phrases with "Daughter" and "Virgin" as Nomen Regens*, eds. John Barton, Reinhard G. Kratz, and Markus Witte, BZAW 447 (Berlin: de Gruyter, 2013), and has been widely adopted by the NAB, the NJPS, and NRSVue English translations. See also, Bruce K. Waltke and M. O'Connor, *An Introduction to Biblical Hebrew Syntax* (Winona Lake, IN: Eisenbrauns, 1990), 153, 226.

Zion is described metaphorically as a *bat*. It is a collective poetical per-sonification of the people.

Although the term *bat* means "daughter," its semantic meaning stresses "young female girl." As an epithet for the city, it has engendered translations such as "Fair Zion," "Lady Zion," and "Miss Zion." It func-tions like a diminutive: "Dear Little Zion" or "Sweet Little Zion," con-noting emotional tenderness or protectiveness toward a female person of lesser power or authority.[6] It has the same linguistic profile and impli-cation as *bat-ʿammî*, which occurs in Lamentations five times, and is understood thus, as "My fair, or, dear, people."

However, many scholars still hold to the conventional understand-ing, whereby in a genitive construction the nomen rectum always quali-fies the nomen regens. The "daughter" here, is a "daughter of Zion."[7] Scholars who read the term this way debate its precise meaning. Many see in it in the remnants of parallel cognate terms where "daughter of City X" can refer to consorts, patron goddesses, and divine daughters.[8] Michael Floyd has proposed that the genitive relationship *bat-ṣiyyon* collectively represents the women of Jerusalem, particularly with respect to the distinctive role that they play in leading the rejoicing and lamentation of the community as a whole.[9] Thus construed, the figure of *bat-ṣiyyon* emphasizes female leadership of public celebration as an important aspect of civic and religious life.

The tenderness and endearment implicit in the reading of *bat-ṣiyyon* as appositional genitive well fits the disposition of the pastoral men-tor developed here, especially in Chapters 1 and 2. However, as will be pointed out later, the pastoral mentor's disposition in Chapter 4 is decid-edly more chiding, and there, the terms *bat-ṣiyyon/-ʿammî* occur four

---

[6]   Berlin, *Lamentations*, 12.

[7]   See F. W. Dobbs-Allsopp, "The Syntagma of Bat Followed by a Geographical Name in the Hebrew Bible: A Reconsideration of Its Meaning and Grammar," *CBQ* 57 (1995): 451–70; Michael H. Floyd, "Welcome Back, Daughter of Zion!," *CBQ* 70 (2008): 484–504.

[8]   Aloysius Fitzgerald, "The Mythological Background for the Presentation of Jerusalem as a Queen and False Worship as Adultery in the OT," *CBQ* 34 (1972): 403–16; Elaine R. Follis, "The Holy City as Daughter," in *Directions in Biblical Poetry*, ed. Elaine R. Follis, JSOTSup 40 (Sheffield: JSOT, 1987), 173–84; Mark E. Biddle, "The Figure of Lady Jerusalem: Identification, Deification and Personification of Cities in the Ancient Near East," in *The Biblical Canon in Comparative Perspective: Scripture in Context IV*, eds. K. Lawson Younger, Jr., William W. Hallo, and Bernard F. Batto, ANETS 11 (Lewiston, NY: Edwin Mellen, 1991), 173–94.

[9]   Floyd, "Welcome Back," 504.

times. Moreover, the phrase *bat-ʾEdom*, in reference to Zion's enemies, appears twice (4:21–22) and in the most acerbic terms, calling into question whether the form is unilaterally one of endearment and tenderness. Additionally, the metaphor of a youthful maiden invoked by reading the form as an appositional genitive is incongruent with the portrayal of *bat-ṣiyyon* throughout as a mother with many children.

The interpretation of Lamentations offered in this volume well resonates with the understanding of the form as genitive construction, traditionally understood. The people are Zion's daughter and Zion is their mother (cf. Isa 66:10–12; 54:1–4; 66:5–9). Put differently, for the people, the entity of Zion is a mothering, nurturing, protecting entity. This embodies the overreliance on Zion theology that this volume claims Lamentations seeks to challenge and reform.

It may be that as the pastoral mentor oscillates between support and critique of *bat-ṣiyyon*, the author has infused his rhetoric with a polysemous epithet that itself can bear both notes of tenderness and also highlight the overreliance the people had upon its "mother" Zion. So as not to forestall either of these latent meanings, the commentary here has adopted the neutral transliteration Bat-Zion/Bat-Ami.

THE NINE STAGES OF BAT-ZION'S SPIRITUAL
REHABILITATION (VV. 9C–22)

Bat-Zion's Naïve Appeal to the LORD (9c)

In v. 9c, the author has Bat-Zion interrupt the pastoral mentor and utter her first cries of the poem: "Look, O LORD, at my affliction, for the enemy has triumphed!" Cries such as this are de rigueur in the Psalms as expressions of piety (e.g., Pss 9:14; 25:18; 119:153). However, in this literary setting, we need to unpack this first plea relative to the subsequent statements she will make as their exchange unfolds. On the one hand the plea accords with the pastoral mentor's theology – the LORD is her only reliable addressee. But on the other, it falls short of his theology in contrast with the successively fuller theodic expressions she reveals in progression. Closely read, Bat-Zion's exhortation demonstrates a naïve misreading of the theological map on a number of cardinal points. In calling out to the LORD and beseeching him to take notice, she espouses the belief that God is unaware that the enemy has triumphed, and hence her call for him to notice. Moreover, Bat-Zion seems to believe that her woes are caused by the enemies of Israel. She does not recognize that the LORD has stood behind all that has happened.[10] Here Bat-Zion reveals that she does not yet share the pastoral mentor's view, stated in v. 5, that her suffering is "because the LORD has made her suffer for the multitude of her transgressions."

This cry may accurately reflect what some community members believed, namely that the LORD is always available to hear Israel's prayers, even following the destruction of Jerusalem and the temple. Indeed, we find that pilgrims bearing tribute to the LORD continued to converge on Jerusalem, even following the temple's destruction (Jer 41:3–4). But no doubt, for other members of the traumatized sixth-century Judean community it was far from clear whether the covenant is still intact. Many passages in Second Isaiah attest to this latent concern. The people of Zion had felt forgotten and forlorn (Isa 49:14). The LORD insists that although he was available, people did not seek him out (Isa 65:1). Thus, the first lesson that the author wishes to instill through the constructed model Bat-Zion, is that they should believe that the LORD is still her potential redeemer. Thus, the first utterance that we hear modeled from Bat-Zion is a plea to God, an implicit affirmation of the covenant, even in the face of the destruction. "Look, O LORD, at my affliction, for the enemy has triumphed!"

Her plea, then, models what the author hopes will be the first step of spiritual rehabilitation for the survivors of the destruction. He does not initially expect the traumatized community to affirm God's role in the destruction, let alone her own. He strives here only to bring his audience to a recognition that, in their anguish, the LORD is the appropriate addressee for them. In turning to the LORD, the constructed figure of Bat-Zion takes a courageous first step which the pastoral mentor wishes to encourage. Now that she has embarked on a path to seek the LORD's assistance, the pastoral mentor will never again in this poem reproach her or remind her of her sin. Instead, he will encourage her to buy in to the theological interpretation of events that he espoused in vv. 5–9b. The way he will do this throughout their exchange is by restating, and, even, amplifying her own sentiments, thereby validating them. We see this for the first time in v. 10 where the pastoral mentor takes Bat-Zion's reference to

---

[10]   Jacob Klein *Lamentations*, 113, astutely notes that Bat-Zion's call, *rə'ēh YHWH 'et-'anəyî*, echoes the language of salvation at the episode of the burning bush (Exod 3:7), where the LORD declares, "I have observed the misery of my people" (*rā'ōh rā'îtî 'et-'ŏnî 'ammî*). It may be that Bat-Zion invokes that seminal story of salvation, but only mistakenly; her predicament here, the result of her own sins, is unlike that of the enslaved Hebrews.

her "affliction" (*'ānəyî*) and the enemy's triumph in v. 9c and fleshes it out (v. 10a–b): "Enemies have stretched out their hands over all her precious things; she has even seen the nations invade her sanctuary." And in v. 10c, the pastoral mentor goes further: "those whom you forbade to enter your congregation." The statement is heavy with implicit puzzlement, bordering on vexation. His statement in v. 10c is the only one in the entire poem he addresses to the LORD, and it is uttered in the presence of Bat-Zion. Put differently, she sees that when she merely referred to her "afflictions" in v. 9c, the pastoral mentor was able to mirror back to her those afflictions in expanded form, and even expressed vexation over the LORD's actions. He has thus further won over her trust that he is aligned with her and creates a safe space for her to question the LORD's actions as well, without fear of reproach.

Bat-Zion Calls Again to the LORD, Despite His Silence (11c)

The pastoral mentor continues to offer positive reinforcement to Bat-Zion by further detailing her plight in v. 11a–b: "All her people groan as they search for bread; they trade their treasures for food to revive their lives." Here, Bat-Zion interjects for a second time (11c): "Look, O LORD, and see how worthless I have become." The plea of 9c "Look, O LORD," is repeated, but now more emphatically, with the addition of "and see." She intensifies her plea precisely because she received no response to her earlier petition. The pastoral mentor responded to her – but the LORD did not. By setting up the exchange between the pastoral mentor and Bat-Zion in this way the author communicates a lesson for his audience of the post-destruction residents of Judah. They are to follow the lead of Bat-Zion; in their abject state, they are to beseech the LORD – as she did in v. 9c. And even though the LORD will not respond, they are to beseech him yet again. Her petition to the LORD in 11c also entails a theodic progression relative to what she had stated in 9c in another fashion. In v. 9c, Bat-Zion wrongly assigned responsibility and agency for her affliction to the conquering armies. Here, in v. 11c, this mistaken ascription is no longer heard.

Bat-Zion Acknowledges, Yet Criticizes the LORD's Role
in Her Affliction (12–13)

Again receiving no response from the LORD, Bat-Zion turns outward for support in v. 12a–b: "Is it nothing to you, all you who pass by? Look and see."

This plea to the passers-by extends through v. 15b. At no point does the pastoral mentor censure her for this. From the perspective of the author, surely it is only acceptable for her to direct her pleas heavenward, to the LORD. By composing a narrative in which Bat-Zion turns outward for support and yet receives no censure from the pastoral mentor, the author signals to his sixth-century audience tacit understanding that the community feels itself abandoned by the LORD. The author creates this turn to the passers-by as a concession, to open a space for Bat-Zion to work things out for herself. She will need to experiment with finding solace from others. In the end, she will only be ignored; within the poem, the passers-by never do respond. She will need to come to the conclusion that there is no one who can bring her comfort other than the LORD. Turning to the passers-by is a momentary but necessary step away from the LORD, one that ultimately enables her to return to him.

The author allows her latitude in this process, and in v. 12c we witness the next stage of her spiritual gestation: "Look and see if there is any sorrow like my sorrow, which was brought upon me, which the LORD inflicted on the day of his fierce anger." From the perspective of the author's theodic theology there is progress here, but it is only partial. Until now, Bat-Zion had laid the blame for her suffering at the hands of the human enemy (v. 9c). Now, for the first time, she comes to a dual recognition: contrary to what she had enunciated in 9c, she now acknowledges that the LORD was, in fact, present and aware of all that transpired. Moreover, she realizes that her affliction was not really at the hands of the enemy as she had earlier suggested in 9c, but, in fact, was, orchestrated by the LORD himself on the day of his wrath.

Nonetheless, this is only a partial step for Bat-Zion. Her understanding does not fully align with the theodic positions staked out by the pastoral mentor. Notice the tone of v. 12c–d: "Look and see if there is any sorrow like my sorrow, which was brought upon me, *which the LORD inflicted on the day of his fierce anger.*" Even as she recognizes that this affliction is divinely orchestrated, her words reveal vexation, even disdain, while expressing, neither remorse for her actions, nor acceptance of responsibility for the results of those actions. Her accusation is thinly veiled: The destruction has been wrought by the LORD, because of his wrath. Note here how Bat-Zion echoes terms and phrases that appeared earlier in the composition. Her cry, "is any sorrow like my sorrow, which was brought upon me, *which the LORD inflicted on the day of his fierce anger*" (*ʾăšer hôgâ YHWH bəyôm ḥărôn ʾappô*) closely matches the pastoral mentor's casting of her sin

and its consequences in v. 5, "Her foes have become the masters; her enemies prosper *because the* LORD *has made her suffer for the multitude of her
transgressions*" (*kî-YHWH hôgāh ʿal rōb-pəšāʿehā*). Bat-Zion polemically
wrestles with the pastoral mentor. By his account, her suffering stemmed
from divine justice. In v. 12c, however, Bat-Zion appropriates his words
and assigns them a new valence. The LORD indeed afflicted her; but it was
out of his wrath, not because she was worthy of such treatment. Here, too,
Bat-Zion receives no censure from the pastoral mentor and her protest is
tolerated. The author of the poem creates a space for Bat-Zion to express
vexation at the LORD.

In v. 13, Bat-Zion details her charge sheet against the LORD: "From on
high he sent fire; it went deep into my bones; he spread a net for my feet;
he toppled me backwards;[11] he has left me stunned, faint all day long." Here
too, Bat-Zion appropriates language of the pastoral mentor. In v. 10, the
pastoral mentor had said that the *enemy* had spread (*pāraś*) his hand over
her treasured things. Here, Bat-Zion recontextualizes that word and argues
that *the Lord* spread (*pāraś*) a net for her feet; in v. 8 the pastoral mentor had
said that the abuse and disparagement of the enemies caused her to "topple
backwards" (*wattāšāb ʾāḥôr*). Here, Bat-Zion charges that the LORD "toppled me backwards" (*hěšîbanî ʾāḥôr*); the pastoral mentor had said in v. 4
that her gates were desolate (*šəʿārêhā šômēmîn*). Here Bat-Zion charges that
the LORD has brought her to desolation (*nətānanî šômēmâ*). In all three of
these allusions, the pastoral mentor had used specific terms to describe the
cruelty of the enemy. Bat-Zion, in her chagrin, questions the assessment of
the pastoral mentor and repurposes those same terms to describe the wrathful cruelty of the LORD. She recognizes the LORD's full involvement in her
demise, but does not yet confront her own agency in that demise. Here,
too, the poet allows his constructed character Bat-Zion to spar verbally with
the pastoral mentor, yet without censure from him. Allowing Bat-Zion to
draw up and verbalize a charge sheet against the LORD of five afflictive acts
all in the presence of the pastoral mentor, allows her to unload her vexation, and provides her relief. The trauma is mediated through the dialogue.
Through her, sixth-century survivors of the destruction learn that they, too,
can unload their own frustration or vexation with the LORD, as a necessary
step toward their own spiritual rehabilitation.

---

[11]   NRSVue reads "he turned me back." I prefer the language of "toppling" because it well
       conveys the word play between v. 8, *wattāšāb ʾāḥôr* and v. 13, *hěšîbanî ʾāḥôr*.

Bat-Zion Acknowledges Her Guilt, But Deems the Punishment Disproportionate (14–15b)

Having unloaded her charges against the Lord in vv. 12–13, Bat-Zion now exhibits spiritual growth as we move on to v. 14a: "My transgressions were bound into a yoke; by his hand they were fastened together." Bat-Zion now understands that she has agency in what has befallen her: Her own offenses have brought her to this state. Yet, at the same time, her spiritual disposition is not yet fully evolved. She elaborates concerning this yoke, made up of her offenses, in vv. 14 and 15: "They weigh on my neck, sapping my strength; the Lord handed me over to those whom I cannot withstand. The Lord has rejected all my warriors in the midst of me; he proclaimed a time against me to crush my young men." Although Bat-Zion recognizes that she has sinned, she surprisingly does not express contrition. Recall that at this stage in the discourse, she is still appealing – not to the Lord – but in light of his silence, to the passers-by of v. 12a. In these verses, she implores them to witness the Lord's disproportionate punishment for her sins. As Charles Miller notes, she once again redirects the audience's attention back to the words of the figure I am calling the pastoral mentor. He had noted in v. 4a that Bat-Zion was distraught by the failure of anyone to come to the appointed feast (*mibbəlî bāʾê môʿēd*). Here, in v. 15b, however, Bat-Zion underscores that it is the Lord who has called a special time (*môʿēd*) to crush her young men, reusing his words to new purpose.[12] Nonetheless, her words demonstrate spiritual development. In vv. 12–13, she cast the Lord as wrathful and made no mention of her agency. In vv. 14–15, she begins to entertain her responsibility, but still vents anger and consternation over the Lord's harsh sentence. The implicit message to the sixth-century audience is that there is a place for members of the traumatized community to express consternation and vexation with the Lord, even while entering a dawning awareness of their own responsibility for what has befallen them.

Bat-Zion Yearns for Closeness with the Lord (16)

In v. 15c, the pastoral mentor offers a short but powerful interjection: "the Lord has trodden as in a winepress the virgin daughter Judah." Recall that following Bat-Zion's exhortation in v. 9c, the pastoral mentor in v. 10 expressed sentiments that amplified what she had said. The same is true

---

12 Miller, "Reading Voices," 403.

here now. His description of the LORD's wrathful actions in 15c goes farther than did her own charges and indictments. She accused the LORD of acting out of anger, even in excess. By casting the LORD as one who tramples on grapes in the context of an assault upon the virgin daughter Judah, the pastoral mentor accuses the LORD of virgin rape.[13] Note that the pastoral mentor makes no reference to Bat-Zion's sins here. His accusations signal to her that he is on her side, expressing vexation and dismay at least equal to her own. Bat-Zion has now turned to the LORD twice and received no response. She has turned to the passers-by at length, and has received no comfort from their quarter either. She is left to ponder her complete abandonment.

This occasions a shift in her address and focus. In v. 16, she reflects to herself, or, perhaps obliquely, to the pastoral mentor in her presence: "For these things I weep; my eyes flow with tears; for a comforter is far from me, one to revive my courage; my children are desolate, for the enemy has prevailed." With Johan Renkema and Erhard Gerstenberger, I understand the phrase *mənaḥēm mēšîb napšî* to imply the definite article "*the* comforter," (contra to the NRSVue) and that this is a reference to the LORD.[14] As Renkema astutely notes, it is not that the comforter does not exist (as per the mention of "any comforter" in 1:2); it is that he exists but is distant, a description apt for the absent LORD.[15] Here, too, it is instructive to note how Bat-Zion appropriates the imagery and language used earlier by the pastoral mentor. In verse 2, the pastoral mentor had said that Bat-Zion sheds tears at night (*bākô tibkeh*), on account of the fact that her lovers – the nations with which she tried to establish relations – turned on her, leaving her no one to comfort her (*'ên lāh mənaḥēm mikol-'ōhăbehā*). Here in v. 16, Bat-Zion redirects the valence of those words. "For *these* things, I weep" (*bôkîyāh*) – not out of desperation on account of the treachery of her former treaty partners. Rather, she sheds tears over the absence of her true source of comfort (*mənaḥēm*) – the LORD. The pastoral mentor had claimed in v. 11 that her people sigh in starvation, surrendering their precious goods to "revive their lives" (*ləhāšîb nāpeš*). In v. 16b, however, she laments the distance of a comforter, literally translated, "who can revive my life" (*mənaḥēm mēšîb napšî*). This recontextualization of his words suggests a spiritual maturation. She seeks for her "soul to be restored." Physical sustenance is not what

---

13   On rape imagery on Lamentations 1, see Guest, "Hiding Behind," 416–19. Guest overlooks the observation made here.

14   Erhard S. Gerstenberger, *Psalms: Part 2 and Lamentations*, FOTL 15 (Grand Rapids: Eerdmans, 2001), 481; Renkema, *Lamentations*, 172.

15   Renkema, *Lamentations*, 172, following Pss 10:1 and 22:2.

is foremost on her mind, but rather the restoration of her relationship with her true source of sustenance, the LORD. And in the absence of her source of sustenance, her children are left desolate before the enemy (16c).

Bat-Zion has made a great stride here, and it is therefore time once again for the pastoral mentor to intercede by validating and amplifying her sentiments (v. 17): "Zion stretches out her hands, but there is no one to comfort her; the LORD has commanded against Jacob that his neighbors should become his foes; Jerusalem has become a filthy thing among them." We can see how this could have been performed as part of a drama. Bat-Zion, pining for the LORD, appeals with hands raised to the heavens, *kî rāḥaq mimmennî mǝnaḥēm mēšîb napšî* "for the comforter is far from me, one to restore my soul!"[16] As has been his wont throughout the poem, the narrator aligns his sentiments with hers and takes them one step further. She expressed loss at the fact that the LORD is distant and provides no comfort. The pastoral mentor escalates the sentiment: not only is the LORD distant and unwilling to comfort her; indeed, it is he who now orchestrates the neighboring powers to afflict her. The pastoral mentor portrays a painful narrative that Bat-Zion must internalize: Even as the LORD is distant as a source of comfort, he is very much present as a vibrant and powerful force, fundamentally in control of historical events.

Bat-Zion Validates the LORD's Judgment (18)

Like v. 15c before, v. 17 functions as a demarcation that helps delineate the stages of Bat-Zion's spiritual maturation. In v. 14a, Bat-Zion recognized that her afflictions were the result of her offenses. But that recognition nowhere approaches the pained contrition she now expresses in 18a: "The LORD is in the right, for I have rebelled against his word!" William Holladay notes that the norm for referring to the LORD as righteous is in direct address, *ṣaddîq ʾāttâ* as found in Ps 119:137; Ezra 9:15; Neh 9:28; Jer 12:1. But Bat-Zion experiences the LORD's distance, and therefore refers to him in third person, *ṣaddîq-hûʾ*.[17] She no longer expresses questioning consternation concerning the harshness of her punishment as she had in vv. 12–15b. She now understands and accepts that she suffers because of her own offenses and that the treatment that she has received is divinely ordained and entirely just. Nonetheless, her development is not yet complete. Although in v. 18a she

---

[16] Similar gestures are found in Lam 2:19; cf. Exod 9:29; Jer 4:31.
[17] William L. Holladay, "Style, Irony, and Authenticity in Jeremiah," *JBL* 81 (1962): 50.

fully vindicates the LORD's actions, she does not call out to him for support. Perhaps she feels that he is so distant that he will not listen. And so in v. 18b, she again turns outward – as opposed to heavenward – for support: "hear, all you peoples, and behold my suffering; my young women and young men have gone into captivity." Alternatively, we may read that she invites the nations to be witnesses to her confession.[18] Although she had earlier turned to passers-by, there is a subtle change here in her address. In v. 12, she had invited passers-by to "Look and see" (*habbîṭû ûrəʾû*) her affliction. Here in v. 18b, although she again implores the nations to see her affliction, she prefaces this by calling upon them to listen – *šimʿû-nā kol-hāʿammîm*. Strictly speaking, there is no affliction for them to *hear*. Rather, the invitation for them to listen is reminiscent of many biblical passages where individuals or entities are called upon to listen as witnesses (Jer 6:18–19; Deut 32:1; Isa 1:2).

From a rhetorical perspective, v. 18 marks a turning point. We have noted the several occasions in this poem on which Bat-Zion echoed and recontextualized the words of the pastoral mentor as she expressed her vexation with the LORD. However, v. 18 marks a pivot, as she fully validates the divine decree against her. From here on, Bat-Zion no longer repurposes his language to serve new polemic purposes. Rather, as her perspective aligns with his, she will echo the pastoral mentor's words, using them toward the same semantic intentions that he had. Moreover, we will see that she also invokes her own earlier words spoken in vexation with the LORD, but now to express her deepened spiritual awareness. In v. 12, she had spoken of "my sorrow" (*makʾōbî*) as an expression of challenge to the LORD. There she implored the passers-by to judge for themselves whether there could be a sorrow as great as hers, which she attributed to the excessive wrath of the LORD. Here, in v. 18, she again turns to outside observers and asks them to note "my sorrow" (*makʾōbî*). However, this time she does so within the context of acceptance and validation of the divine judgment. The crowning touch of this validation is in her invocation of the pastoral mentor's words in v. 5. The pastoral mentor had stated earlier "the LORD has made her suffer for the multitude of her transgressions; her children have gone away (*hāləkû šəbî*), captives before the foe." For the pastoral mentor, the captivation and exile of her children are the surest signs that Bat-Zion has sinned. She concludes her confession in v. 18 by exclaiming, "my young men and young women have gone into captivity" (*hāləkû baššebî*). By echoing his words from verse 5 at the end of v. 18 in a verse of confession and contrition, Bat-Zion affirms and adopts his position.

---

[18]   Klein, *Lamentations*, 124.

Bat-Zion Concedes the Futility of Turning to Other Nations (19)

Verse 19 carries forth the alignment between Bat-Zion's dawning awareness and the earlier exclamations of the pastoral mentor. The question
that has plagued her throughout – to whom shall she turn for support – is
now resolved positively. The pastoral mentor had suggested that she erred
in turning to other nations – lovers – in covenant. This was stated in v. 2:
"among all her lovers, she has no one to comfort her; all her friends have
dealt treacherously with her; they have become her enemies." In v. 19a, Bat-
Zion now realizes this as well: "I called to my lovers, but they deceived me."
When she states *qārā'tî lam'ahăbay hēmmâ rimmûnî* she is admitting her
folly, and essentially arriving at full semantic agreement with the pastoral
mentor's use of similar language in v.2, *eîn-lāh mǝnahēm mikkol-'ohăbêhā
kol-rē'êhā bāgǝdû bāh*. As Johan Renkema righty notes, none of the nations
respond to Bat-Zion's plea in v. 18b, and thus she concludes that she must
address her petitions to the LORD alone.[19]

Bat-Zion Expresses Her Spiritual Distress (20)

The penultimate stage of Bat-Zion's spiritual maturation begins in v. 20a.
For the third time in the poem she beckons God to notice, but we ought to
notice the change that she has undergone. In vv. 9c and in 11c, she beckoned
God to note her *physical suffering*. Specifically, in v. 11b, the proximate cause
of her beckoning the LORD had been the gnawing hunger her people experienced: "All her people groan as they search for bread; they trade their treasures for food to revive their lives (*lǝhāšîb nāpeš*). Look, O LORD, and see
how worthless I have become." We noted how, at those early stages, she was
not yet capable of the soul searching necessary for proper understanding:
She assigned blame to the nations, and did not yet comprehend her own
responsibility for her afflictions. Now, for a final time, she will call upon the
LORD to see, to take note. Once again, the call to the LORD comes in the
wake of a depiction of hunger in vv. 19b–c: "my priests and elders perished
in the city while seeking food to revive their lives" (*wǝyāšîbû 'et-napšām*).
But unlike in v. 11c, this time her cry to the LORD does not focus upon her
material needs and her starved depredation. Instead, she cries out, "Look,
O LORD, at how distressed I am; my stomach churns; my heart is wrung
within me *because I have been very rebellious*." The distress that she beckons

---

[19]   Renkema, *Lamentations*, 186.

the LORD to note is not primarily her physical distress, as before, but her spiritual distress. Her stomach turns at the thought of her betrayal; she has turned a new heart and seeks to reconnect.[20]

Bat-Zion Calls to Avenge Her Suffering (21–22)

In v. 20c, Bat-Zion cries out, "In the street the sword bereaves; In the house it is like death.," and this cry elicits the final stages of her maturation, beginning in v. 21. In v. 18, she had called to the nations to heed her suffering. But none came to her aid or to offer sympathy. This she now concedes: "They heard how I was groaning, with no one to comfort me. All my enemies heard of my trouble; they are glad that you have done it." Her words, "with no one to comfort me" (*'ên mənaḥēm lî*) aligns her voice with that of the pastoral mentor, who had stated in v. 2, "she has no one to comfort her" (*'ên-lāh mənaḥēm*). Having now realized the futility in finding comfort from the nations, she now calls for vengeance: "Bring on the day you have announced, and let them be as I am."

Some commentators see this as "ugly and repugnant," but nonetheless "a convenient and necessary outlet for the anger and rage that the catastrophe and its attendant suffering ignite."[21] However, we may also view the call for vengeance as the pinnacle of her spiritual maturation in terms of the theological implications it bears. Having spent the better part of her remarks – vv. 12–20 – addressing the passers-by, Bat-Zion concludes that her only true savior is the LORD. He *is* listening, even as he does not immediately respond. Put differently, Bat-Zion's call for vengeance is a constructed avowal that the LORD may still wish to act on Israel's behalf. From here, her final call expresses an affirmation of God's power and does so with an eye to the future, unprecedented within the poem. The enemies, as she points out in v. 21, have the upper hand and exult in it. Nonetheless, she proclaims her faith in the LORD's capacity to effect a reversal of fortunes. We can see how here, too, Bat-Zion revisits language she had used earlier. Words she initially said in criticism of the LORD are now repurposed and uttered in trust of the LORD. When she initially calls for revenge in v. 21d, she does so saying, "Bring on the day that you have announced (*hēbē'tā yôm-qārā'tā*),

---

[20]   On bodily pain and psychological suffering in the Hebrew Bible, see Paul M. Joyce and Diana Lipton, *Lamentations through the Centuries*, WBBCS (Chichester: Wiley-Blackwell, 2013), 59–60.

[21]   Dobbs-Allsopp, *Lamentations*, 73.

and let them be as I am." In doing so, she reverses the semantic intent of the divine proclamation as she had expressed it v. 15a. There, she despaired of the LORD saying, "He proclaimed a time against me (*qārā ʿalay môʿēd*) to crush my young men." The notion of God proclaiming days of judgment is recontextualized from one of rejection of the LORD to one of affirmation of his justice and capacities.

Her conclusion, in v. 22, strikes a theological balance: "Let all their evil doing come before you, and deal with them as you have dealt with me because of all my transgressions." On the one hand, Bat-Zion affirms her belief in the LORD, his power, and his relationship with Israel. Yet, in calling for revenge, she in no way mitigates her own responsibility and acknowledges that she has been the cause of all that has befallen her. Here, again, the reuse of language is telling, and her voice aligns with his. The pastoral mentor had said that destruction had come "because the LORD has made her suffer for the multitude of her transgressions" (*ʿal rōb-pəšāʿêhā*). This onus she now fully owns, claiming, "As you have dealt with me because of all my transgressions" (*ʿal kol-pəšāʿāy*). She further amends her former posture by reassigning the semantic intent of her own earlier language. In v. 12, she had challenged the passers-by to reflect whether "there is any sorrow like my sorrow, which was brought upon me" (*ʾăšer ʿôlal lî*), which the LORD inflicted on the day of his fierce anger. There, she exclaimed these words critically and could not accept the LORD's judgment. Here, Bat-Zion echoes these same terms, but this time in affirmation of the LORD's execution of justice: "and deal with them (*wəʿôlēl lāmô*) as you have dealt with me (*kaʾăšer ʿôlaltā lî*)." Her call for revenge – with all of its attendant theological affirmations – while bearing the onus of her own sins is the ultimate stage of Bat-Zion's spiritual rehabilitation. It is to this posture that the author wishes to advance his suffering audience of sixth-century Judean survivors. He is under no delusion and realizes that continuing misery does not allow for a hopeful end, let alone a happy one. And thus, his constructed figure Bat-Zion reaches this plateau, but only amid deep apprehension (v. 22b–c): "deal with them as you have dealt with me because of all my transgressions; for my groans are many, and my heart is faint."

CONCLUSION

For the traumatized sixth-century Judean audience, grieving on the one hand and spiritually adrift on the other, the path taken by the constructed Bat-Zion could serve as a model to help them navigate through difficult times. The soul-searching necessary to reach the proper theological perspective could not be achieved in one move. Through the agency of his constructed representative, the pastoral mentor, the author nurtures a relationship of confidence building with his audience, through the constructed figure of Bat-Zion. He seeks to guide her through nine progressive stages of awareness. In the first and most elementary stage, she turns to the Lord in v. 9c. Yet she is still incapable of affirming either the Lord's role in her affliction or of hers. In spite of divine silence to her plea, she advances to the second stage by nonetheless turning to the Lord again in v. 11c, and in v. 12c reaches the third stage, when she comprehends that what has stricken her is not the fortitude of the earthly adversary but divine wrath. But the Lord's actions seem harsh to her, and it is only in v. 13a that we are witness to a fourth stage: an understanding that the Lord's wrath is not arbitrary, but a response to her own offenses. To her, his identity seems to be akin to that of the Grim Reaper. She evolves to a fifth stage in v. 16b, where she realizes that God was once, and perhaps, again, could be, a partner, one who comforts her and revives her spirit. Turning to the passers-by has failed to bring her support. That potential to receive divine succor and comfort propels her toward a sixth stage, one of passionate contrition in v. 18a. The seventh stage of spiritual rehabilitation comes in v. 19 as she concedes the futility of appealing to the nations, and that her redemption will come from the Lord alone. The eighth stage of her development arrives in v. 20 when she appeals for the Lord to notice her spiritual desire to reconnect, and not merely to redress her physical needs. Finally, she affirms her faith that in spite of the chaos that surrounds her and with his temple violated, the Lord is an appropriate addressee to mete out justice and avenge her enemies. These are the stages the author wishes to see his audience traverse, as modeled by the figure of Bat-Zion in Lamentations 1, a drama of spiritual rehabilitation.

As noted in the introduction, recent commentary to Lamentations has sought to place its various voices – some theodic and others anti-theodic – on equal footing. Scholars have noted that this reading strategy offers the gendered voice of Bat-Zion a place of pride alongside the male narrator. There is no question that Bat-Zion in Lamentations 1 is one of the most vocal female characters in the Hebrew Bible. Reading her in such a fashion renders this text a highly appealing and useful one for many modern readers.

According to one scholar, the author of Lamentations embodies protest in the female figure of Bat-Zion because, "a woman's voice, according to the cultural code of Lamentations can achieve expressivity but not reflection."[22] However, the interpretation offered here suggests a different take on the gendered role played by Bat-Zion. Bat-Zion emerges as a potential heroine for sixth-century Judeans. Not solely because she launches protest against the LORD, although she is given space to do so. Rather, she emerges as a heroine precisely because she demonstrates the capacity to engage in deep and difficult reflection and to evolve in her understanding of the LORD and her connection with him.

Reading the voices of Lamentations 1 in this hierarchic fashion has several advantages over the more recent readings that place all the voices on equal footing as the voice of the author. These readings admit that they are unable to account for the progression of the dialogue between the narrator and Bat-Zion; why each says what it says at a given juncture. These readings, further, are unable to offer a clear and distinct characterization of the ideology of the two protagonists, as each voices both theodic and anti-theodic sentiments. Reading this chapter as a culture script designed to shape meaning for a traumatized community resolves these issues. What emerges is a carefully scripted evolution in Bat-Zion's theology, with the pastoral mentor as her protagonist as she develops, as he no longer mentions her sins once she embarks on her path, beginning at v. 9c. Finally and most significantly, the reading proposed here allows for the double-voicing, the reverberations of speech from one character to the next to be charted on a steady course: so long as Bat-Zion resists the claims made by the pastoral mentor, she repurposes his words in polemic fashion. Once she adopts his narrative of the destruction, she echoes his language, but now with the same semantic meanings with which he had expressed them. Finally, we see that Bat-Zion herself repurposes her own speech, turning phrases once expressed in consternation at the LORD and using them later as expressions of contrition. Bat-Zion comes to adopt the metanarrative espoused by the pastoral mentor: trauma will be mediated not by setting things right in the world, but by setting things right in the self.

---

[22]   Alan L. Mintz, *Hurban: Responses to Catastrophe in Hebrew Literature* (New York: Columbia University Press, 1984), 6.

2 Dispelling Delusions I: The LORD and His Love for Zion

¹ How the LORD in his anger
　　has humiliated*f* daughter Zion!
He has thrown down from heaven to earth
　　the splendor of Israel;
he has not remembered his footstool
　　in the day of his anger.

² The LORD has destroyed without mercy
　　all the dwellings of Jacob;
in his wrath he has broken down
　　the strongholds of daughter Judah;
he has brought down to the ground in dishonor
　　the kingdom and its rulers.

³ He has cut down in fierce anger
　　all the might of Israel;
he has withdrawn his right hand from them
　　in the face of the enemy;
he has burned like a flaming fire in Jacob,
　　consuming all around.

⁴ He has bent his bow like an enemy,
　　with his right hand set like a foe;
he has killed all those in whom we took pride
　　in the tent of daughter Zion;
he has poured out his fury like fire.

⁵ The LORD has become like an enemy;
　　he has destroyed Israel.
He has destroyed all its palaces,
　　laid in ruins its strongholds,

f　2.1 Meaning of Heb uncertain

50

and multiplied in daughter Judah
    mourning and lamentation.

⁶ He has broken down his booth like a garden;
    he has destroyed his tabernacle;
the LORD has abolished in Zion
    festival and Sabbath
and in his fierce indignation has spurned
    king and priest.

⁷ The LORD has scorned his altar,
    disowned his sanctuary;
he has delivered into the hand of the enemy
    the walls of her palaces;
a clamor was raised in the house of the LORD
    as on a day of festival.

⁸ The LORD determined to lay in ruins
    the wall of daughter Zion;
he stretched the line;
    he did not withhold his hand from destroying;
he caused rampart and wall to lament;
    they languish together.

⁹ Her gates have sunk into the ground;
    he has ruined and broken her bars;
her king and princes are among the nations;
    guidance is no more,
and her prophets obtain
    no vision from the LORD.

¹⁰ The elders of daughter Zion
    sit on the ground in silence;
they have thrown dust on their heads;
    they put on sackcloth;
the young girls of Jerusalem
    have bowed their heads to the ground.

¹¹ My eyes are spent with weeping;
    my stomach churns;
my bile is poured out on the ground
    because of the destruction of my people,[g]

---

[g]   2.11 Heb *the daughter of my people*

because infants and babes faint
in the streets of the city.

¹² They cry to their mothers,
"Where is bread and wine?"
as they faint like the wounded
in the streets of the city,
as their life is poured out
on their mothers' bosoms.

¹³ What can I say for you, to what compare you,
O daughter Jerusalem?
To what can I liken you, that I may comfort you,
O virgin daughter Zion?
For vast as the sea is your ruin;
who can heal you?

¹⁴ Your prophets have seen for you
false and deceptive visions;
they have not exposed your iniquity
to restore your fortunes
but have seen oracles for you
that are false and misleading.

¹⁵ All who pass along the way
clap their hands at you;
they hiss and wag their heads
at daughter Jerusalem:
"Is this the city that was called
the perfection of beauty,
the joy of all the earth?"

¹⁶ All your enemies
open their mouths against you;
they hiss, they gnash their teeth,
they cry: "We have devoured her!
Ah, this is the day we longed for;
at last we have seen it!"

¹⁷ The LORD has done what he purposed;
he has carried out his threat;
as he ordained long ago,
he has demolished without pity;
he has made the enemy rejoice over you
and exalted the might of your foes.

[18] Cry aloud[h] to the LORD!
  O wall of daughter Zion!
Let tears stream down like a torrent
  day and night!
Give yourself no rest,
  your eyes no respite!

[19] Arise, cry out in the night,
  at the beginning of the watches!
Pour out your heart like water
  before the presence of the LORD!
Lift your hands to him
  for the lives of your children,
who faint for hunger
  at the head of every street.

[20] Look, O LORD, and consider!
  To whom have you done this?
Should women eat their offspring,
  the children they have borne?
Should priest and prophet be killed
  in the sanctuary of the LORD?

[21] The young and the old are lying
  on the ground in the streets;
my young women and my young men
  have fallen by the sword;
in the day of your anger you have killed them,
  slaughtering without mercy.

[22] You invited my enemies from all around
  as if for a day of festival;
and on the day of the anger of the LORD,
  no one escaped or survived;
those whom I bore and reared,
  my enemy has destroyed.

INTRODUCTION

Lamentations 2 has long confounded expositors. All agree that it tells of great destruction by the LORD, with a focus on the privations of starvation.

---

[h] 2.18 Cn: Heb *Their heart cried*

All agree that the narrator speaks for most of the chapter (vv. 1–19), with Bat-Zion concluding the chapter with words of bitterness to the Lord (vv. 20–22). The interpretive crux here stems from the fact that the narrator catalogues the destructive acts of the Lord, and yet never mentions Israel's sins. In fact, on one occasion (2:14), the narrator alludes to the role of the false prophets in deluding the people, seemingly removing the burden of guilt from them. This is in stark contrast to Chapter 1, where, as we saw, Zion's sinful past is openly discussed across the entire chapter (Lam 1:5, 8–9, 14, 18, 20, 22). Yet, at the same time, the narrator himself never expresses objection to the Lord's total obliteration of Jerusalem. These ambiguities beg for a nuanced understanding of the religious typology being addressed here.

To identify the community of believers addressed by this chapter, their beliefs and their dispositions, I turn once again to an illustration from the Second World War. In his memoir detailing his experiences at the Mauthausen concentration camp in Austria, Joseph Drexels, a Catholic, reports seeing etched into a wall of a prison cell the words, *Wenn es einen Gott gibt muß er mich um Verzeihung bitten* – "If there is a God, He will have to beg my forgiveness."[1] These words give voice to a precarious religious posture of an inmate oscillating, teetering between two positions. On the one hand, he has witnessed and endured collective mass trauma and unimaginable suffering. His apparently prior assumption that there is a God in this world is no longer a given. But on the other hand, if he is to maintain that God exists, he can no longer conceive of that deity as a benevolent and just God, as he had before. This is a God with whom he can be – indeed, must be – angry. This is a God, whom – if he exists – must be confronted and even held accountable. And thus, the inmate oscillates between two poles or positions: either he will abandon his belief in a God altogether or else he will engage him in vexation and protest.

This, I would claim, is a good devotional profile of the community our author seeks to address and transform in Lamentations 2. This is an audience that believed that the Lord benevolently and unconditionally protects his elected people Israel and his elected temple. These residents of Jerusalem believed that they were serving the Lord. They would swear in his name (Jer 5:2). They claim that they possess his Torah, meaning his teachings, broadly speaking (Jer 8:8). They instilled great faith in their priests, sages, and prophets as conduits toward connection with the Lord and as

---

[1]   Joseph Drexels, *Rückkehr unerwünscht: Joseph Drexels "Reise nach Mauthausen und" der Widerstandskreis Ernst Niekisch*, ed. Wilhelm Raimund Beyer (Stuttgart: Deutsche Verlags-Anstalt, 1978), 124. My thanks to the Collections and Specialist Library of the Mauthausen Memorial for this reference.

agents who lead them in the proper worship of him (Jer 18:18; Ezek 22:26). Moreover, they believed that the LORD would not allow Jerusalem to fall (Jer 5:12; 14:13; 23:17; Ezek 13:1–10; 22:28) and that anyone – such as Jeremiah – who claimed that the LORD would, in fact, destroy Jerusalem was a heretic, as he denied the LORD's special providence for Israel. And therefore, politically, such a person should be deemed a rebel, for he counseled surrender to the Babylonian enemy (Jer 11:21; 23:9; Jer 26:1–24; 38:4).

Finally, these were people who held an abiding belief in the sanctity of Jerusalem and of the temple. This entailed a conviction that the temple vessels that had been carted off to Babylon would be returning soon (Jer 27:16; 28:2–4). And it meant that the buildings of Jerusalem – not just the temple, were collectively the abode of the LORD, and therefore would not be conquered (Jer 7:4). Within this belief system, the LORD is unconditionally benevolent to his elected people Israel and his elected site Jerusalem.

It is therefore no wonder that when Jeremiah prophesizes that the LORD will bring doom, there are people cited as saying (Jer 5:12), "It is not he; neither shall evil come upon us; neither shall we see sword nor famine" (KJV). The God that Jeremiah was portraying was simply one they could not fathom. Jeremiah explicitly calls out their proclivity to misconstrue their relationship with the LORD, perceiving it as much closer and loving than it really was at that point (Jer 3:3–4): "you have the forehead of a prostitute; you refuse to be ashamed. Have you not just now called to me, 'My Father, you are the friend of my youth.'"

In Lamentations 2, the author takes on this mindset – this religious typology. The author seeks to dispel their notions about the LORD and his love for Zion with a diametrically opposite view: The LORD, in fact, is the agent responsible for Jerusalem's immeasurable suffering. He seeks to open the lid on their assumptive world and to shatter it, by exploring – and exploding – their various beliefs about divine providence, Zion, and election. But our author realizes that much like the inmate at Mauthausen who left the inscription of the wall of his cell, the residents of Zion will have a hard time embracing the LORD on the terms that he lays out – as one who can does bring Israel great suffering. They, like the inmate at Mauthausen, will seek to either abandon such a god, or otherwise confront him in anger. There is no option here of dwelling on Israel's sins.[2]

---

[2]   It is instructive to note that in the Psalms, communal laments rarely acknowledge sin as a possible cause for Israel's misery (see Pss 9–10; 42–44; 74; 77; 80; 89; 102; 123; 137). See discussion in Rom-Shiloni, *Voices from the Ruins*, 342.

The author's aim in this chapter is not merely to rebut. His aim is to transform. To rebuke is easy. But to have that rebuke heard and assimilated is an accomplishment that requires great sensitivity and wisdom on the part of the censuring party. To transform his audience, our author must approach this effort with a sympathetic understanding of how the traumatized community will assimilate the shattering of their assumptive world.

Given the theological proclivities I outlined earlier, I proceed to unpack what that assimilation might have looked like. Through his agent, the pastoral mentor, our author will tell them that, in fact, they were not serving the LORD at all; that their priests, sages, and prophets deceptively misrepresented the LORD. He will tell them that the temple's association with the LORD was never a guarantor for its impregnability, let alone for the surrounding structures of Jerusalem. But most importantly, he will dispel their belief in an always protecting and benevolent god. He will tell them that, in fact, the LORD has acted against them with fury and is the agent ultimately responsible for what has befallen them.

That last point in particular – that God is not with them, but against them – is an incredibly difficult notion to assimilate. The book of Jeremiah is a witness to just how difficult it was to convince people of this notion. As noted in the introduction, we should not assume that because their own prophets got everything wrong, they concluded that Jeremiah was right. There is no record in Jeremiah of the people remorsefully approaching him following the destruction and acknowledging the fulfillment of his prophecies. Cognitive dissonance is an incredibly powerful force. The traumatized community could easily adopt a relatively comforting delusion: In reality, our assumptive world was correct – the LORD would not choose to harm Israel or Jerusalem. If the Babylonians destroyed the temple and the city, then it is because they – and possibly their god – prevailed. This would allow them to maintain a belief in a perhaps weakened notion of the LORD, but one that still viewed the LORD as the champion of Zion. However, the notion that, in fact, the LORD had turned on them in the most excessive and cruel fashion would be very difficult to assimilate.

Our author realizes that audiences standing at the precipice of apostasy – here, outright rejection of the LORD – are incapable of hearing rebuke. But our author also realizes that anger can be managed in either destructive or constructive ways. Anger toward God, as a form of spiritual struggle, carries the potential for maladjustment as well as growth.[3] He recognizes what contemporary studies of the psychology of religion have taught us: that anger against God requires resolution. And in the first place, this requires acknowledging and communicating these negative feelings toward God.[4] Protest responses are not simply behavioral expressions of anger toward God. To the extent that protest behaviors reflect assertiveness, autonomy, engagement, or ongoing attempts to process feelings, they can constitute an active coping style.[5] The alternative is that the anger gives way to a process of repression and emotional distancing from God. And so in Lamentations 2, we read of an encounter between the pastoral mentor and Bat-Zion in which he encourages her to embark on a constructive path of expressing her vexation and anger with the LORD.

From the author's perspective, anger at the LORD cannot be the endgame of Israel's spiritual journey in the wake of the destruction, even as it is an ameliorative station along the way. From Chapter 2, the author will move to the account of the *geber* in Chapter 3, where the *geber* speaks about his own experience of anger with the LORD and will suggest to the survivors a more accepting stance.

Structurally, our chapter bears strong similarities to Chapter 1. Here, again, the pastoral mentor opens with a long soliloquy that takes up about half the chapter. And here, too, the purpose of his soliloquy is twofold, as it was in Chapter 1: Through it, the pastoral mentor gains credit with Bat-Zion by expressing empathy. But the soliloquy is also a platform for the author to lay out his interpretation of events. It is a vehicle for him to express the stance he would like Bat-Zion to adopt for herself. Like Chapter 1, this chapter concludes and reaches climax in its last three verses with a speech by Bat-Zion. Many key phrases that we encountered in Chapter 1 are echoed and repurposed here in Chapter 2. Both chapters are arranged as a 22-verse acrostic, and both chapters exhibit a chiastic arrangement that extends through every verse of the chapter.[6]

---

3   Julie J. Exline et al., "Anger toward God: Social-Cognitive Predictors, Prevalence, and Links with Adjustment to Bereavement and Cancer," *Journal of Personality and Social Psychology* 100 (2011): 131.

4   Julie Juola Exline and Alyce Martin, "Anger toward God: A New Frontier in Forgiveness Research," in *Handbook of Forgiveness*, ed. Everett L. Worthington, Jr. (New York: Routledge, 2005), 82.

5   Julie J. Exline, Steven J. Krause, and Karen A. Broer, "Spiritual Struggle among Patients Seeking Treatment for Chronic Headaches: Anger and Protest Behaviors toward God," *Journal of Religion and Health* 55 (2016): 1732.

6   See my study, Joshua Berman, "Criteria for Establishing Chiastic Structure: Lamentations 1 and 2 as Test Cases," *Maarav* 21 (2014): 51–69.

The chapter unfolds in three parts. In vv. 1–12, the pastoral mentor stakes his claim that it is the Lord who is responsible for the destruction. He details the Lord's wrathful acts in a way that demonstrates empathy with her horror as she hears this. In vv. 13–19 – and for the only time in the book – the pastoral mentor expressly turns to Bat-Zion and addresses her. Indeed, these are the verses that are the strongest proof that the narrator of Lamentations is not merely a bystander or a reporter, but one who seeks to guide her. Finally, in vv. 20–22, Bat-Zion responds in an outburst to the Lord.

THE PASTORAL MENTOR REVEALS THE LORD'S WRATHFUL NATURE (VV. 1–12)

In vv. 1–12, the pastoral mentor details the destruction the Lord has wrought. It is the opening move to dispel their belief in an unconditionally loving God. The author employs 27 terms of anger in reference to the Lord's destructive force in vv. 1–8 alone. This contrasts with what we saw in Chapter 1. There, too, the Lord acted in anger, as chronicled in detail by Bat-Zion and by the pastoral mentor in 1:12–15. As Lee notes, it is a regular trope to find in the prophets that God's wrath burns like fire. But this is always depicted as a response to sinful behavior (e.g., Isa 9:18–21; Hos 7:4–7; Jer 5:14).[7] Here, in Chapter 2, no charge is leveled against Bat-Zion and this in a text unrivaled in its detailed and sustained depiction of the Lord's destructive wrath. The point of this chapter is not that Bat-Zion has sinned. The point of the chapter is that Bat-Zion has heretofore harbored a convenient but delusional notion of covenant and election, and must learn to recognize the painful dynamics of his intervention in Zion's affairs.

Following an introductory verse, v. 1, the passage comprises three parts that move geographically from outside of Jerusalem, moving progressively closer to the epicenter of the pain. The first part, vv. 2–5, describes the Lord's destruction of Judah, generally. Moving closer in, the second part, vv. 6–10, details the Lord's destruction of Jerusalem. The third part, vv. 11–12, focuses on the height of suffering: starving children at the bosoms of their mothers.

Throughout, the Lord's destructive anger is marked through a theme relentlessly pursued at every point – the theme of reversal: the contrast between the former realities of glory that were considered normative according to Zion theology, and the new reality where all has been undone.

---

7   Lee, *The Singers of Lamentations*, 138.

At the same time, however, that the pastoral mentor inculcates a new perspective for Bat-Zion to consider, he does this without any of the chiding typically found in Jeremiah. Following the destruction, when the people are suffering, a different tone is the order of the day. Even as the pastoral mentor dispels her theological assumptions, he does so with empathy. He presents the true reality of the Lord's wrath from a standpoint of shock, a standpoint that no doubt would mirror her own.

The Pastoral Mentor's Introduction (1)

The theme of reversal is already evident in the first action attributed to the Lord in v. 1, that in his anger he *humiliated* daughter Zion. The key word, *yāʿîb*, here has generated much discussion, as it is a hapax. The NRSVue here follows those who see it as meaning to humiliate or disparage, as in the Arabic *ʿyb*.[8] Some maintain that it is a *hiphil* form, and is related to *tôʿēbâ*, abomination, and this is how the Aramaic Targum understood the phrase, that the Lord *abhorred* daughter Zion.[9] Others have pointed to the origin of the word as related to cloud, *ʿāb*, and read that the Lord "clouded" daughter Zion, which is to say that he has engulfed her.[10] Whether the Lord "humiliated," "abhorred," or "engulfed," the point here is that he did this to "daughter Zion," using a term of endearment. The self-perception of the survivor community is that they are, as the prophets had told them, endeared to the Lord. The pastoral mentor jarringly awakens them to his interpretation of reality: even the once-beloved can be humiliated/abhorred/engulfed by the Lord of Israel. Yet at the same time, he has couched the statement as an expression of astonishment: "How the Lord in his anger has humiliated daughter Zion!" His shock and bewilderment well express their own dawning recognition that it was, indeed, the Lord who had done this.

In many passages in the Hebrew Bible, God's presence in a cloud is a sign of his merciful presence (Exod 24:15–18; 40:34–38; 1 Kgs 8:10–11).[11] The overturning of Zion theology – their theology – is semantically achieved through an inversion of the trope: God's palpable presence in a cloud is repurposed from one of beneficence to one of disdain and destruction. Reversal of their prior theology continues in v. 1b. What the Lord has

---

[8]   Klein, *Lamentations*, 140.
[9]   Hillers, *Lamentations*, 96; Berlin, *Lamentations*, 66.
[10] Renkema, *Lamentations*, 216.
[11] Salters, *Lamentations*, 112.

thrown down is not merely "Israel," or "sinful Israel," but rather "the splendor of Israel." The clause may refer to the temple, which is described using the same term "splendor" (*tif ārâ*) in Isa 64:10, or to Jerusalem. And the "divine footstool" in v. 1c can likewise refer to the temple or to the ark inside it.[12] Salters astutely points out that *yiśrāēl* cannot refer to the northern kingdom, as that had ceased to exist more than a century earlier. *Tif eret yiśrāēl*, then, he rightly concludes, refers to Israel's storied place.[13]

As with many prophecies, the first verse here functions as a portent of the themes that will arise in the subsequent verses of the composition.[14] The final stich of v. 1 speaks of the acts the LORD has done in "the day of his anger," an inversion of the "Day of YHWH" found in many prophetic books; the ultimate day of salvation becomes one of judgment.[15] The following verses of the soliloquy will amplify all the ways in which this day of the LORD's anger stands in diametric opposition to the salvation the Judean community had come to expect from the LORD on the foretold, "Day of YHWH." The verse presages what we shall see in all the subsequent verses of the soliloquy: a staccato listing of actor-victim phrases – about Israel generally ("splendor of Israel") in vv. 2–5, about Jerusalem and the temple ("did not remember his footstool") in vv. 6–10, and about Bat-Zion, herself, the stand-in for the residents of Jerusalem (the LORD "has humiliated daughter Zion") in vv. 11–12. Finally, we observe in this verse a subtle shifting of verbs from perfect forms that describe a concrete and concluded past ("He has thrown down from heaven to earth the splendor of Israel") to imperfect forms, as in *yā'îb*, which can just as readily be read with a durative sense: He humiliates/abhors/engulfs, and following Salters, I interpret these as ongoing actions.[16] God's "clouding" of Israel – whatever its precise meaning – is a process that is continuing as the pastoral mentor speaks.

The LORD's Destruction of His People Judah (2–5)

The pastoral mentor begins in earnest detailing the destruction of Judah in a way that challenges the delusional theology that perhaps the LORD is not responsible for this catastrophe; perhaps he was overpowered, or

---

12   Lee, *The Singers of Lamentations*, 141.
13   Salters, *Lamentations*, 114.
14   For example, with regard to the place of Isa 1 as the opening chapter of the book, see Brevard S. Childs, *Isaiah*, OTL (Louisville: Westminster John Knox, 2001), 16.
15   Isa 2:1–4:1; Isa 19; Amos 3–5; Jer 4:5–31; Zeph 1:3–3:8; Joel 2:2; Ezek 30:3.
16   Salters, *Lamentations*, 113.

otherwise absent. In this regard, v. 2b contains a particularly striking term. In the NRSVue translation, the phrase *higgîaʿ lāʾāreṣ* is rendered as a *hiphil* verb – "he has brought down to the ground in dishonor the kingdom and its rulers," and this is how Salters understands the phrase.[17] However, the Masoretic Text signals a break (*atnaḥ*) following the word "to the ground." Moreover, the phrase *higgîaʿ lāʾāreṣ* literally translates "he *arrived* on the ground." Jacob Klein correctly parses the verse as follows:

> *in his wrath he has broken down the strongholds of daughter Judah.*
> *He **arrived** on the earth.*
> *He debased the kingdom and its rulers.*[18]

The reading is tantalizing as it is unusual for Scripture to describe the Lord's immanence in such a way (cf. Gen 11:5; 18:21; Exod 3:8). Why does Scripture express the Lord's presence in such anthropomorphic terms at this moment of the obliteration of Judah? Dobbs-Allsopp notes that in the Lamentation Over Ur and in the Lamentation Over Sumer and Ur, Enlil, the high god of the pantheon, decrees the destruction of Ur and several other Mesopotamian cities, thus mandating their respective patron deities of the city to abandon their respective sanctuaries. It is their abandonment that allows their destruction.[19] Seen in this light, our author's emphasis could not be clearer: The destruction of Judah in no way signals the Lord's abandonment of the land because of the decree of another god, or on account of his weakness. In fact, Judah is destroyed, precisely because the Lord is fully present and at work.[20]

Verses 2–5 continue to detail the inversion of the fortune and circumstances Bat-Zion had come to expect and ascribe this inversion to the Lord's activity. The author poetically achieves this by cleverly repurposing a series of terms that elsewhere are aligned semiotically with salvation, but are here inverted. In v.3, the pastoral mentor cries that the Lord has cut down the *qeren*, the "might" of Israel. As Dobbs-Allsopp notes, the

---

[17]   Salters, *Lamentations*, 118.
[18]   Klein, *Lamentations*, 141.
[19]   F. W. Dobbs-Allsopp, *Weep, O Daughter*, 45. The motif of cities or their structures lamenting is common in the Sumerian lamentations. See "Lamentation over the Destruction of Ur," trans. S. N. Kramer, *ANET*, 455–63. See Berlin, *Lamentations*, 75.
[20]   It is interesting to note that in Jeremiah's prophecies against the nations, he depicts the national gods and their idols as having either gone into exile or as having crashed down at the time of destruction (Jer 48:7; 49:3; 50:2; 51:47). See Rom-Shiloni, *Voices from the Ruins*, 309–10.

term *qeren* is normally associated with deliverance (Pss 89:24; 132:17).[21] The LORD's "right hand" is normally synonymous with salvation (Exod 15:6, 12; Ps 89:13; Isa 41:10.)[22] Yet in v. 3, the LORD draws away his protective right hand from before the enemy and even draws the bow with the right hand in v. 4.

These verses also continue the reversal of Day of YHWH imagery. Isaiah had said of Israel's Assyrian foe, "The light of Israel will become a *fire* and his Holy One a *flame*, and it will *burn* and *devour* his thorns and briers in one day (Isa 10:17)." Here in v. 3, these terms are repurposed: "He has *burned* like a *flaming fire* in Jacob, *consuming* all around."[23] Assis notes that Jeremiah had called on the LORD to empty his wrath upon the oppressors of Israel (Jer 10:25), but that here in v. 4, the LORD pours out his fury against Zion.[24] In more beneficent times, God had "multiplied" his blessing (Gen 15:1; 16:10; 26:4; Deut 1:10; 7:13; Isa 51:2). However, in v. 5, he "multiplies" mourning and lamentation.[25]

The LORD's Destruction of His City and Temple (6–10)

If vv. 2–5 upended Bat-Zion's understanding of the election of Israel/Judah, in vv. 6–10, the pastoral mentor challenges and overturns her conception of the LORD's election of Jerusalem and his own temple – the putative symbols of his own greatness. According to v. 6, the LORD has broken down his *own* booth like one would uproot a garden. This opening stich of v. 6 is somewhat ambiguous, and others prefer to read that the temple was like a temporary hut, easily overturned.[26] Not only has he turned against his own symbols in the spatial realm – the temple – but also the celebrations of his rule in the temporal realm, "the LORD has abolished in Zion festival and Sabbath." Moreover, not only have the festivals been abolished, but in v. 7, the pastoral mentor completes the reversal. For the heathen conquerors of his temple, "a clamor was raised in the house of the LORD *as on a day of festival.*" In

---

[21]   Dobbs-Allsopp, *Lamentations*, 82; Salters, *Lamentations*, 120.

[22]   Salters, *Lamentations*, 120. See Pss 16:11; 18:36; 63:9; 118:15; 138:7. Particularly, germane for our context is that the LORD's right hand grants Israel the land; see Pss 44:3; 78:54; 80:16; Zeph 1:18.

[23]   Renkema, *Lamentations*, 228.

[24]   Assis, *Lamentations*, 102.

[25]   Salters, *Lamentations*, 128.

[26]   Klein, *Lamentations*, 146. Dobbs-Allsopp, *Lamentations*, 85, notes that similar imagery comparing destroyed temples to dilapidated booths abandoned after the harvest are found in Mesopotamian laments as well.

a further blow to Bat-Zion's delusion of connectedness to the LORD, the pastoral mentor maintains that the LORD himself is responsible for destroying all agents of connection and communion with him (vv. 6c–7a): "in his fierce indignation [he] has spurned king and priest. The LORD has scorned *his* altar, disowned *his* sanctuary." The progression inward, from Judah (vv. 2–5) to Jerusalem (vv. 6–7), now begins to move directly toward her, and the LORD's agency in her own suffering. In vv. 7–9, he details how the LORD strikes at "*her* palaces" (v. 7); "*her* gates" (v. 8); "*her* bars," "*her* king and princes," and "*her* prophets" (v. 9). From a rhetorical perspective, I note the exquisite semantic reversal pulled off by the author in v. 8. Here, the pastoral mentor says that the LORD extended a plumb line to execute his plans of his destruction. Exegetes have questioned the employ of this image, as the plumb line is used in building as a vertical reference line to ensure a structure is centered. But in the upside-down world of Lamentations 2, a plumb line can be poetically repurposed to engineer a demolition, the "un-building" of the city. The apex of this process of debunking their prior beliefs is in v. 9c, where the pastoral mentor notes there is no instruction – *torah*, in the language of the text – and that her prophets obtain no vision from the LORD. I take this here to be a repudiation of the community's prior beliefs. When the pastoral mentor exclaims "guidance [*torah*] is no more" he refers to the instruction, or *torah* of God the false prophets claimed to possess, as Jeremiah put it (Jer 2:8), "Those who handle the *torah* did not know me," and (8:8), "How can you say, 'We are wise, and the *torah* of the LORD is with us,' when, in fact, the false pen of the scribes has made it into a lie?" The sentiment continues in v. 9c, "and *her* prophets obtain no vision from the LORD." The pastoral mentor here does not bemoan the cessation of prophecy. Rather he empathically describes her stupefied state – she must now reckon with the fact that those in whom she trusted, "*her* prophets" have nothing to offer her. The fact that v. 9c begins "*and* her prophets ..." suggests that when the pastoral mentor exclaims in v. 9b, "*torah* is no more" that this *torah* is likewise of a dubious nature, from the perspective of the pastoral mentor.[27]

---

[27] The semantic matching between "her prophets" and *ḥazôn* here is matched in v. 13 where the root of *ḥazôn* and the term "your prophets" are the focus of the pastoral mentor's attention to false prophecy. The shared semantic field suggests that here as well, the prophets under question are the false prophets. See also the same term "her prophets" in 4:13, where the context similarly suggests the false prophets.

**A CLOSER LOOK: MESOPOTAMIAN LAMENTS AND THE BOOK
OF LAMENTATIONS**

Outside of the Hebrew Bible laments over the destruction of holy cities
and temples are found only in Mesopotamian literature. The early and
classic form of these laments first appeared in the Old Babylonian period
(ca. 2000–1950 BCE). Specimens exist from five Sumerian laments composed in the wake of the destruction of the holy cities and temples of
Sumer following the demise of the Third Dynasty of the kingdom of
Ur. Two of these – the *Lamentation Over Ur* and the *Lamentation Over
Sumer and Ur* – were composed a short time after the fall of the city
when the memory of the destruction was still alive in the consciousness
of the people.[28]

These laments were composed against the backdrop of the restoration and renovation of the destroyed temples in southern Babylon by
the kings of Isin. They hoped to base their authority in the religious
establishment and to prove in the eyes of the masses that they were the
new legitimate rulers of Sumer. According to most scholars, the laments
served a one-off cultic purpose: to appease the wrath of the god during
the period of the removal of the rubble of the old shrine, prior to the
rebuilding of the new temple. Some maintain that these laments were
said following the renovation of the temple and that their purpose was
to ensure that the wrath of the gods would abate and that no further
destruction would ensue.[29]

These laments share many motifs found in the book of Lamentations.
These include the desolation of the highways during occupation and
destruction, mass death by sword, famine during siege, foxes prowling
over ruins, capture of the king and his imprisonment, desecration and
torching of the temples, pillaging of the temple treasury, cessation of the
cult, the cessation of holiday celebration, destruction of the kingdom and
its strongholds, the abuse of elders and priests, and the enslavement of
the masses. Common to both are also issues of ideology. The destruction
is understood as a divine decree that cannot be changed or averted and
the marauding armies are viewed as agents of the gods in fulfilling this

---

[28]   On the former, see Nili Samet, *The Lamentation over the Destruction of Ur*, MC 18 (Winona
      Lake, IN: Eisenbrauns, 2014); on the latter, see Piotr Michalowski, *The Lamentation over
      the Destruction of Sumer and Ur*, MC 1 (Winona Lake, IN: Eisenbrauns), 1989.

[29]   Klein, *Lamentations*, 16.

decree. Gods leave their temples before they are destroyed. Four of the poems in Lamentations end with a plea or a request. The Mesopotamian laments conclude with a plea for the restoration of the temple and resumption of the cult.[30]

These similarities have led some scholars to believe that Lamentations borrows this form from the Sumerian laments.[31] Despite the nearly 1500 years between the destruction of Ur and the destruction of Jerusalem, not to mention the geographic distance between them, these scholars point to a tradition of lament that continues in Mesopotamia into Neo-Assyrian and Neo-Babylonian times, which could have afforded the Israelites exposure to these traditions. Based on the Mesopotamian model of lamenting as the rebuilding of the shrine ensues, some scholars maintain that the poems of Lamentations were written during the preparations for the rebuilding of the Second Temple under Zerubbabel.[32] However, this position has been the subject of challenge. Unlike the Sumerian laments, the poems of Lamentations express no notion of the LORD returning to his temple. Moreover, the elements of protest in Lamentations 1 and 2 are incongruous with the aim of appeasing the wrath of the god by lamenting the destruction of his temple and city, as in the Sumerian laments.

Other scholars entirely dismiss any connection between the Sumerian laments and the book of Lamentations. For these scholars, similarities in content stem from similarity of situation. And while they recognize that these works share common phrases, these are not unique to Lamentations and to Mesopotamian laments, but are, rather, widely found throughout the Bible, particularly in the Torah and in the prophetic literature.[33]

---

[30]   W. C. Gwaltney, Jr., "The Biblical Book of Lamentations in the Context of Near Eastern Lament Literature," in *Scripture in Context II: More Essays on the Comparative Method*, eds. William W. Hallo, James C. Moyer, and Leo G. Perdue (Winona Lake, IN: Eisenbrauns, 1983), 191–211.

[31]   Samuel Noah Kramer, "Lamentation over the Destruction of Nippur," *Eretz Israel* 9 (1969): 90.

[32]   Edward L. Greenstein, "The Book of Lamentations: Response to Destruction or Ritual of Rebuilding?" *Religious Responses to Political Crisis in Jewish and Christian Tradition*, eds. Henning Graf Reventlow and Yair Hoffman, LHBOTS 444 (New York: T&T Clark, 2008), 52–71.

[33]   Thomas F. McDaniel, "The Alleged Sumerian Influence upon Lamentations," *VT* 18 (1968): 198–209.

Indeed, there are significant differences that distinguish them as well. In Lamentations, the destruction is the decision of a single god who abandons his temple out of his own volition. Destruction is punishment for sins of the people, who have abrogated their covenantal obligations. In the Sumerian laments, destruction is the random decision of the gods and predicated on the axiom that earthly kingship must move from city to city; no city can claim eternal rule. The decision is usually against the wishes of the local patron god, who is subordinate to the higher divine power above him, and he must depart his temple, against his wish. The Sumerian laments are usually composed in stanzas and include an antiphon, which suggests that these compositions served a cultic purpose and were recited by a priest and a choir of lamenters. By contrast, Lamentations bears no liturgical or cultic markers, and thus it is hard to determine whether or not these poems were originally composed for cultic or liturgical purposes.

In contrast with the relatively brief poems in Lamentations that are appropriate for public reading, the Sumerian laments are of great length (200–500 lines per poem). These include a narrative portion employing mythic and epic elements, and specifics about the ruling king and the conquering nation. In these works, the earthly events unfolding are of secondary significance relative to the deliberations of the Sumerian gods on high, whose actions, reactions, and feelings at the time of the destruction are noted in great detail.

Critically, the Sumerian laments are purely cultic prayers, offered to the god after he has already returned to his temple that is in the process of restoration, or once it has been rebuilt from its rubble. These prayers are recited only to appease the wrathful god as the rubble of his former temple is removed, or alternatively to ensure that the god will not again abandon his temple in the future. In Lamentations, by contrast, the people are still in desperate straits. Restoration of the people to the land and the rebuilding of the temple are nowhere mentioned and are far off the horizon.

In the final verse of his account, v. 10, the pastoral mentor shifts gears, poetically speaking. Verses 2–9 employ a consistent staccato array of clauses in which the verb of destruction precedes the object of destruction. The subject in nearly all of these clauses is the LORD. In v. 10, the LORD is nowhere mentioned. The focus shifts here in a climactic way to the epicenter of the pain – the people themselves. The pastoral mentor has painted a panoramic interpretation of what has transpired, moving from Judah/Israel (vv. 2–5), to Jerusalem (vv. 6–9), and now finally and ultimately to the very human suffering of Bat-Zion and her starving children. Renkema aptly observes that the verbs in the previous verses are perfects and express what has already transpired. Verse 10 is rendered with imperfect verbs and gives more of a sense of the present state, the consequence. Lee is correct that the action slows down and intensifies.[34] The NRSVue nicely captures this enduring moment: "The elders of daughter Zion sit on the ground in silence; they have thrown dust on their heads; they put on sackcloth; the young women of Jerusalem have bowed their heads to the ground." The verse also gives an overview of the suffering, encapsulating in a merismus the extremes of the spectrum – from the maidens to the elders.[35]

THE PASTORAL MENTOR BREAKS DOWN
IN EMPATHY (VV. 11–12)

Having expressed in awe the destructive acts of the Lord (vv. 1–9) and the crushed state of the people (v. 10), the pastoral mentor himself now succumbs and breaks down and joins the other traumatized mourners on the ground. After 27 clauses in which the consequences of the Lord's fury have been made clear, the pastoral mentor now focuses his attention toward the epicenter of Bat-Zion's inverted world – the starving children at their mother's empty bosoms (vv. 11c–12). The emotional empathy that the pastoral mentor feels toward Bat-Zion is matched in his appropriation of her own expressions of suffering. She had stated in v. 1:20 "my stomach churns," and he now echoes that same phrase, "my stomach churns" (v. 11) in empathy.[36] On the one hand, his account of the Lord's

---

[34]　Lee, *The Singers of Lamentations*, 146.
[35]　Berlin, *Lamentations*, 71.
[36]　Renkema, *Lamentations*, 268, suggests the effusive account here indicates that it is Bat-Zion speaking. However, most expositors, rightly in my opinion, understand that this is the narrator who is speaking. The proof for this is in v. 11b, "my bile is poured out on the ground because of the *destruction of my people*." The NRSVue has done a poor job, though at preserving the original full Hebrew phrase *šeber bat-ʿammî*, which many translations render as "the destruction of the daughter of my people." The phrase "daughter of my people" is a term of endearment often uttered by Jeremiah. Within Lamentations, the construct "daughter-x" is never used by Bat-Zion, but only by the pastoral mentor (1:6; 2:1, 4, 8, 11, 13, 18; 3:48; 4:3, 6, 10, 22).

targeted destruction in vv. 1–10 signals to Bat-Zion that she has misinter-
preted the events that have befallen her. Explicitly, however, the pastoral
mentor's tone over these verses is empathic. He sees the LORD's destructive acts from a victim perspective. He does not lecture her, but rather
shares in her astonishment and bewilderment. Dobbs-Allsopp is correct
that nowhere here do we see any sign of God's experience of injury; his
anger is one-dimensional.[37] The depiction reflects the human experience
of that overwhelming anger. Yet, at the same time, the depiction of the
LORD's anger never explicitly indicts the LORD as behaving excessively in
the way that Bat-Zion had claimed in 1:12.

The empathy he wishes to express and thereby win over her trust reaches
a head, here in vv. 11–12. Verse 12 is the most graphic in the chapter. The
rhetorical focus here is not on starving children, though they are plainly
in view. Rather, it is upon the suffering of the mothers as they vainly try to
nourish them. The word "mother" both opens the verse ("they cry to their
mothers …") and closes it ("… on their mothers' bosoms"). It is not merely
that the children cry out. It is that their mothers are pained at hearing them.
This is all quite deliberate. The author's aim is not to chronicle the LORD's
indiscriminate destructive force and to question its morality. The author's
aim – through his surrogate, the pastoral mentor – is to empathize with
Bat-Zion's anguish and to lead her to express it fully. She is the focus. What
we witness here is not death, but the wrenching process of dying in slow
motion. Throughout 11 verses, the pastoral mentor has described many travesties. Initially, these were expressed in single stich segments, clause after
clause. Verses 11c–12 are the most sustained images the pastoral mentor
paints before us.

Note here the rhetoric of starvation. On the one hand, there is nothing to
eat. Adele Berlin notes that the norm is for scripture to refer to basic food-
stuffs as *dāgān wətîrōš*. However, here, the babies cry for *dāgān wāyayin* –
tîrōš(fresh wine, must)spoils easily, whereas fully fermented wine can be
stored. But now, even the wine has been spent.[38] And yet, strangely, there
is also voracious eating occurring in this chapter at the same time. The
NRSVue reads in v. 2: "The LORD has *destroyed* without mercy all the dwellings of Jacob." But the word *billaʿ* here is better translated as "swallowed up"
(cf. KJV). And in like fashion, the LORD "swallows up" Israel and "swallows
up" all her palaces (2:5). He did not withdraw his hand from "devouring"

---

[37]   Dobbs-Allsopp, *Lamentations*, 81.
[38]   Berlin, *Lamentations*, 72. On wine as a drink for the famished, see 2 Sam 16:2.

(*ballēaʿ* 2:8). The LORD's fire consumed (*ʾākəlâ*) all around (2:3). And so, while the LORD's activities constitute five acts of consumption, swallowing and devouring, small babies cry out for lack of anything at all to eat. The pastoral mentor thereby projects to Bat-Zion that he shares in her vexation with the LORD's conduct.

THE PASTORAL MENTOR APPEALS TO BAT-ZION (VV. 13–19)

The contention that the respective speeches of the pastoral mentor and of Bat-Zion are said in each other's presence, and in response to one another finds its anchor in verses 2:13–19, as here the pastoral mentor addresses Bat-Zion in direct and explicit fashion.

The Conventional Reading: A Call to Pray to the LORD (13–17)

What does the pastoral mentor wish to achieve through this address? With broad consensus, scholars have assessed the purpose of the address in a single fashion, but one, which upon examination is problematic. The consensus reads these verses as an argument to Bat-Zion that she has no one to turn to for comfort other than the LORD.[39] These scholars note that in v. 13 the narrator argues that she has no one to comfort her. From there, in vv. 14–16, the narrator devotes a verse apiece to three parties: in v. 14, the narrator addresses the failure of the false prophets to save Jerusalem; in v. 15, he relates the astonished and mocking reactions of the passers-by to her plight, while in v. 16, he details the taunting celebrations of the conquerors. For the consensus, the narrator introduces these parties to alert Bat-Zion that there are no potential saviors on the horizon: neither the prophets, nor the bystanders, nor the conquerors of Jerusalem will save her.[40] Finally, in v. 18, by this reading, the narrator calls upon Bat-Zion to appeal to the LORD as the sole true source of comfort.

The proposal is attractive, because within the author's own theology, the ideas conveyed are true ones: Bat-Zion truly has no source of comfort other than the LORD, and it behooves her, therefore, to seek him out. However, while the basic sentiment underlying this reading accords with the author's own theology, it is a forced reading when applied to these seven verses. In v. 13, the narrator does not state that the LORD is her only

[39] Dobbs-Allsopp, *Lamentations*, 78; Berlin, *Lamentations*, 73.
[40] Dobbs-Allsopp, *Lamentations*, 78.

source of comfort. In fact, the narrator nowhere mentions the LORD here at all. Moreover, rather than explicitly underscoring that the LORD is her source of comfort (cf. Isa 51:12) the pastoral mentor actually states here that there is *no one* to heal her: "For vast as the sea is your ruin; who can heal you?"

The consensus reads that in vv. 14–16, the narrator details three potential sources of comfort for her – the false prophets, bystanders, and the vanquishers – only to demonstrate with each that they will fail to offer her that comfort. However, this stretches cogency. Did Bat-Zion really need to be reminded that the marauding conquerors of Jerusalem (v. 16) would not serve as comforters? To illustrate with a modern point of reference, did Jewish survivors of the Holocaust need to be reminded that the Nazis would offer them no comfort? The suggestion itself borders on insult and on the absurd. The same is true as well when we consider the passers-by of v. 15 as potential healers. Indeed, in contemporary parlance, one can speak of a passer-by on the street who offers a helping hand as a Good Samaritan. But such an understanding of the bystanders in v. 15 is anachronistic and tone-deaf to the employ of the trope of passers-by at sites of destruction elsewhere in the Bible. At all times, the bystanders serve solely to adumbrate the astonishing nature of a vanquished party's demise. Thus, Jeremiah says with regard to Judah (18:16): "[they make] their land a horror, a thing to be hissed at forever. All who pass by it are horrified and shake their heads." Concerning the fall of Edom, the prophet says (Jer 49:17): "Edom shall become an object of horror; everyone who passes by it will be horrified and will hiss because of all its disasters." And concerning Babylon, the prophet exclaims (Jer 50:13), "everyone who passes by Babylon shall be appalled and hiss because of all her wounds." Moreover, the suggestion that passers-by might provide Zion comfort is improbable from a second standpoint. In contemporary circumstances, a passer-by might indeed help a stranger in need. But that would usually be an individual stranger assisting an individual in distress, or in small parties. But individuals who pass by or through Jerusalem are simply too few in number to bring comfort to a city of traumatized survivors. What need would there be to alert Bat-Zion that random travelers will not offer her salvation and comfort?

However, most problematic for the consensus reading is v. 17. Within the consensus reading, we would expect that after the narrator has claimed that there is no one to comfort her, and has ostensibly demonstrated the futility of seeking out comfort from three potential candidates, he would now, in contrast, highlight the proper address for her to seek comfort – the LORD. Instead, however, in v. 17, the narrator presents the LORD in diametrically opposite fashion: "The LORD has done what he purposed; he has carried out his threat; as he ordained long ago, he has demolished without pity; he has made the enemy rejoice over you and exalted the might of your foes." Casting the LORD as one who demolishes without pity, and who consciously delivers Israel into the hands of her enemies, is to identify him as anything but the source of comfort.

A CLOSER LOOK: THE ORDER OF THE HEBREW ALPHABET

The first four poems of the book of Lamentations are acrostics. Yet while the MT version of Chapter 1 follows the order of the letters familiar to us, with the *'ayin* verse (1:16) preceding the *peh* verse (1:17), in the subsequent three chapters, we find the reverse order: the *peh* verse (or verses, in the case of Chapter 3) precedes the *'ayin* verse. The version of Chapter 1 found in the Dead Sea Scrolls (4QLam) brings the order of verses into line with the subsequent chapters: the *peh* verse precedes the *'ayin* verse.

Epigraphic inscriptions from Iron Age Israel can help us explain the variance between the order of the letters *peh* and *'ayin* found in at least three of the four acrostic chapters of Lamentations and the ordering of *'ayin* before *peh* with which we are familiar today. A common inscription – ubiquitous across the region – is the *abecedary*, an onomatopoeia that connotes an inscription containing solely the letters of the alphabet. Within West Semitic languages employed outside of the land of Israel, such as Ugaritic and Aramaic, the order of the alphabet found in abecedaries is *'ayin–peh*, as found in Ugaritic inscriptions at Tell Ras Shamra on the Syrian coast from ca. 1300 BCE and an eighth century BCE Aramaic inscription at Tell Ḥalaf in northeastern Syria. By contrast, within the land of Israel during the Iron Age, three abecedaries have been found that can be securely dated. These are the 'Izbet Ṣarṭah inscription (ca. 1200 BCE), a potsherd found in an Israelite settlement in Western Samaria; the Kuntillet 'Ajrud inscription, a jar fragment from northeastern Sinai that dates from ca. 800 BCE; and most recently an abecedary inscribed in stone in a tenth century BCE structure at Tel Zayit, just north of Lachish, in Judah. All three of these feature the order *peh–'ayin*.

This may well have been the prevalent, if not dominant order of these letters in Israel during the Iron Age.[41]

In post-exilic inscriptions, however, the order of the letters is always *'ayin–peh* – the order with which we are familiar today. What may have led the *'ayin–peh* order to gain traction with the return of the exiles, and thereafter throughout the period of Persian period Yehud? We know that exiles returning to Judea from Babylon were deeply influenced by the host culture in which they had resided. Their spoken vernacular was Aramaic, not Hebrew. They referred to the months of year using the Babylonian names of the months, rather than the ordinal number of the month as found in the Torah. It is reasonable to surmise that exiled Judeans had adopted the Aramaic alphabet in use in Babylonia and continued to use it in Israel upon their return, even when writing in Hebrew.[42]

If the version of Chapter 1 contained in 4QLam reflects the original composition, then all four acrostics contained in Lamentations – a work of the sixth century BCE – reflect the epigraphic tradition attested by the Iron Age abecedaries. If the MT ordering of the verses in Chapter 1 is true to the original composition, then Lamentations stands as a witness to a period of fluidity in which there were more than one accepted orderings of the letters of the Hebrew alphabet.[43]

A New Proposal: A Call to Reject the False Prophets (13–17)

I propose an alternative interpretation of the narrator's address to Bat-Zion. Following vv. 11–12, Bat-Zion can see that her interlocutor understands her pain and even shares in it. He ascribed all of this misery to the hands of Lord, thereby challenging her most basic premises about the Lord and

---

[41] On these inscriptions and the development of the alphabet, see Aaron Demsky, "Researching Literacy in Ancient Israel – New Approaches and Recent Developments," in *"See, I Will Bring a Scroll Recounting What Befell Me" (Ps 40: 8): Epigraphy and Daily Life from the Bible to the Talmud; Dedicated to the Memory of Professor Hanan Eshel; with 60 Figures*, eds. Esther Eshel and Yigal Levin, JAJSup 12 (Göttingen: Vandenhoeck & Ruprecht, 2014), 89–104.

[42] Mitchell First, "Using the *Pe–Ayin* Order of the Abecedaries of Ancient Israel to Date the Book of Psalms," *JSOT* 38 (2014): 476.

[43] Frank Moore Cross, "Studies in the Structure of Hebrew Verse: The Prosody of Lamentations 1:1–22," in *The Word of the Lord Shall Go Forth: Essays in Honor of David Noel Freedman in Celebration of His Sixtieth Birthday*, eds. Carol L. Myers and M. O'Connor, ASOR Special Volume Series 1 (Winona Lake, IN: Eisenbrauns, 1983), 148.

his relation to her. But how can she know his interpretation of events to be true? How can she know that this wasn't simply the doings of the attacking nations? Perhaps the LORD still views Israel with benevolence but could not prevail. Convincing her of the validity of his epistemology is the purpose of his address to her in vv. 13–17.

This will be a painful process for her, and so in v. 13, the pastoral mentor seeks to earn her emotional trust by giving expression himself to what she surely feels: that her suffering is incomparable (cf. 1:12): "What can I say for you,[44] to what compare you, O daughter Jerusalem? To what can I liken you, that I may comfort you, O virgin daughter Zion? For vast as the sea is your ruin; who can heal you?" Indeed, the notion of comfort is raised here. But the LORD is not mentioned. The only agent interested in comforting her is our pastoral mentor, and he is dismayed that the depths of her suffering are beyond his capacity to comfort.

Close reading of vv. 14–17 reveals that the pastoral mentor seeks to prove the validity of his interpretation of events by demonstrating the error of the false prophets and by proving that the prophets Jeremiah and Ezekiel were correct in their prognostications, down to the details. The climax of his argument will be in v. 17 when he declares, "The LORD has done what he purposed; he has carried out his threat; as he ordained long ago." It is his task in vv. 14–16 to show her that, in fact, this is so. The things the LORD had said "long ago" have indeed transpired.

The pastoral mentor begins in v. 14: "Your prophets have seen for you false and deceptive visions; they have not exposed your iniquity to restore your fortunes but have seen oracles for you that are false and misleading." The consensus view of which I spoke earlier interprets this verse to mean that the prophets will not succeed in comforting her. But the verse does not speak of comfort. Indeed, it speaks of nothing prospectively – what will or will not happen. Rather it speaks entirely to the question of Bat-Zion's epistemology. She had bought into what the prophets were selling – false and deceptive visions. These declared not only that no harm would befall Jerusalem, but that the LORD would not bring harm to Jerusalem (Jer 23:17): "They declare to men who despise Me: 'the LORD has said: 'All shall be well with you'"(NJPS). Their prophecies were in line with the long-standing tradition

---

[44] On the unusual form *mâ-ʾăʿîdēk* Salters, *Lamentations*, 152, rightly points as a parallel to Jer 49:19 where *yōʿîdēnnî* and *kamônî* are set in parallel, where both mean "to what are you comparable?"

of Zion theology that God protects Jerusalem and the Davidic dynasty as found in Pss 2; 46; 48; 76.[45]

There is a deep connection between this verse and the climactic point of his argument in v. 17, when the pastoral mentor says "The LORD has done what he purposed, he has carried out his threat; as he ordained long ago." That claim is general, and it is difficult to say that the pastoral mentor refers to any one prophecy specifically. However, among the prophecies the pastoral mentor has in mind, could be the words of Ezekiel (12:24–25): "For there shall no longer be any *false vision* or flattering divination within the house of Israel. But I the LORD will speak the word that I speak, and it will be fulfilled. It will no longer be delayed, but in your days, O rebellious house, I will speak the word and fulfill it, says the LORD GOD." The Hebrew for "false vision," *ḥăzôn šāwʾ*, closely matches the term the pastoral mentor uses in v. 14: "Your prophets *have seen for you false* and deceptive visions," *ḥāzû lāk šāwʾ*. The pastoral mentor invokes the false prophets here to demonstrate that the theological bearings she adopted from the false prophets are now themselves, "falsified," to use a term from epistemology. The pastoral mentor invokes the prophecy from Ezekiel to demonstrate that Ezekiel was right when he said the LORD will orchestrate events such that the visions of the false prophets will go unfulfilled, and Jerusalem will be sacked.

However, the pastoral mentor knows that he is walking a fine line. Even as he decries the corrosive impact of the false prophets, he is careful to draw blame away from Bat-Zion. Given the enormity of her theological delusion, she is not in a position now to hear about the full extent of her culpability. And hence he speaks of her almost as a victim herself, one who was duped. The false prophets are the ones primarily to blame. The visions they fed you were "deceptive"; the words they fed you were "misleading," or, even as per the NKJV, "delusions." The main issue here is not Bat-Zion's culpability. The pastoral mentor's primary goal is to convince her that she was duped and must now accept his interpretation of events – that the LORD brought on the calamity through which she now suffers.

From here and for reasons that are not initially clear, the pastoral mentor invokes the passers-by, in v. 15: "All who pass along the way clap their hands at you; they hiss and wag their heads at daughter Jerusalem: 'Is this the city that was called the perfection of beauty, the joy of all the earth?'"

45   Renkema, *Lamentations*, 283.

The clapping, hissing, and head-wagging have been alternatively described as expressive of astonishment, horror, and derision, and there may be elements of all these here.[46] But how does this contribute to the pastoral mentor's argument that her previous beliefs were delusional and that the LORD was responsible for her downfall? Adele Berlin astutely notes that the passers-by not only express astonishment, but that the author has projected onto them the Zion theology belief in the inviolability of Jerusalem.[47] The expression that Jerusalem had been "the joy of the earth" is expressed in Ps 48:2–3 [48:1–2 ET]: "Great is the LORD and greatly to be praised in the city of our God. His holy mountain, beautiful in elevation, is the joy of all the earth." Jerusalem is called the perfection of beauty in Ps 50:2: "Out of Zion, the perfection of beauty, God shines forth." Put differently, for the pastoral mentor, the passers-by provide verbal testimony to the fact that the conceptions of old no longer hold. Hearing their testimony, Bat-Zion must let go of the premise that the LORD of Zion always relates to her with benevolence.

However, there is a more profound and textually layered reason for invoking the passers-by at this junction in the chapter, immediately following the critique of the false prophets in v. 14, and here, too, I turn to an intertextual close reading. Verse 15 echoes the words of Jeremiah concerning the misdirection of the false prophets and the catastrophic results it would engender (Jer 18:15–16): "But my people have forgotten me; they burn offerings to a delusion; *they make them stumble*[48] in their ways, in the ancient roads, and have gone into bypaths, not the highway, making their land a horror, a thing to be hissed at forever. All who pass by it are horrified and shake their heads." Reading with the MT, the medieval rabbinic exegete R. David Qimhi understands that the word *wayyakšilûm*, "*they* make them stumble" refers to the council of the false prophets.[49] The consequence of this, Jeremiah had said, is that "passers-by" (ʿôbēr ʿālêhā), will "hiss" (šərîqôt), and will wag their heads" (wəyānîd bərōʾšô). These are the terms that the pastoral mentor employs to describe the passers-by here: "All who pass along (ʿôbrê) the way clap their hands at you; they hiss (šārəqû) and wag their heads (wayyānîʿû rōʾšām)."

---

[46]   See discussions in Renkema, *Lamentations*, 290; Berlin, *Lamentations*, 74.

[47]   Berlin, *Lamentations*, 73.

[48]   This follows the Hebrew, as well as the Greek, Syriac, and Vulgate translations. NRSVue reads here: "they have stumbled."

[49]   Most modern commentators following LXX to read "and they stumbled." See discussion in Jack R. Lundbom, *Jeremiah 1–20: A New Translation with Introduction and Commentary*, in AB 21A (New York: Doubleday, 1999), 822.

Invoking the language of the prophecy in Jeremiah 18 achieves the pastoral mentor's goal. He will state in v. 17 that "the LORD has done what he purposed; he has carried out his threat; as he ordained long ago." Bat-Zion will now be able to judge for herself the veracity of the pastoral mentor's words. Jeremiah had said that the false prophets would lead Jerusalem to stumble so greatly that one day passers-by would hiss and wag their heads in astonishment. The pastoral mentor encourages Bat-Zion to note that this has now come to pass.

Just as the passers-by offered oral testimony that demonstrated the error of Bat-Zion's former beliefs, so, too, do the enemies, in v. 16: "We have *devoured* her! Ah, *this is the day* we longed for; at last we have seen it!" They attest to the inversion of the Day of the LORD. It has now become *their* day. The contrast surrounding feasting and famine continues. While Jerusalemites starve, they "devour." Jacob Klein astutely notes that v. 16a, "All your enemies *open their mouths* against you" (*pāṣû ʿālayik pîhem*) is elsewhere used to describe the devouring of savage animals as in Ps 22:14 [ET 13]: "they open wide their mouths at me (*pāṣû ʿalay pîhem*), like a ravening and roaring lion."

Throughout Lamentations, enemies and foreigners are oft-mentioned but rarely heard (cf. 4:15). Yet in vv. 15–16, Bat-Zion hears from two sets of foreigners, the passers-by in v. 15 and the enemies in v. 16. I have argued that both are constructed to dispel Bat-Zion's rosy version of Zion theology. Upon closer structural inspection of these two verses, we can see that they are designed in parallel as a diptych:

	Verse 15 – Passers By	Verse 16 – Enemies
a	They clap their hands at you— all who pass along the way	They open their mouths at you— all your enemies
b	they hiss and wag their heads at daughter Jerusalem:	they hiss, they gnash their teeth,
c	"Is this the city that was called the perfection of beauty, the joy of all the earth?"	they cry: "We have devoured her! Ah, this is the day we longed for; at last we have seen it!"

I have taken liberties with the NRSVue translation and have adjusted the opening stich of each verse to conform to the syntax of the Hebrew. In each, the depiction opens in the *a* stich with a verbal clause that focuses on a limb (hands; mouth) and its action, followed by the subject (passers-by;

enemies). In each, the *b* stich opens with hissing and the gesture of an additional limb (heads; teeth). In the *c* stich, the foreigner offers an exclamation about the lowly state of Jerusalem.

I noted that v. 15, with its focus trained on the passers-by, alludes to the words of the prophet concerning passers-by in the wake of the destruction in Jer 18:15–16 and represents a fulfillment of that vision. The sacking of Jerusalem, of course, is foretold in many prophetic passages, and v. 16, with its focus trained on the exultation of the enemy, does not resonate semantically with any particular prophecy we possess. The verse does, however, strike quite a parallel with the description of the LORD's furious destruction of Judah and Jerusalem in vv. 1–9. The enemies here in v. 16 exclaim, "We have devoured!" (*billaʿănû*). Earlier in the chapter it was the LORD himself who "devoured" three times in the pastoral mentor's litany (2:2, 5[2x], 8). The enemy gloats here, "Ah, *this is the day* we longed for; at last we have seen it!" This was how the pastoral mentor described the LORD's delivery of Jerusalem into the hands of her enemies (2:7): "he has delivered into the hand of the enemy the walls of her palaces; a clamor was raised in the house of the LORD *as on a day of festival.*" The pastoral mentor wishes Bat-Zion to internalize that when he speaks of "enemies" in 16a, these are nothing but an extension of the power behind them, the enemy that is the LORD himself, who as per 2:3, "has withdrawn his right hand from them in the face of the enemy" and as per 2:4, who "bent his bow like an enemy, with his right hand set like a foe" and in 2:5, "has become like an enemy."

To this point, the pastoral mentor has claimed that there is proof that the destruction was not random, nor truly instigated by Judah's enemies, but rather is a conscious, guided act of God. The first proof (v. 14) is that the false prophets have themselves been proven false, as predicted by Jeremiah. The second (v. 15) is that the astonished abhorrence registered by the passers-by is, too, not only the fulfillment of a prophecy but of a prophecy that said this would be the consequence of following the false prophets. And in the third verse (v. 16), Bat-Zion is called upon to realize that the surface reality of enemies rejoicing at her expense is but a cover for divine activity empowering them in the first place.

This is all tied together in verse 17: "The LORD has done what he purposed, he has carried out his threat; as he ordained long ago, he has demolished without pity; he has made the enemy rejoice over you and exalted the might of your foes." As noted earlier, the verse hardly makes the case that the LORD is now her source of comfort. It goes to great pains to explicitly lay out that he is directing her misery. I demonstrated earlier that v. 15, where the pastoral mentor describes the reactions of the bystanders, was, in fact, a reference to a prophecy against the false prophets, and the same is true of our verse as well. Following an extended reprimand of the false prophets in Jer 23:9–17, the LORD says (Jer 23:20): "The anger of the LORD will not turn back until he has executed and accomplished the intents of his mind." The phrase "executed … intent of his mind" in the Hebrew reads *'ad-'ăśōtô … məzimôt libbô*. These very words are echoed in v. 17a here: The LORD has done what he has purposed, *'āśāh YHWH 'ăšer zāmām*. At first glance, it appears that within Lamentations 2, the false prophets are a focus of a single verse, 2:14. However, our close reading with attention to the prophetic texts it references demonstrates that the mediation on the false prophets here is far more sustained. This is not merely because of the severity of their actions. Rather it is because of the stubborn persistence of their message and its sway over Bat-Zion. The pastoral mentor seeks to wean her away from that hopeful thinking, and thus repeatedly demonstrates its utter error and futility.

The NRSVue renders 17b, "he has carried out his *threat*; as he ordained long ago." The word in question here is *'emrātô*, and the NRSVue is an outlier here, with most translations rendering the term more literally, "his word." However, in the Psalms, the word has the connotation of clarity, purity, and trustworthiness (Pss 12:7; 18:31; 105:19; 119:123; Prov 30:5). This establishes a contrast between the words of the LORD and the words of the false prophets, which were termed in v. 14 "false," "deceptive," and "misleading." The *trustworthy words* that the LORD pronounced are those summarized in the next stich: "he hath thrown down, and hath not pitied" (KJV). These two terms, *hāras* and *lō' hāmāl*, refer to specific prophecies concerning the sacking of Jerusalem. Jeremiah's calling card is that he is to forewarn that the LORD will destroy or throw down (*lahărōs*) (Jer 1:10; cf. 31:28; 42:10). Ezekiel repeatedly warns that the LORD will not pity (*hāmal*) the wicked city (Ezek 5:11; 7:4, 9; 8:18; 9:5, 10).

The Pastoral Mentor Urges Bat-Zion to Express Vexation to the LORD (18–19)

The pastoral mentor has spoken uninterrupted for 17 verses and in vv. 18–19 reaches his denouement by turning to Bat-Zion with a call to action. However, the first two stichs of v. 2:18 have presented commentators with an interpretive crux, resulting in varied understandings of this call. A literal presentation of the Hebrew of these two stichs yields the following:

"*Their heart cries to God / wall of daughter of Zion /* Let tears stream down like a torrent day and night / give yourself no rest / your eyes no respite." To make sense of how these stichs cohere, expositors struggle with four questions:

– Who is the narrator addressing in v. 18a? Does he reflect to himself, or does he speak to Bat-Zion?
– Whose heart is it that cries to the LORD?
– In v. 18b, what or whom is the "wall of Bat-Zion"?
– What is the connection between stich a and stich b?

Some have proposed emendation of the text, but all textual witnesses reflect the Hebrew of the MT. With Johan Renkema, I maintain that the agent whose heart cries out to God is the starving children.[50] These, recall, were the focus of the pastoral mentor's impassionate missive in vv. 11–12. There is also morphological evidence for this reading. The phrase "their heart" is a single word in Hebrew *libbām*, employing the third-person masculine plural possessive suffix – *ām*. This is used four times with regard to the starving children in v. 12 – *ləʾimmōtām* – "to their mother" [2x]; *bəhitʿaṭṭəpām* – "in their faint"; *napšām* – "their soul." When the pastoral mentor urges Bat-Zion to turn to the LORD in vv. 18–19, it is with these miserable children in mind. Indeed, in v. 19, the pastoral mentor explicitly calls upon Bat-Zion to appeal to the LORD on behalf of her young children, and thus it is reasonable to read here in v. 18a that it is they whose heart cries out to the LORD.

Some understand "the wall of Bat-Zion" to mean the LORD himself and that the import of the two stichs taken together is that "their heart cries out to the LORD, the wall of Bat-Zion."[51] However, we have already encountered within our chapter the phrase "wall of Bat-Zion" and it is from that reference that we should take our cue (2:8): "The LORD determined to lay in ruins *the wall of daughter Zion*; he stretched the line; he did not withhold his hand from destroying; he caused *rampart and wall to lament; they languish together*." The mourning wall is an anthropomorphism and refers to those who wail at the wall or in the gates – it is the residents of Jerusalem themselves. And thus, I read v. 18 as a plea to Bat-Zion, or here, "the wall of Bat-Zion": "Their heart cries to the LORD! Wall of daughter Zion – let tears stream down like a torrent day and night; give yourself no rest, your eyes no respite." If the pastoral mentor implores her to do so, it implies that she does

---

50   Renkema, *Lamentations*, 311.
51   Renkema, *Lamentations*, 311; Provan, *Lamentations*, 76.

not now do so of her own accord. It suggests that Bat-Zion has shut down emotionally as a defense mechanism. In *Man's Search for Meaning*, Viktor Frankel observed that in his experience as an inmate at Auschwitz, new arrivals quickly reached a stage of what he calls "emotional death," whereby witnesses to even the most gut-wrenching scenes became inured and incapable of experiencing disgust, horror, or even pity.[52]

Indeed, there is even textual support for this reading. In v. 10, the pastoral mentor said that, "The elders of daughter Zion sit on the ground in silence" (*iddəmû*). It is that silence that the pastoral mentor now wants to break: "Give yourself no rest (lit. 'silence' *tiddōm*), your eyes no respite!"[53] The pastoral mentor wants Bat-Zion to engage her pain: "Let tears stream down like a torrent day and night! Give yourself no rest, your eyes no respite!" Note that in v. 18, the pastoral mentor makes no request that she engage *the* LORD. First, she must engage *herself*, her own pain, rather than continuing to suppress it. For in escaping her pain, she also escapes having to confront the LORD. Only by reengaging her pain, will a path be opened for her to begin engaging the LORD, once again. Indeed, in calling upon her to weep incessantly, the pastoral mentor calls upon her to weep even as he does, as recorded in v. 11, "My eyes are spent with weeping ... because of the destruction of my people, because infants and babes faint in the streets of the city." The pastoral mentor implores her to reconnect with the experience of pain and loss that she herself had registered in Chapter 1, when she attested, (1:16), "*For these things I weep; my eyes flow with tears;* for a comforter is far from me, one to revive my courage; my children are desolate, for the enemy has prevailed."

In v. 19, the pastoral mentor implores Bat-Zion to channel this pain toward an appeal to the LORD on behalf of her children: "Arise, cry out in the night, at the beginning of the watches! Pour out your heart like water before the presence of the LORD! Lift your hands to him for the lives of your children, who faint for hunger at the head of every street." But what sort of an appeal is it? Although some understand it simply as a plea for mercy,[54] the LORD's merciful grace has not been a subject of this chapter. In fact, v. 17 insisted that the LORD tears down and does not pity. Others understand the narrator's call as a

---

[52]   Viktor E. Frankl, *Man's Search for Meaning*, Harold S. Kushner, foreword, Part 1 trans. by
        Ilse Lasch, William J. Winslade, afterword (Boston: Beacon, 2006), 21–22.
[53]   Renkema, *Lamentations*, 319.
[54]   Renkema, *Lamentations*, 309.

plea for her to confess.[55] But Bat-Zion's transgressions have not been a focus in this chapter. In fact, in v. 14, the only verse to explicitly mention Bat-Zion's misdeeds, the pastoral mentor said that Bat-Zion had been duped by the false prophets and that they were to blame for not alerting her to her transgressions. Instead, I note with Todd Linafelt that the narrator appeals to Bat-Zion to reengage her emotions so that she will turn to the Lord *in protest*.[56] I noted at the outset the inmate at Mauthausen who incised the epitaph "if there is a God, he will have to beg me for forgiveness." We explored that inmate's alienation from the Almighty; his previously held image of God as a God of grace and mercy had been shattered by the events he saw and experienced. If he was to affirm the existence of the Lord and his capacity to intervene in events, then the only disposition he was prepared to take was that of protest. The same holds true here. Bat-Zion's delusions that God is always merciful to Israel have now been dispelled by the pastoral mentor. To accept his interpretation of events leaves her, therefore, in a place of anger against the Lord. The author knows that given her reality, only two choices stand before her. She may either abandon the Lord or channel her anger into an engagement of protest. The pastoral mentor seeks to push her toward the latter.

The language of v. 19 does not give a clear indication of what sort of appeal the pastoral mentor has in mind, although some of the terms here, are used elsewhere to imply protest and bitterness. His call to her *rōnnî* simply means "to cry out." But in Ps 88:3, it has the connotation of crying out to the Lord in bitterness and consternation: "let my prayer come before you; incline your ear to my cry" *rinnnātî*. The appellant builds his argument until it concludes in vv. 14–18:

> [14] O Lord, why do you cast me off?
>   Why do you hide your face from me?
> [15] Wretched and close to death from my youth up,
>   I suffer your terrors; I am desperate.
> [16] Your wrath has swept over me;
>   your dread assaults destroy me.
> [17] They surround me like a flood all day long;
>   from all sides they close in on me.
> [18] You have caused friend and neighbor to shun me;
>   my companions are in darkness.

---

[55] Bier, *Perhaps There Is Hope*, 94; Bergant, *Lamentations*, 78.
[56] Linafelt, *Surviving Lamentations*, 56.

The pastoral mentor tells Bat-Zion to *"pour out your heart* like water," and this image, too, can sometimes express a spirit of bitterness, as we find with Hannah (1 Sam 1:15–16): "I have been *pouring out my soul* before the Lord. [16] Do not regard your servant as a worthless woman, for I have been speaking out of my great anxiety and vexation all this time." The pastoral mentor wishes for Bat-Zion to engage her pain and to engage her Lord. But her bitterness leaves no possibility of her beseeching a Lord of mercy, let alone expressing contrition. He is angry with her and she is angry with Him. The idea finds expression in a beautiful semantic apposition in our poem. The Lord had poured out his fury at her "like fire" (2:4). She will seek the moral high ground through the employ of a counterimage – "Pour out your heart *like water*." Our pastoral mentor has urged her to express her bitterness to the Lord, and this she does – with a vengeance – in vv. 20–22.

BAT-ZION'S CHARGE SHEET AGAINST THE LORD (VV. 20–22)

Verses 20–22 are the climax of the chapter. The constructed character of Bat-Zion responds to the pastoral mentor's heeding and approaches the Lord.[57] As this composition is a didactic tool that seeks to forge a new script of meaning for the traumatized community, we need to see these verses not merely as expressions of what survivors of the destruction are thinking and feeling. Rather, we need to consider them as a desideratum; these are the expressions that our author wishes the community to express. He wishes for them to adopt the theology that the Lord, in fact, brought all this upon them. And aware that this is likely to engender anger among some community members, the author constructs Bat-Zion's angry comments as a first step toward a constructive engagement with the Lord. Offering this active coping style to the community provides them standing and a vehicle through which to process feelings, and I read these verses with an eye toward how this is accomplished.

Earlier we saw that many commentators understood the references to the false prophets, the bystanders and the enemies in vv. 14–16 as references to a priori sources of comfort that the narrator believes are unable to deliver.

---

[57] Salters, *Lamentations*, 178, understands that these are the words that the narrator implores Bat-Zion to proclaim. However, most commentators, rightly in my view, understand that change in voice reflects a shift to words said now by Bat-Zion herself.

These commentators interpret vv. 20–22 as a vindication of their position, and see here a plea for mercy to the LORD on behalf of her starving children, or as an attempt to move the LORD to intercede.[58] However, there is no appeal to mercy here; in fact, Bat-Zion makes no request of the LORD at all. Rather, as others have proposed, what she expresses here is best understood as protest.[59]

Her opening claim is a highly pregnant one: "Look, O LORD, and consider! To whom have you *done* this?" The Hebrew word for *done* here is *'ôlaltā*. In assonance, it closely resembles the word for infant, *'ôlēl*, which has appeared twice in this chapter. The first is in v. 11, when the pastoral mentor shares in Bat-Zion's emotional torture "because *infants* (*'ôlel*) and babes faint in the streets of the city." The word appears a second time in v. 19, when the pastoral mentor implores Bat-Zion: "Lift your hands to him for the lives of your *infant* children (*'ôlālayik*)." And it appears for a third time, here in v. 20: "Should women eat their offspring, the children (*'ôlălê*) they have borne?" In short, when she asks in v. 20a "to whom have you done (*'ôlaltā*) this?," she has in mind, first and foremost, the starving children (*'ôlālîm*), and their tormented mothers. In challenging the LORD, Bat-Zion reveals that she has accepted the pastoral mentor's interpretation of events: It truly is the LORD, who is responsible for such unimaginable suffering.

And yet at the same time, we may interpret that Bat-Zion is still clinging to her previous belief in unswerving divine providence and in the LORD's benevolent relationship with Israel. As Adele Berlin rightly notes, Bat-Zion's opening question, "Look, O LORD, and consider! To whom have you done this?" may not refer narrowly to the starving infants and their tormented mothers. Rather, it may be understood as challenging how the LORD could act so toward his own elected people.[60] This interpretation whereby she still clings to her prior beliefs well fits the final stich of the verse: "Should priest and prophet be killed in the sanctuary of the LORD?" She relates to the temple here as a structure unimpacted by Israel's behavior. The temple is the temple *of the* LORD: she apparently still cannot accept that the LORD would allow such atrocities to occur there. Moreover, as Yaakov Klein has rightly noted, she seems to be invoking here the understanding that the temple of the LORD is the ultimate safe sanctuary from judgment and danger (Exod 20:14; 1 Kgs 2:28), this in contrast to what Jeremiah had

---

[58]   Renkema, *Lamentations*, 317–20.
[59]   Linafelt, *Surviving Lamentations*, 56.
[60]   Berlin, *Lamentations*, 77.

warned that the LORD would not allow his temple to become a safe haven for the wicked (Jer 7:10).[61] Further, Bat-Zion challenges the LORD, "Should priest and prophet be killed in the sanctuary of the LORD?" But just who are these prophets? Klein is right when he notes that these were the false prophets that the pastoral mentor disparaged in v. 14.[62] Put differently, it seems that she still puts some stock in these figures as representatives of the LORD and cannot accept that he would do this to those that represent him.

The rhetoric of v. 20 serves to empower Bat-Zion and grant her limited standing. In chapter 1:11, Bat-Zion uttered the statement, "Look O LORD, and see" (*rǝʾēh YHWH wǝhabbîṭâ*), but in a manner that was plaintive and supplicant, appealing to the LORD's mercy: "All her people groan as they search for bread; they trade their treasures for food to revive their lives. Look, O LORD, and see how worthless I have become." The same words now, however, in 2:20a, have been repurposed: Look, O LORD, and consider! To whom have you done this? Should women eat their offspring, the children they have borne? Should priest and prophet be killed in the sanctuary of the LORD?" Here, I would maintain that the NRSVue translation of *habbîṭâ* as "consider" is too restrained and that the phrase is better rendered "Look, O LORD and behold!" Bat-Zion is no longer in a mode of supplication. Rather, she demands of the LORD that he notice and acknowledge what he has done. The rhetorical questions in vv. 20b–20c are further empowering statements. As questions put forth to the LORD, they, too, implicitly, demand a response. The emotion here matches that found on the cell wall at Mauthausen: If this is God's doing, then, he must beg my forgiveness – an insistence that the LORD acknowledge and respond to the justice of her demand.

In v. 21b, the protest intensifies as Bat-Zion moves from rhetorical questioning to outright accusation. Verse 20 had focused on moral and theological outrage. Verse 21 expresses Bat-Zion's personal pain: "*my* young women and *my* young men have fallen by the sword." I read v. 21c slightly differently than the NRSVue translation in greater accord with the accusatory tone of the Hebrew: "You kill in the day of your anger; you slaughter, you show no mercy." The phrase "the day of your anger" harkens back to the opening verse of the chapter, "he has not remembered his footstool *in the day of his anger.*" It highlights the inversion of the trope of the Day of YHWH – now turned against Israel herself. Bat-Zion's terms "*slaughtering without mercy*" brings the theme of eating and devouring to its head. The

---

61   Klein, *Lamentations*, 160.
62   Klein, *Lamentations*, 162.

Hebrew word *ṭābaḥ*, slaughter, often means slaughtering for a festive meal (e.g., 1 Sam 25:11). As we noted earlier, the LORD's destruction of Jerusalem is depicted with several terms of "eating" and "devouring" (2:2–3, 5[2x]), even as Bat-Zion's infants perish from starvation. Bat-Zion's charge sheet in these final verses of Chapter 2 up the ante – mothers consume the flesh of their own children, as the LORD prepares a feast of slaughter.[63]

In the ultimate verse, v. 22, the festive motif continues its reversal: "You invited my enemies from all around as if for a day of festival; and on the day of the anger of the LORD, no one escaped or survived." Bat-Zion had been raised to expect the Day of YHWH as it is found in the prophetic literature – as the day when the LORD would avenge Israel against its heathen enemies. But instead, the LORD takes out his vengeance against Israel. The final strophe brings a crescendo to the entire chapter: "those whom I bore and reared, *my enemy* has destroyed." But just who is her enemy (s.)? It may refer collectively to the invading conquerors. However, in the singular, it may signal that Bat-Zion has resigned herself that the "enemy" is, as the pastoral mentor himself had said, none other than the LORD himself (2:3–4[2x], 5). In vv. 20–22a, Bat-Zion addressed the LORD directly. However, vv. 22b–c are no longer expressed as direct address; she now speaks *about* the LORD, not *to* him: "on the day of the anger of the LORD, no one escaped or survived; those whom I bore and reared, my enemy has destroyed." Dobbs-Allsopp is correct to interpret that the shift rhetorically signals that she slowly turns to walk away.[64] The chapter concludes with Bat-Zion at the precipice: Is she engaging the LORD, albeit in protest – but engaging nonetheless? Or has her anger and despair consumed her, as she distances herself from him?

CONCLUSION

In Chapter 1, the author addressed himself to those who yet harbored some notion that the LORD could indeed punish Zion for her sins, but for whom the suffering engendered by the destruction of Jerusalem was too great. He wished to model for her a path back to connection with the LORD, and therefore the pastoral mentor needed to explore the dynamics of her misdeeds, especially in vv. 5, 8–9. Thematically, Chapter 2 strikes different chords for a different audience, an audience that believed that the LORD's election of

---

[63] Klein, *Lamentations*, 162; Berlin, *Lamentations*, 76.
[64] Dobbs-Allsopp, *Lamentations*, 102.

Zion was unconditional. In Chapter 2, the pastoral mentor scarcely touches on Bat-Zion's responsibility for her downfall, save for a highly oblique reference in v. 14. Here, the pastoral mentor must earn her trust by expressing full empathy with Bat-Zion's pain, even as he stakes his claim that it was the LORD who acted deliberately to bring her downfall. In nearly exclusive fashion, vv. 1–9 portray the LORD as the enemy with only one scant reference to human enemies (v. 4). Dalit Rom-Shiloni notes that the idea that God alone is attacking Israel appears nearly twice as often as the notion that God is sending enemy troops in Jeremiah and five times more often in Ezekiel and that the distribution and extremity of these passages underscores that they are of a polemical nature.[65] The same is true here in Lamentations 2, as the author seeks to dispel any notion that the conquering armies arrived solely on their own accord.

In Chapter 1, where the thematic focus was on reestablishing a connection with the LORD, the author cast the figure of Bat-Zion primarily as an abandoned woman in search of support and comfort. In Chapter 2, the thematic focus shifts to those who have had their assumptive theology shattered and must come to grips with a LORD who destroys. It addresses those community members who may waver between anger at the LORD and abandonment of him altogether. And to represent these traumatized remnants, Bat-Zion is cast as a mother suffering through the starvation of her little children – and whose anger and resentment, therefore, are at a fever pitch. In Chapter 1, the model Bat-Zion progresses from step-to-step digesting and assimilating her own responsibility for her downfall, which paves the way for her to appeal to the LORD (vv. 20–22) in recognition of her culpability. In Chapter 2, Bat-Zion experiences no sense of responsibility. She moves only from a place of alienation from the LORD to one of encounter and protest.

Constructive protest, however, is but a first step toward repairing the relationship between Bat-Zion and the LORD. Ultimately, the anger of protest must reach resolution. It is toward this goal that the author moves forward in Chapter 3.

---

[65]   Rom-Shiloni, *Voices from the Ruins*, 269, 308.

3 Redirecting Zion's Anger: The *Geber* as Model

¹ I am one who has seen affliction
  under the rod of God'sⁱ wrath;
² he has driven and brought me
  into darkness without any light;
³ against me alone he turns his hand,
  again and again, all day long.
⁴ He has made my flesh and my skin waste away;
  he has broken my bones;
⁵ he has besieged and enveloped me
  with bitterness and tribulation;
⁶ he has made me sit in darkness
  like the dead of long ago.
⁷ He has walled me about so that I cannot escape;
  he has put heavy chains on me;
⁸ though I call and cry for help,
  he shuts out my prayer;
⁹ he has blocked my ways with hewn stones;
  he has made my paths crooked.
¹⁰ He is a bear lying in wait for me,
  a lion in hiding;
¹¹ he led me off my way and tore me to pieces;
  he has made me desolate;
¹² he bent his bow and set me
  as a mark for his arrow.
¹³ He shot into my vitals
  the arrows of his quiver;

ⁱ 3.1 Heb *his*

¹⁴ I have become the laughingstock of all my people,
   the object of their taunt songs all day long.
¹⁵ He has filled me with bitterness;
   he has sated me with wormwood.
¹⁶ He has made my teeth grind on gravel;
   he has made me cower in ashes;
¹⁷ my soul is bereft of peace;
   I have forgotten what happiness is;
¹⁸ so I say, "Gone is my glory
   and all that I had hoped for from the Lord."
¹⁹ The thought of my affliction and my homelessness
   is wormwood and gall!
²⁰ My soul continually thinks of it
   and is bowed down within me.
²¹ But this I call to mind,
   and therefore I have hope:
²² The steadfast love of the Lord never ceases,[j]
   his mercies never come to an end;
²³ they are new every morning;
   great is your faithfulness.
²⁴ "The Lord is my portion," says my soul,
   "therefore I will hope in him."
²⁵ The Lord is good to those who wait for him,
   to the soul that seeks him.
²⁶ It is good that one should wait quietly
   for the salvation of the Lord.
²⁷ It is good for one to bear
   the yoke in youth,
²⁸ to sit alone in silence
   when the Lord[k] has imposed it,
²⁹ to put one's mouth to the dust
   (there may yet be hope),
³⁰ to give one's cheek to the smiter
   and be filled with insults.
³¹ For the Lord will not
   reject forever.
³² Although he causes grief, he will have compassion
   according to the abundance of his steadfast love;

---

[j]   3.22 Syr Tg: Heb *Lord, we are not cut off*
[k]   3.28 Heb *he*

³³ for he does not willingly afflict
 or grieve anyone.
³⁴ When all the prisoners of the land
 are crushed under foot,
³⁵ when justice is perverted
 in the presence of the Most High,
³⁶ when one's case is subverted
 —does the LORD not see it?
³⁷ Who can command and have it done,
 if the LORD has not ordained it?
³⁸ Is it not from the mouth of the Most High
 that evil and good come?
³⁹ Why should any who draw breath complain
 about the punishment of their sins?
⁴⁰ Let us test and examine our ways
 and return to the LORD.
⁴¹ Let us lift up our hearts as well as our hands
 to God in heaven.
⁴² We have transgressed and rebelled,
 and you have not forgiven.
⁴³ You have wrapped yourself with anger and pursued us,
 killing without pity;
⁴⁴ you have wrapped yourself with a cloud
 so that no prayer can pass through.
⁴⁵ You have made us filth and rubbish
 among the peoples.
⁴⁶ All our enemies
 have opened their mouths against us;
⁴⁷ panic and pitfall have come upon us,
 devastation and destruction.
⁴⁸ My eyes flow with rivers of tears
 because of the destruction of my people.[l]
⁴⁹ My eyes will flow without ceasing,
 without respite,
⁵⁰ until the LORD from heaven
 looks down and sees.
⁵¹ My eyes cause me grief
 at the fate of all the young women in my city.

---

[l] 3.48 Heb *the daughter of my people*

⁵² Those who were my enemies without cause
    have hunted me like a bird;
⁵³ they flung me alive into a pit
    and hurled stones on me;
⁵⁴ water closed over my head;
    I said, "I am lost."
⁵⁵ I called on your name, O Lᴏʀᴅ,
    from the depths of the pit;
⁵⁶ you heard my plea, "Do not close your ear
    to my cry for help, but give me relief!"
⁵⁷ You came near when I called on you;
    you said, "Do not fear!"
⁵⁸ You have taken up my cause, O Lᴏʀᴅ;
    you have redeemed my life.
⁵⁹ You have seen the wrong done to me, O Lᴏʀᴅ;
    judge my cause.
⁶⁰ You have seen all their malice,
    all their plots against me.
⁶¹ You have heard their taunts, O Lᴏʀᴅ,
    all their plots against me.
⁶² The whispers and murmurs of my assailants
    are against me all day long.
⁶³ Whether they sit or rise—see,
    I am the object of their taunt songs.
⁶⁴ Pay them back for their deeds, O Lᴏʀᴅ,
    according to the work of their hands!
⁶⁵ Give them anguish of heart;
    your curse be on them!
⁶⁶ Pursue them in anger and destroy them
    from under the Lᴏʀᴅ's heavens.

INTRODUCTION

Chapter 3 is the most enigmatic of Lamentations' five poems. The main difficulty stems from the question of the speaker or speakers across its sixty-six verses. Verses 1–21 and vv. 52–66 are said in the first person, although from strikingly different perspectives. The lament in vv. 1–21 is self-reflective meditation on the cruelty of the Lᴏʀᴅ, while vv. 52–66 are a plea to him for salvation from affliction. Verses 22–39 are a manifest of wisdom sayings purporting the righteousness of the Lᴏʀᴅ and the limitations of human understanding. Verses 40–47 are said in the first-person plural and comprise a confession, if one tinged with bitterness. Verses 48–51 comprise the only passage that resembles anything seen in the first two chapters of Lamentations. Here, a first-person singular voice decries the suffering of "Bat-Ami" (v. 48), similar to the cries of the pastoral mentor in 2:11–13.

The interplay of voices, juxtaposing vastly different theological perspectives and foci of content, has naturally spawned a wide range of interpretation. For some, these elements are too disparate to be bridged in a synchronic reading and must be considered a patchwork of liturgical passages that were never intended to be co-joined in the fashion we have before us.[1] However, the acrostic structure of the poem undermines this approach. It seems that for all of its disparate elements, the poem was constructed as unified whole.

The linchpin for any interpretation of Lamentations 3 surrounds the identity and function of the constructed character *haggeber*, who introduces himself to us straight away in v. 1, and whom most expositors see as the voice responsible for, minimally, vv. 1–21 and 52–66. One understanding of the *geber*, already found in rabbinic midrash, sees the afflicted *geber* as personified Israel or Zion.[2] Such personification of Israel is a poetic convention we find in Ps 129:1–3, although there, unlike here, the male sufferer is explicitly identified as a metaphor for Israel. A second opinion sees the *geber* as a concrete individual sufferer, but one whose persona is a fluid personality that vacillates between its manifestation as an individual and its manifestation as the collective Israel. By this reading, the travails the *geber* endures that are detailed in vv. 1–21 and in vv. 52–66 parallel the travails of the community, and thus the *geber* is able to segue to a plural voice in vv. 40–47. This understanding of the *geber* resembles modern interpretations of the suffering servant of Isaiah (Isa 52:13–53:12), where the servant of the LORD is the prophet who brings the LORD's word to the people, and who's life parallels that of the downtrodden and afflicted Israel.[3] However, these interpretations are challenged by the fact that at least at two junctures, the first-person speaker casts himself as distinct

[1] Kraus, *Klagelieder*, 53–59; Claus Westermann, *Lamentations: Issues and Interpretation*, trans. Charles Muenchow (Minneapolis: Fortress, 1994), 168–69, 191–93.
[2] Midr. *Eichah Rabbah* 3:1; Gottwald, *Studies in the Book*, 39–42; Albrektson, *Studies in the Text*, 126–28; Salters, *Lamentations*, 105.
[3] Jill Middlemas, "Did Second Isaiah Write Lamentations III?," *VT* 56 (2006): 505–25; Gordis, *Lamentations*, 170–74. The idea is already found in the medieval commentary of the rabbinic exegete Joseph Ibn Kaspi.

with reference to the community of Zion. In v. 14, the sufferer sets himself apart saying, "I have become the laughingstock of all my people, the object of their taunt songs all day long," and in v. 48, he casts himself as distinct from the people, saying, "My eyes flow with rivers of tears because of the destruction of my people."

For this reason, most expositors interpret the speaker in vv. 1–21 and 52–66 as a lone individual, a member of the people of Zion, but also distinct from them. He portrays his own struggle to relate to the LORD as a model for the traumatized people following the destruction. The narrator here offers many clues through which expositors have tried to determine his identity. Considering that this figure believes that he has the authority to address the people on such weighty theological issues, some scholars have surmised that the *geber* might be Joachin,[4] or a nonspecific Judean king, or a noble.[5] These, however, have few clues internal to the text of Lam 3 to substantiate them.[6]

A popular approach in recent scholarship sees the *geber* as "an every-man": a literary construct of a figure of spiritual dimensions who seeks to draw from the lessons of his own suffering to enlighten a path forward for Zion.[7] Some scholars see here a figure constructed from a template of ideas and phrases from the book of Job.[8] Broadly speaking, the similarity is clear enough: the *geber*, like Job, struggles to understand how God could subject him to such suffering. The parallel is witnessed through a number of linguistic similarities as well. Job himself is referred to by the epitaph *geber* at many junctures (Job 3:3, 23; 4:17; 14:14; 22:2; 33:29; 34:7, 9). Both perceive the LORD's pursuit in terms of being subjected to wild animals (3:10; Job 10:16). Like the *geber*, Job is the target of the LORD's arrows (3:12; Job 16:12–13). The LORD force feeds the protagonist bitter items (3:15; Job 9:18). Like the *geber*, Job decries that the LORD has erected a barrier to his prayer (3:8; Job 3:23). The *geber* is subject to the taunts of his enemies, as Job is (3:14; Job 30:9).

---

4   M. H. Segal, "Lamentations 3" [Hebrew], *Tarbiz* 11, (1939): 1–16; N. W. Porteous, "Jerusalem-Zion: The Growth of a Symbol," in *Verbannung und Heimkehr: Beiträge zur Geschichte und Theologie Israels im 6. und 5. Jahrhundert v.Chr. Festschrift Wilhelm Rudolph zum 70. Geburtstage dargebracht von Freunden und Kollegen,* ed. Armilf Kuschke (Tübingen: Mohr, 1961), 244–45.

5   Renkema, *Lamentations,* 349–51.

6   For an overview of opinions, see Salters, *Lamentations,* 185–86.

7   Dobbs-Allsopp, *Lamentations,* 106–8.

8   Hillers, *Lamentations,* 122–23; Berlin, *Lamentations,* 84–86. The connection to Job is first intimated in Midr. *Eichah Rabbah* 3:1.

Paradoxically, though, the *geber* also enunciates the theology put forth by Job's friends. Like the friends, the *geber* maintains that the pious sufferer must accept the trials and tribulations that the LORD bestows upon him (3:24–27; Job 5:16–18). God is responsible for the suffering, but will eventually bring healing as well (3:32; Job 5:18). Like Job's friends, the *geber* is certain that the LORD would never perpetrate an injustice (3:33–36; Job 8:3). And like Job's friends, the *geber* believes that the bad as well as the good emanates from the LORD (3:38; Job 2:10).[9] The upshot of all these parallels is that the author of Lamentations 3 has crafted his work less with the figure of Job in mind as with his eponymous book as a resource.

Overwhelmingly, however, the clues about the *geber* internal to the text of Lamentations 3 suggest an affinity with the life of Jeremiah. These begin with specific tribulations common to the *geber* and to Jeremiah. Each suffers derision from his fellow countrymen (Lam 3:14; Jer 20:7). Each was hounded and chased (Lam 3:52; Jer 20; 26:8, 24), and in the end was imprisoned in a pit (Lam 3:53; Jer 38:6). In Lam 3:28, the *geber* is given the advice to "sit alone" *bādād*, as does the prophet (Jer 15:17). Moreover, the range of genres employed by each is remarkably similar. Thus, we find in both works individual expression of affliction caused by enemy and the LORD (Lam 3:1–20, 52–65; cf. Jer 15:10–21), and communal expression of penitence (Lam 3:40–42; cf. Jer 14:7, 20) and of pain (Lam 3:42–47; cf. Jer 14:8–9, 18– 22).[10] Jeremiah employs the personal lament more than any other prophet (Jer 4:10; 6:10–11; 11:18–20; 12:1–4; 15:10, 15–18).[11] The *geber* pines over Jerusalem in terms practically lifted from the text of Jeremiah. The *geber* exclaims "My eyes flow (*tērad ʿênî*) with rivers of tears because of the destruction of my people (*ʿal-šeber bat-ʿammî*). My eyes will flow without ceasing (*wəlōʾ tidmeh*), without respite" (Lam 3:48–49). These words well fulfill what the prophet was told (Jer 14:17): "You shall say to them this word: Let my eyes run down with tears night and day, and let them not cease (*tēradnâ ʿênay dimʿâ laylâ wəyômām wəʾal-tidmênâ*), for the virgin daughter of my people (*bat-ʿammî*) is struck down with a crushing blow (*šeber*), with a very grievous wound." The trope of the righteous

---

9 Berlin, *Lamentations*, 85–86; Klein, *Lamentations*, 211–14.
10 Mark Boda, "The Priceless Gain of Penitence: From Communal Lament to Penitential Prayer in the 'Exilic' Liturgy of Israel," *HBT* 25 (2003): 65. A comprehensive table of linguistic parallels between Lamentations and Jeremiah is available in Gabriel H. Cohn, *Studies in the Five Megillot* [Hebrew] (Jerusalem: The Jewish Agency for Israel – Eliner Library, 2006), 175–84.
11 Lee, *The Singers of Lamentations*, 167.

sufferer who absorbs abusive taunts is oft found in the Hebrew Bible (e.g., Job 12:4; Pss 69: 8–10; 119:25), but the linguistic parallel of Lam 3:14 to Jeremiah 20:7 is striking. The *geber* says, "I have become the laughingstock of all my people (*hāyîtî śəḥōq ləkol-ʿammî*), the object of their taunt songs all day long (*nəgînātām kol-hayyôm*)," as much as the prophet in Jeremiah laments, "I have become a laughingstock all day long; everyone mocks me (*hāyîtî liśḥôq kol-hayyôm*)."

For some, these parallels are proof positive that the *geber*, and indeed, the author of the poem, is none other than Jeremiah himself.[12] For others, the author of Lamentations 3 marshals the persona of Jeremiah as a model of how to handle disaster.[13] We cannot determine with certainty the author responsible for Lamentations 3. We can, however, determine the impression that the constructed figure of the *geber* imprints upon the readers or listeners of this work. These audiences would have understood that the *geber* speaks to them with the authority of a figure like Jeremiah. To be sure, not all of the details that the *geber* shares about his travails align neatly with what is known about the prophet Jeremiah from his eponymous book. Some, in fact, align more neatly with the tribulations ascribed to the figure of Job.

With all this in mind, I construe the figure of the *geber* and the pivotal role he plays in this chapter as follows: the *geber* of Lamentations 3 is the same speaker as the constructed narrator of Chapters 1 and 2, the figure that I have called the pastoral mentor.[14] In Chapter 3, the pastoral mentor picks up where Chapter 2 left off. There, as we saw, the pastoral mentor had encouraged Bat-Zion to channel her anger constructively and appeal to the LORD (2:18–19). Bat-Zion indeed addressed the LORD, but more in confrontation and imprecation than in appeal. She is unable to overcome her resentment for what she now understands is what the LORD has done to her. This is where the pastoral mentor now steps in – to attempt to take her beyond her resentment.

Here in Chapter 3, he will share his own experiences of suffering and consternation with the LORD (vv. 1–18) and model for her how he himself overcame these feelings and reoriented himself toward the LORD (vv. 22–39). This culminates with his call to her to follow suit (vv. 40–41). In Chapters 1 and 2, he had appealed to her as mentor to mentee, from a position situated

---

[12] Among medieval commentators, these include Rashi and Ibn Ezra in their respective commentaries to 3:1. See also Wiesmann, *Die Klagelieder*, 44–84.

[13] Gottwald, *Studies in the Book*, 37–46.

[14] The position that the speaker here is the same as the narrator of chs. 1 and 2 is proposed as well in Provan, *Lamentations*, 80–81; House, *Lamentations*, 404–8.

as a distinct other. In vv. 3:40–41, however, he shall call to her from within, using a plural and hence inclusive voice: "Let us test and examine our ways and return to the Lord. Let us lift up our hearts as well as our hands to God in heaven." However, as we shall see, Bat-Zion accedes to his call only half-heartedly and rejects the model he had adduced from his own bitter experience with the Lord (vv. 42–47). The pastoral mentor laments her inability to see things as he does (vv. 48–51) and realizes he must tack in a different direction if he is to reach her. He goes on to repudiate virtually every point he had made in his earlier exhortation of vv. 21–39 and crafts a lament (vv. 52–66) tailored to address the spirit and the woes that she had detailed (vv. 42–47) in her rejoinder of his earlier position.

THE PASTORAL MENTOR'S PERSONAL VEXATION WITH THE LORD (VV. 1–20)

In the opening soliloquy of Chapter 3, the pastoral mentor details his suffering at the hands of an unnamed jailer, who only in v. 19 is identified explicitly as the Lord himself. But more than just despair, the pastoral mentor here vents vexation. We hear in his voice profound chagrin that the Lord does not relate to him as he should. The pastoral mentor expects that the Lord will protect him, and instead the Lord is his adversary. To be sure, his torture is perpetrated by unmentioned human agents. But the human perception is that it is the Lord who is responsible. The theological stance is well expressed by the testimony of a survivor of the Treblinka extermination camp following the Second World War: "I expect a great many people like myself felt at the time of their suffering that God was doing it to them. When we suffer pain, we're all ego and self-centered. When it's happening to you, you think God must be right there and He is responsible."[15]

The constructed figure of the pastoral mentor shares his vexation in order to earn credit with Bat-Zion. From a thematic perspective, the disillusionment he expresses parallels the theological shock of Bat-Zion in Chapter 2. There, we noted that the people had bought into Zion theology. The Lord had chosen Zion the place and Israel the people, and could therefore be counted upon for deliverance and protection. We noted there that over the first ten verses of Chapter 2, the pastoral mentor not only details the Lord's

[15]   Reeve Robert Brenner, *Faith and Doubt of Holocaust Survivors* (New York: Free Press, 1980), 127.

hand in Jerusalem's downfall, but expresses this in a fashion that underscores just how contrary this was to Bat-Zion's expectations. The pastoral mentor moves to the fore at the opening of Chapter 3 to earn her trust and credit by demonstrating that he knows just what she is experiencing, for he experienced the same vexation himself.

That the author wishes us to read Chapter 3 as a direct continuation of Chapter 2 is evident from the poetic structure of the pastoral mentor's soliloquy in vv. 1–18. We noted that in Chapter 2, the author details God's wrathful hand in a relentless sequence of some two dozen clauses of destruction, usually verbal clauses of divine actor and human victim. The same is true in the pastoral mentor's missive in 3:1–18, where the LORD's destructive hand is likewise portrayed through a litany of some two dozen clauses, most of them likewise detailing the divine actor and the human victim. Just as Zion's sin is nowhere mentioned in 2:1–10, so, too, the pastoral mentor in 3:1–18 nowhere contemplates that his predicament stems from sin.

Verse 1 forms a bridge with several connections back to Chapter 2. The pastoral mentor, who self-identifies here as "the *geber*" – a righteous follower of the LORD (Pss 34:9; 37:23; 40:5) – says that he has seen the affliction of the LORD's wrathful rod. This may simply refer to the tribulations he details in the following verses. But the term "have seen affliction" (*rā'â 'ŏnî*) is a pregnant one. After all, it was Bat-Zion, in her very first words in the book, who exclaimed (1:9), "Look, O LORD, at my affliction, (*rə'ēh YHWH 'et-'onəyî*) for the enemy has triumphed!" Her expectation was that the LORD would respond, but as we saw, her call was met only with divine silence. When the pastoral mentor underscores that *he* "has seen the affliction" of God's rod, he implicitly expresses his vexation that he seems to be the only one noticing her affliction, to the LORD's exclusion.[16] Moreover, it was Bat-Zion who had called upon the LORD using the verb *rə'ēh* at the conclusion of Chapter 2 (2:20): "Look, O LORD, and consider! To whom have you done this? Should women eat their offspring, the children they have borne? Should priest and prophet be killed in the sanctuary of the LORD?" Her call is met with divine silence and the text of Lamentations moves on to the opening verse of Chapter 3, where the pastoral mentor intimates that

16   Wilhelm Rudolph, *Das Buch Ruth, Das Hohe Lied, Die Klagelieder*, in KAT XVII 1–3 (Gütersloh: Mohn, 1962), 235; Renate Brandscheidt, *Gotteszorn und Menschenleid: Die Gerichtsklage des leidenden Gerechten in Klgl* 3, TTS 41 (Trier: Paulinus-Verlag, 1983), 71; Renkema, *Lamentations*, 353.

he is there for her – *he* has seen the affliction the LORD has wrought.[17] As Dobbs-Allsopp notes, elsewhere in the Hebrew Bible, it is only the LORD who "sees affliction" (*rō'eh 'onî* - Exod 3:7; 4:31; Job 10:15; Pss 9:13; 31:7), but here, the LORD, seemingly, sees no more.[18] The "affliction" that only the pastoral mentor "sees," affliction whose source is the LORD himself, launches a theme that will carry us throughout vv. 1–18: Expectations of the LORD are dashed, and his behavior is contrary to expectation. His experience mirrors that of Bat-Zion in Chapter 2, who had held fast to a belief in the salvific grace offered by Zion theology, only to witness the LORD acting in a diametrically contrary manner. The pastoral mentor signals to Bat-Zion that he is intimately familiar with the vexation she experiences with the LORD by invoking the word *'ebrātô* in v. 1: "the rod of *God's wrath.*" This same term is used and in the same form near the outset of the portrayal of the LORD's acts of destruction in 2:2: "in *his wrath* he has broken down the strongholds of daughter Judah."

The *rod* (*šēbeṭ*) of his wrath, is, likewise, an image that conveys the vexation of the LORD acting counter to expectations and initiates what will be a recurring theme in this soliloquy: the inversion of the metaphor of the LORD as shepherd. The rod in Ps 23:4 offers comfort, and the psalmist sees himself under the LORD's pastoral care (cf. Ps 23:4; Ezek 20:37; Mic 7:14). In our verse, however, the pastoral mentor suffers the blows of that rod, which now becomes the rod of discipline (cf. Job 9:34; 21:9; Ps 89:32; Isa 10:5).[19] Inversion of the shepherding imagery continues in v. 2. The pastoral mentor charges, "he has *driven* (*nāhag*) and *brought* (*wayyōlak*) me into darkness without any light." The term *nāhag* as the shepherd's driving of the sheep is found in Gen 31:18, Exod 3:1; 1 Sam 23:5; Isa 11:6; Job 24:3 and together with the verb *hālak* in Isa 63:13–14. For the pastoral mentor, the divine shepherd who should be driving his faithful flock toward nourishing pastures (Ps 23:2–3) and guiding the pious through darkness (23:4) instead drives him to a dark abyss. The NRSVue reads the end of the verse *ḥōšek walō'-'ôr*, "into darkness without any light," but grammatically preferable and adopted widely is the translation found in the New King James Version, "in darkness and not in light." Rendered thus, the stich draws our attention to the theme of the LORD's beneficent behavior inverted.

[17] Lee, *The Singers of Lamentations*, 169.
[18] Dobbs-Allsopp, *Lamentations*, 111. See similarly Gen 29:32; 31:42; 1 Sam 1:11; Ps 9:14.
[19] Pierre J. P. Van Hecke, "Lamentations 3, 1–6: An Anti-Psalm 23," *SJOT* 16 (2002): 268–69.

Verse 4 continues the twin themes of expectations of the LORD reversed in general terms, and the inversion of the divine shepherd trope in particular. "Flesh" and "bones" elsewhere are conduits of divine grace, as in Ps 34:20–21[ET 19–20], "Many are the afflictions of the righteous, but the LORD rescues them from them all. He keeps all their bones; not one of them will be broken." And with regard to flesh, Job 10:11–12: "You clothed me with skin and flesh and knit me together with bones and sinews. You have granted me life and steadfast love." Here, however, the LORD lays waste to the pastoral mentor's flesh and bones: "He has made my flesh and my skin waste away; he has broken my bones." Moreover, the LORD as divine shepherd cares for the broken bones of his sheep (Ezek 34:16), and bad shepherds are those who fail to do so (Ezek 34:4; Zach 11:16). In v. 2:9, the LORD broke (*šibbar*) the bars of Zion's gates, and here, he likewise breaks (*šibbar*) the bones of the pastoral mentor.

Verse 6 continues these themes. In Psalm 23, the pious poet is able to walk through dark valleys guided by the LORD, whose goodness and mercy will allow him to dwell (*wəšabtî*) for the rest of his life. In v. 3:6, however, the LORD himself forces the pastoral mentor to dwell *hôšîbanî* in darkness.[20] Elsewhere in the Psalms (113:8), we find the LORD providing for the pious by seating them (*ləhôšîbî*) with the princes of the people. In v. 7, the LORD walls him in, or literally "fences" him in (*gādar baʿădî*). This, too, is a term that elsewhere connotes the protective measures a shepherd takes to fence in his sheep (Zeph 2:6; cf. Num 32:16), and generally, the terms *bānâ*, "to build up" and *gādar*, "fence in," have providential meanings in Amos 9:11.

In verse 8, the pastoral mentor claims that when he cries out to the LORD, his prayer is stopped-up, or shut out (*śātam təfillātî*). The pastoral mentor then is "boxed in" not only from all sides, but figuratively from above as well. Calling out to the LORD (*zāʿaq*) and crying out to him (*šāwaʿ*) are elsewhere actions that draw divine response and salvation (Pss 18:5–7; 22:6; 30:3–4; 34:16; 107:13–14; 145:19). Here, those expectations are dashed. It isn't merely that the LORD has not heard his call, *lōʾ šāmaʿ* (as per Amos 5:23). Here, the LORD *blocks* prayer; stops it up. In v. 9, the term "fencing in" is again used as a term of persecution rather than a term of salvation. Elsewhere, the LORD watches protectively over the pathways of the supplicant (Pss 119:105; 142:4), but here, "he has made my paths crooked." Protective shepherds shield their sheep from lions and bears (1 Sam 17:34–35; Amos 5:19; cf. Ezek 34:5; cf.

---

[20]   Van Hecke, "Lamentations," 271.

Ps 22:22). But in v. 10, the pastoral prophet sees the LORD himself as the lion and the bear, stalking him out as prey.

A stark parallel to the fate of Zion in Chapter 2 is seen in vv. 12–13. "He bent his bow" (*dārak qaštô*) at the beginning of v. 12 is the same phrase that we find in 2:4, "He has bent his bow (*dārak qaštô*) like an enemy, with his right hand set like a foe." That the pastoral mentor has become a laughing-stock among his people and an object of their taunts aligns his own experience with that of Bat-Zion in Chapter 2, who likewise suffered taunts and jeers by the enemies and the passers-by in 2:15–16.

In 3:15, the verbs "filled" and "sated" are deliberately misused; one is not filled with bitterness, nor sated with wormwood. The normal expectation of the LORD is that through the language of "filling" *śābēaʿ* he will nourish the pious (Jer 31:14; Pss 65:5; 81:17; 107:9; Isa 58:10–11), and through the language of *rāwâ* sate them as well, as found in the image of the LORD as shepherd in Ps 23:5 (cf. Pss 36:9; 66:12; 132:15; 136:25). Thus, the pastoral mentor's experience of debasement matches that of Zion in 2:15–16.

In v. 17, the pastoral mentor reaches the nadir of his despair. This difficult verse has engendered multiple renderings. NRSVue, like many translations, renders the first stich of the verse, "my soul is bereft of peace," an understanding already found in the Aramaic Targum. However, this is syntactically problematic and requires the revocalization of the verb to a third-person feminine passive. Moreover, every occurrence of the verb *zānaḥ* in the Hebrew Bible refers to abandonment by God (e.g., Lam 2:7; Pss 44:10; 60:3), and the verb is never used to connote that an entity is "bereft" of something, as proposed by the NRSVue translation.[21] It is therefore preferable to read the verb as a second-person masculine, as does the New King James Verions: "You have moved my soul far from peace", just the opposite of what the Psalmist expresses using these very terms, "He has redeemed my soul in peace" (NKJV Ps 55:19[ET 18]).[22] Many expositors have been reluctant to translate the stich in this fashion, because the entire soliloquy has referred to the LORD only obliquely, in the third person. However, I would maintain that as the pastoral mentor arrives at this summation of his situation, he now turns to God in chagrin. Indeed, he does exactly what Bat-Zion did at the close of Chapter 2: After having suffered blow after blow, she

[21]   Klein, *Lamentations*, 181.
[22]   Rudolph, *Die Klageliede*, 231; Albrektson, *Studies in the Text*, 138; Renkema, *Lamentations*, 379; Klein, *Lamentations*, 181.

finally turned to the LORD in vexation, in an accusatory tone (2:20–22). We see here how the pastoral mentor crafts his soliloquy to align his difficult encounter with the LORD to match the experience of Bat-Zion in Chapter 2. The pastoral mentor signals to her that he himself has been through the religious experience that she currently endures. Both are left without hope.

Verse 18 concludes the speech with a resolution. NRSVue translates "so I say, 'Gone is *my glory*, and all that I had hoped for from the LORD'," but the word *niṣḥî* literally means "my eternity," and is better understood as rendered by Rashi and many modern translations as "my endurance," or "my future."[23] The word for "hoped" – a noun in the Hebrew, *tôḥaltî* – stems from the root *yāḥ'al*, which means to wait. The pastoral mentor sees in the LORD nothing that will help him endure. Elsewhere, the pious are able to place hope *tôḥelet* in the LORD (Pss 38:16; 39:8). But now, the pastoral mentor has no more hope in the LORD. This is the first time in the poem that the pastoral mentor has named the LORD, and Adele Berlin is certainly correct when she comments, "the literary strategy here is to name God just at the turning point, when, on the one hand, God seems most remote and, on the other hand, just as he is about to become the main topic of discourse."[24] And here, too, we see a parallel between the pastoral mentor's discourse in Chapter 3 and Bat-Zion's in Chapter 2. In vv. 2:20–21, Bat-Zion addressed the LORD accusingly. By 2:22, she no longer addressed him, but only referred to him in third person, signaling her distancing from him: "On the day of the anger of the LORD, no one escaped or survived; those whom I bore and reared, my enemy has destroyed." The same holds true here. The pastoral mentor turned accusingly to the LORD in 3:17, but by 3:18 can only speak about him in the third person: so I say, "Gone is my endurance, and all that I had hoped for from the LORD." He is now distanced from the LORD.

In v. 19, the pastoral mentor finds himself now divorced from God, and alone in his suffering. This verse and the one that follows are an intense moment of reflection. The Aramaic Targum, as well as many modern English translations read the opening verb of the verse as an imperative, a call to God to remember. However, the word *zəkār* is best understood as a noun, as rendered by the NRSVue, "the *thought* of my affliction." Moreover, nothing in the previous verses would suggest that the pastoral mentor could now suddenly turn to the LORD in prayer. Indeed, as per 3:8,

---

23   Provan, *Lamentations*, 89.
24   Berlin, *Lamentations*, 92.

prayer at this point is stopped up, blocked. In the earlier verses of the poem, the progression of images was high-paced; each strophe detailed a new and seemingly crueler act by the LORD rained down upon the pastoral mentor. In vv. 19–20, the tempo slows to a standstill as the pastoral mentor contemplates his divorce from the LORD, left only to ruminate about his suffering (3:20): "My soul continually thinks of it and is bowed down within me." The "bowed down soul" is a phrase that suggests utter depression (cf. Pss 42:6, 12; 43:5).[25] The pastoral mentor may have moved on from the LORD. But this provides him with no liberation, let alone relief from his suffering. Rather, it leaves him mired in his suffering and with no hope at all. This is the nadir of the predicament he has detailed until now.

THE PASTORAL MENTOR RECONSIDERS HIS PREDICAMENT (VV. 21–39)

Realizing that his divorce from the LORD leaves him in utter despair and depression, the pastoral mentor begins to assimilate a dawning recognition. This is intimated by v. 21: "But this I call to mind, and therefore I have hope." The Hebrew *ašîb el-libbî* is actually stronger than the translation here. It has the connotation of "this I shall *retort* or *counter* to my heart." We hear the pastoral mentor beginning to seek a way out of his despondency and paralysis and to articulate a reason to backtrack from his statement in v. 18 that he had lost all hope in the LORD.[26] But what could bring about such a change of heart? The reflections of two Holocaust survivors interviewed by Reeve Robert Brenner in his study, *The Faith and Doubt of Holocaust Survivors*, offer valuable insight. One reflected, "It occurred to me then, as it does now, that there might have been psychological benefits to believe in God and put one's complete trust in Him and that's the explanation why more Jews did not forsake their God in the death camps. It was better to believe than not believe. Maybe believing in God even helped some to survive."[27] Another attested that, "If I went ahead and challenged God and my challenge was victorious then I would be all alone. I would have been utterly alone in the camps, and I could not have survived."[28]

---

[25] Albrektson, *Studies in the Text*, 142; Provan, *Lamentations*, 91.
[26] This follows Renkema, *Lamentations*, 382 and the medieval rabbinic expositors who read the verse as introducing what follows. As Klein, *Lamentations*, 183, notes "this" usually refers to what follows (e.g., Lev 6:2, Ezek 36:37).
[27] Brenner, *Faith and Doubt*, 96.
[28] Brenner, *Faith and Doubt*, 102.

As he reconsiders his predicament, the pastoral mentor's mode is not prayer – he does not address the LORD at all. Distanced now from the LORD, he considers him from the outside in, as it were. And so he meditates *about* the LORD, rather than appealing *to* him. His words are almost a voice he hears from outside that addresses him; the voice of his own religious conscience. This is evident from v. 24a: "'The LORD is my portion,' *says my soul.*" Verses 21–39 are an internal musing between himself and his religious conscience. Although we find these precise formulations nowhere else, the passage gives the sense that he is invoking, or, perhaps, recalling a sapiential creed. It is also worthy to note how his internal discourse differs from a seemingly similar composition, the wisdom psalm of Psalm 37. Consider 37:7: "Be still before the LORD, and wait patiently for him; do not fret over those who prosper in their way, over those who carry out evil devices." The thrust of the verse is highly similar to what we will see here in 3:26: "It is good that one should wait quietly for the salvation of the LORD." Or, consider what we find in Ps 37:34: "Wait for the LORD and keep to his way, and he will exalt you to inherit the land; you will look on the destruction of the wicked," which is similar to what we find here in v. 25: "The LORD is good to those who wait for him, to the soul that seeks him." However, in Psalm 37, those messages are addressed to a poetic "you." There is suasion created by the text, as the psalter addresses the reader. But in the sapiential creed of Lam 3:22–39, the pastoral mentor never frames his discourse as an explicit address to another. Any "you" in his words would need to be Bat-Zion, and that would establish a kind of hierarchy between himself as mentor and her as mentee that he is looking to dissipate. He prefers, therefore, to lay out the arguments and express their beneficiary as "one" rather than as "you." The rhetorical purpose here is deliberate. He lays bare his own inner ruminations about the LORD, providence and justice in order to allow her to "overhear" him and to reach her own conclusions, as we shall see in vv. 40–47.

His opening reflection in v. 22 is that the innate virtues of the LORD are loving kindness, *ḥesed* and mercy, *raḥămîm*. Most importantly, they are exhibited over the long term; they are not always evident immediately. They "never cease" and "never come to an end." And even when an entire period is characterized by divine absence and suffering, this should not foreclose hope for the future: "they are new every morning; great is your faithfulness" (3:23). The LORD's mercy and loving kindness are not issued or measured in long periods of time; rather in the divine economy, each day is a new frame of divine providence and what happened yesterday need not dictate what will happen today. In this most hopeful note, we see the pastoral mentor addressing the

LORD for the only time during this sapiential rumination: "they are new every morning; great is *your faithfulness*." In v. 24, the pastoral mentor continues the conversation with himself. His "soul" now states – as if it is distinct, and outside of "himself" – that the LORD is "my portion." One scholar has astutely noted that in several passages, we see that referring to a king as "one's portion" is an acceptance of their dominion (2 Sam 19:44; 20:1; 1 Kgs 2:16).[29] This then is the logic of the verse's two stichs: Since my soul prevails over me to accept his dominion, I am now in a position to have hope – to wait. In v. 21, the pastoral mentor said, "this I call to mind, and therefore I will have hope," *ʿal-kēn ʾôḥîl*. The second stich of v. 24 is more emphatic, *ʿal-kēn ʾôḥîl lô*, "therefore I will hope *in him*." Now that the pastoral mentor has accepted the LORD's dominion, he will now proceed to entertain a more theologically challenging proposition, namely that the suffering itself accrues reward to the sufferer. This understanding is achieved in progressive stages.

In the *ṭet*-stanza, the pastoral mentor expounds on the added benefits of waiting and hoping for the LORD while suffering. According to v. 25, the LORD is good to those who hold out hope for him; the very stamina they reveal will be a source of merit. He is good to the "soul that seeks him." He is not immediately accessible; the soul toils to seek him, and thereby earns merit. Verse 26 offers an elaboration and a corrective of v. 25. It is good to not merely wait in hope for the LORD, as per v. 25; v. 26 says that "It is good that one should wait *quietly* for the salvation of the LORD." This translation of the NRSVue misses some of the rhetorical force of the verse, which I would render, "It is good that one should wait – and keep silent – *wayāḥîl wədûmām* for the salvation of the LORD." Waiting is one thing. But the suffering is unbearable. The challenge that accrues the most merit is to bear the suffering in silence, to bottle the desire to challenge the LORD's authority. Moreover, the sufferer no longer merely waits for "him" as per vv. 24 and 25. Rather, they ought to bear their suffering – in silence – all while certain of the impending salvation *of the Lord*.

Verse 27 continues the progression. The NRSVue translates the verse, "It is good for one to bear the yoke in youth," but this misses an emphasis at the beginning of the verse. Its literal translation would read, "It is good for *the pious man (laggeber)* when he bears a yoke in his youth." In truth, the word *laggeber* is superfluous, and could have been omitted with no loss of meaning: "It is good for *one* when he bears a yoke in his youth." However, explicit

29 Yehiel Zvi Moskowitz, "Lamentations" [Hebrew], in *Five Megillot*, Da'at Miqra', (Jerusalem: Massad Harav Kook, 1990), 24.

mention of the *geber* lends the verse a self-reflective dimension. After all, the speaker is none other than he who introduced himself in v.1 as "the *geber*." Here, the pastoral mentor engages in self-criticism and preaches to himself that it is insufficient to hope and even insufficient to do so while steadfastly remaining silent. It is best to, literally, "lift" (*yiśśā*) the yoke. This goes beyond *bearing* it, as per the NRSVue; he must actively embrace his suffering and lift the yoke. Both verses 26 and 27 open with the word *ṭôb*, "it is good," and this creates a cumulative effect from one verse to the next: it is good to suffer in silence; in fact, it is good to actively embrace and lift the yoke of suffering.

Verse 28 progresses further. The NRSVue reads: "to sit alone in silence when the LORD has imposed it," but many modern translations correctly read the opening words as "*Let him* sit alone and be silent." The end of the verse *kî nāṭal ʿālāyw* has been understood as rendered in the NRSVue, by most modern translations and by most medieval rabbinic expositors, as well, "when the LORD has imposed it."[30] However, all ancient translations render the phrase to read "… as he bears it upon himself." This reading is compelling because v. 27 already spoke of the yoke being borne or raised by the sufferer himself, and thus there is a chronological disjoint if the poet states that it is now that the LORD places it upon him. Thus, v. 28 makes more sense if it speaks of a sufferer who has already lifted the yoke and now bears it.

Verse 29 reveals just how precarious this spiritual balance can be for the silent sufferer. As the burden grows for the sufferer, so, too does the questioning and the urge to challenge, grow for him as well. To this, the wisdom voice inside the pastoral mentor counsels, "let him put dirt or dust into his mouth, perhaps there is hope" suggesting that blasphemy could erupt at any moment and must literally be blocked up.[31] As Mark Stone so aptly notes, the word "perhaps" signifies that the confident theodic rhetoric of 3:22–28 is beginning to unravel, as the stich "perhaps there is hope" underscores wavering conviction.[32] The highest level of virtuous suffering is reached in v. 30, where the voice of wisdom counsels that the sufferer should actively embrace his suffering in an act of submission: "give one's cheek to the smiter and be filled with insults," in the sense of being sated. When slapped, he should turn his cheek to receive more slaps. The denigration and debasement that he endures should "fill" him. In this, the pastoral mentor reconsiders his earlier utterance

---

30 Klein, *Lamentations*, 189.

31 I read here an imperative at the beginning of the verse, contra to the reading of the NRSVue, "to put one's mouth to the dust (there may yet be hope)."

32 Mark P. Stone, "Vindicating Yahweh: A Close Reading of Lamentations 3.21–42," *JSOT* 43 (2018): 92.

in v. 15 considering his treatment at the hands of the LORD, "He has filled me with bitterness; he has sated me with wormwood." His words also repurpose and change the valence of difficult experiences suffered by Bat-Zion to this point in the book. After all, it was Bat-Zion who "sat alone" (1:1), and who had a yoke of suffering placed upon her (1:14). The pastoral mentor to this point is still involved in his personal introspection and has yet to issue his call to action to Bat-Zion with regard to her own distress. Nonetheless, by repurposing these words from Chapter 1, he already implicitly beckons her to reconsider the meaning of the experiences she has endured.

Verse 31 is an inflection point. Verses 24–30 explored the theological experience of suffering from the perspective of the sufferer and the steps – physical and mental – that he needs to take in response to what the LORD has decreed for him. Verses 31–38 leave the realm of the sufferer and explore the world of the LORD; when suffering is experienced below, what is experienced above? Verse 31 is an inflection point because it equally attends to both realms. Unlike vv. 24–30, v. 31 says nothing explicit about the sufferer: "For the LORD will not reject forever." It speaks about the LORD more directly than the earlier verses do. Yet, at the same time, the sufferer is everywhere present in this verse, because it speaks of the LORD's rejection, or abandonment, and that is a human experience.

Verses 32–33 portray the LORD's disposition as the sufferer endures his suffering. He indeed causes grief, but this is only a prelude to the greater loving kindness he will display. And this is because of "his heart", in v. 33, which has no desire to bring grief. For the pastoral mentor, this is important as he construes his own suffering and the LORD's role in it. But he shares this aloud because his aim is for Bat-Zion to consider these lessons as well. Verse 33 should lead Bat-Zion to acknowledge the LORD's hand in bringing the destruction. Yet, on the other hand, it should also bring her to the belief that the LORD, in his real essence, is a God of love, who looks forward to moving past the necessity of punishment. It is that aspect of the LORD that the pastoral mentor wishes Bat-Zion to focus upon, even as she suffers.

Verses 34–36 are often said to champion the LORD's sovereignty and omniscience, and this they do. But rhetorically, the poet here is up to more than that. Notice first that these are verses not about all forms of suffering, but of abuses of power: the imprisoning king or tyrant in v. 34; the judge who skews judgment in a trial in v 35; either a judge or the opposing side to a judgment in v. 36. Note, further, that in all three verses, the syntax bears no explicit subject. The abusing agent is never named. Rather, we hear of, "when prisoners are crushed under foot" (v. 34); "when the due justice of a man is turned aside" (v. 35); "when one's case is subverted" (v. 36). The focus in these depictions of abuse is on the victim, not the perpetrator. The abusing agent is hidden in these, because at the end of the day, the lesson for the sufferer is to understand that his suffering comes from above, even as human agents carry out the LORD's will. At the same time, the sufferer who feels abandoned (as per the insistence of v. 31) is here reassured that at all times, his suffering is noticed. Even when he is but one of a multitude of prisoners trampled under-foot or the victim of a travesty of justice, "Does the LORD not see it?" (v. 36). This is not merely a statement of the LORD's justice, or omniscience. It is a statement of the LORD's caring involvement with each and every person, even as they suffer. The sufferer can take solace that his suffering is noticed.

The pastoral mentor concludes his meditation in vv. 36–39 with four rhe-torical questions.

The poetic tool of rhetorical questioning empowers the audience. Even as it foreordains only one proper answer, it encourages the listener to arrive at that conclusion on their own. The questions build in progression. Verse 36 advances the proposition of the LORD's omniscience: "when one's case is subverted – does the LORD not see it?" Verse 37 moves a step further – all that happens in the world is because he has ordained it: "Who can com-mand and have it done, if the LORD has not ordained it?" From here, v. 38 is the natural corollary. Since all that happens has been ordained from heaven, this, perforce, includes the things we perceive as good as well as those things we perceive as bad: "Is it not from the mouth of the Most High that evil and good come?" And because of the statements made earlier in v. 33, that the LORD would never willingly afflict people without cause, the only conclu-sion is that human suffering is the result of sin (v. 39): "Why should any who draw breath complain about the punishment of their sins?"

THE COMMUNITY DISMISSES THE CALL OF
THE PASTORAL MENTOR (VV. 40–47)

In vv. 40–47, we witness a sudden switch to a plural voice. Several propo-sitions have been advanced to identify this voice. Some scholars read this voice to be the voice of the *geber*, but now speaking in the name of the peo-ple.[33] Other scholars maintain the change in voice is a change in persona, and that we now hear the people speaking.[34] Both of these opinions seek to

---

[33]   Dobbs-Allsopp, *Lamentations*, 123–24; Berlin, *Lamentations*, 95.
[34]   Lee, *The Singers of Lamentations*, 176; Assis, *Lamentations*, 187.

interpret vv. 40–47 as an integral unit; they both maintain that the shift to a plural voice – which will revert to the voice of the *geber* in the singular, from v. 48 on – must be the voice of a single agent.

These positions are challenged, however, by the deep dissonance we see between the sentiments expressed in vv. 40–41 and those expressed in vv. 42–47. Verses 40–41 are nearly euphoric in their theodic embrace of the LORD: "Let us test and examine our ways and return to the LORD. Let us lift up our hearts as well as our hands to God in heaven." And the opening stich of v. 42 seems to follow suit: "We have transgressed and rebelled." Yet, immediately – mid-verse – the sentiment changes, and radically so. In the ensuing five and a half verses, this plural voice lays eight charges at the feet of the LORD, the most damning of which is that he kills without pity (v. 43). What's more, between v. 42a "We have transgressed and rebelled," and the sudden shift thereafter, there is not even the presence of a conjunction to indicate or mediate the transition.[35] Note how different this is from how our poet handles transition of mood and theological inclination in an earlier passage. In vv. 1–18, the pastoral mentor leveled a litany of charges at the LORD, ultimately foreswearing him in v. 18. Only in v. 21 does he express that perhaps there is hope. Verses 19–20 are a two-verse intermezzo, during which the pastoral mentor takes stock of his position having given up the LORD and now left with no hope, in silent pain. No such intermediary bridge exists between the seeming euphoria of vv. 40–42a and the despondency bordering on anger of vv. 42b–47. Adele Berlin and Frederick Dobbs-Allsopp maintain that we are hearing the narrator across all of vv. 40–47 but that he is "overwhelmed by the harshness" of the destruction and this explains the shift in the middle of v. 42.[36] But that explanation fails to explain the exuberance expressed in vv. 40–41 to embrace the LORD and return to him. Why was the pastoral mentor not overcome with the harshness of the destruction in those verses? If, indeed, this is what drives the pastoral mentor in vv. 42–47, what emotional or theological bromide could possibly have shielded or deluded him earlier?

The question is compounded if we follow those who maintain that the speaker throughout vv. 40–47 is the people as a whole. The dissonance between vv. 40–41 and vv. 42–47 presents itself here, too. Moreover, it raises the question of why or how the people would have adopted the embracing position of vv. 40–41 in the first place. For Adele Berlin and Frederick

---

[35] This, contra to Dobbs-Allsopp, *Lamentations*, 124.
[36] Berlin, *Lamentations*, 96; Dobbs-Allsopp, *Lamentations*, 123.

Dobbs-Allsopp, there is good reason to believe that the pastoral mentor has adopted that position in those verses. After all, he had engaged in a reflective mediation about the Lord and suffering that stretched back to v. 21, perhaps even back to the beginning of the chapter. However, if the people as a whole were so stirred by his words that they collectively called for a cleansing and a return to the Lord, as per vv. 40–41, what suddenly broke for them in the middle of v. 42?

Jacob Klein suggests that it is the *geber* who speaks in vv. 40–41, calling upon Zion to turn to the Lord in supplication and in penance. From v. 42, however, what we read is the text of the prayer he wishes Zion to utter. However, here, too, we are hard pressed to reconcile the eager embrace that he proposes in vv. 40–41 with the dour and bitter expression that he putatively scripts for the people to say in the subsequent verses. Klein maintains that the bitterness and focus on suffering here is designed to arouse the mercy of the Lord.[37] Contrast vv. 42–47, however, with other examples of penitential prayers that weave elements of lament and penance, such as Ezra 9:5–15 and Neh 9:6–38. These prayers exhibit much greater balance between the elements of lament and the elements of penance, whereas Lam 3:42–47 contains three words of contrition in v. 42a, and five and a half verses of bitterness. In fact, the final two verses of this putative collective prayer, vv. 46–47, seem not to be directed to the Lord at all: "All our enemies have opened their mouths against us; panic and pitfall have come upon us, devastation and destruction."

Instead, I follow the interpretation offered by Elizabeth Boase. For Boase, vv. 40–41 are spoken by the *geber*.[38] They represent the culmination of his rumination. Indeed, the entirety of the chapter has been building to these very verses. The pastoral mentor has traced his own internal reckoning of suffering and the role of the Lord in it. By v. 39, he comes to the conclusion that the Lord is a Lord of compassion and mercy, to whom one may appeal but only if there is penance for the sins that are the source of suffering. The *geber*, for Boase, switches to the plural voice in vv. 40–41 because he is now inviting the community of Zion to join him and to apply the lessons he deduced from his own travails now upon theirs, as a collective unit. In Chapters 1 and 2, he coaxed and guided Bat-Zion from the vantage point of an authority figure standing apart from her, even as he commiserated with her. Here, he changes rhetorical tactic and appeals to the community from

---

[37]   Klein, *Lamentations*, 197–98.
[38]   Boase, *The Fulfillment of Doom?*, 223.

within, as one of their own. This is why the sentiment in vv. 40–41 is exuberant – for exuberant embrace of the LORD through penance is the natural posture to adopt when one takes to heart the sapiential lessons of vv. 21–39. The pastoral mentor is hopeful that the perspective that he brought to his own suffering will now be adopted by the community broadly with regard to their misery, and that they will now go on to engage the LORD with a new approach. According to Boase, the plural voice that we hear in v. 42, and extending until v. 47, is that of the community of Zion, and stands in tension with the voice that has spoken until now, which I have interpreted as the voice of the pastoral mentor. What drives Boase to split the passage of the plural voice of vv. 40–47 into two (40–41 and 42–47) is the highly dissonant disposition that we find in each.

The pastoral mentor's exhortation begins in v. 40. His rhetoric here matches the logic of the previous four rhetorical questions. By exhorting, "Let us test and examine our ways and return to the LORD," he does not lay a specific accusation at the feet of the community. He encourages them to conduct an examination. There is an echo here of v. 2:14. When the pastoral mentor speaks of returning to the LORD, *wənāšûbâ ʿad-YHWH*, it invokes what he had said the false prophets had failed to do: "they have not exposed your iniquity to restore your fortunes" *ləhāšîb šəbûtēk*, which is rightly translated in the Douay-Rheims version as, "they have not laid open thy iniquity, to excite thee to penance."

In verse 41, the pastoral mentor calls for the community to join him, "Let us lift up our hearts as well as our hands to God in heaven," where the phrase *niśśā ləbābēnû el-kappayim* echoes his own call to Bat-Zion from v. 2:19, "Lift your hands to him for the lives of your children," *śəʾî ʾēlayw kappyik*, further buttressing the understanding that the pastoral mentor orchestrates his messages here in Chapter 3 in order to address the state of Bat-Zion in Chapter 2. The Hebrew of v. 41 literally reads, "Let us lift our hearts toward our hands, toward God in heaven." It is as if the hearts are instructed to follow the hands. The gesture of the hands does not stem from the heart. Rather, the pastoral mentor is aware that enacting this gesture is not simple for the community; it is not where they are at. And so, effectively, the pastoral mentor encourages them to raise their hands to the LORD – even if it is mechanical – but to thereafter bring their hearts to follow their hands. The pastoral mentor implicitly recognizes that the LORD is distant – he is in heaven – a nod to the distance from him the people feel at this time.[39]

---

[39]   Assis, *Lamentations*, 191.

The people, however, entirely reject the pastoral mentor's exhortation and demonstrate the flaws of his argument. Verses 42–47 tell a running, chronological story: the story of the people's experience of punishment and sense of abandonment by God. In v. 42, they do half-heartedly "confess": "We have transgressed and rebelled, and you have not forgiven." This is half-hearted, because these are the only words of contrition they express. A full-throated expression of remorse would resemble the laments of contrition found in Ezra 9 or in Nehemiah 9. But it is, nonetheless, sincere. They are prepared to adopt the pastoral mentor's narrative that they have transgressed and rebelled. However, they are unprepared to believe that contrition will improve their lot. What blocks the people from engaging in remorse whole-heartedly and in extended fashion is the conviction that it is too late; that there is nothing that can deliver them from their doom; that the LORD has shut the gates of repentance. It is this condition that they now detail.

Following their confession in v. 42a, they immediately note that the LORD did not forgive (*lōʾ sālāḥtā*), which would be better translated, "did not pardon"; that is, since there was transgression and rebellion, the LORD found no basis to pardon Judah. In v. 43, the people lay their charge directly at the LORD's feet: "You wrapped yourself with anger and pursued us, killing without pity."[40] That final stich, "killing without pity" *hāragtā lōʾ ḥāmālətā* demonstrates that the community still retains the sentiments expressed at the end of Chapter 2. In v. 2:21, Bat-Zion said, "in the day of your anger you have killed them, slaughtering without mercy," *hāragtā bəyôm appekā, tābaḥtā lōʾ ḥāmaltā*. In both 2:21 and 3:43, the statement that the LORD "kills *without pity*" expresses the vexation of dashed hopes for how the LORD would conduct himself. The expectation of the LORD was that he would be a God of compassion. The opening stich of v. 43, "You wrapped yourself with anger" *sakkōtâ bāʾap* also demonstrates a line of continuity with Bat-Zion's experience of the LORD in Chapter 2. In v. 2:1, the pastoral mentor stated that the LORD had "clouded" *yāʿîb* Bat-Zion in his anger, a point reiterated at several junctures in his soliloquy (2:3, 4, 6). With the medieval rabbinic exegete Rashi, we may read here in v. 43 that it is the LORD who is covered with anger, and thus inaccessible to the people. This is the central theme of the community's missive: Contrition will serve no purpose because the LORD is hopelessly distant from us.

---

[40]   I have emended the NRSVue, which reads here, "You have wrapped …". Biblical Hebrew has no clear perfect form and I read these verses to tell a narrative that progresses rather than a series of continuing states.

Verse 44 is the crux of Bat-Zion's claim. Several biblical passages stress that when the sinner repents, the Lord is there and ready to receive him back with warm embrace (Ps 32:5; Jer 18:5–12; Isa 55:7). And it is in that spirit that the community could open v. 42 with words of confession. But there is no follow up because the community is convinced that the Lord is not attentive, or, as it were, not listening. He is, as per the previous verse, "clouded over" with anger. This is now stated even more explicitly in v. 44: "you have wrapped yourself with a cloud so that no prayer can pass through." As Adele Berlin and Miriam Bier argue, repentance could be effective, if only it could get through.[41] The community's words offer subtle but implicit criticism of the pastoral mentor. When the community states that its prayers were blocked, it alludes to what he had said about his own experience, as stated in v. 8, "though I call and cry for help, he shuts out my prayer." The community echoes or invokes no other trope from his original soliloquy as much as this one. It is as if the community has failed to hear anything the pastoral mentor has said, other than his lament that his prayer is blocked by the Lord himself – to this, and this alone, they can relate.

In v. 45, the charge sheet expands. One scholar astutely notes that the root *māʾas* is paired as the opposite of *bāḥar*, choseness, in Isa 41:9: "You are my servant; I have chosen you and not cast you off." Thus, here in 3:45, the community intimates that the Lord has done the opposite of what was expected of him: Rather than choosing Israel, he has rejected Israel.[42] Many scholars have understood that when the community says in v. 3:45, "You have made us filth and rubbish among the peoples," that they speak about those in exile.[43] However, it could equally be that the community's decrepit state within the ruins of Judah has also earned the scorn of the nations to which they refer. This is explicitly expressed in v. 46, "All our enemies have opened their mouths against us." These words are clearly a throwback to 2:16: "All your enemies open their mouths against you; they hiss, they gnash their teeth, they cry: 'We have devoured her! Ah, this is the day we longed for; at last we have seen it!'"

While vv. 42–45 are framed as second-person addresses of the Lord, there is no second-person discourse in the final two verses of their lament, vv. 46–47. It may be that the community members simply rue woefully aloud among themselves. More likely, however, is that since the pastoral

---

[41]　Berlin, *Lamentations*, 96; Bier, "*Perhaps There Is Hope*," 129.
[42]　Assis, *Lamentations*, 193.
[43]　Salters, *Lamentations*, 255.

mentor spoke in their presence throughout the chapter and finally appealed to them, in vv. 46–47, they now expresses their final thought about the LORD, back to him. They can no longer speak to the LORD; only about the LORD, specifically of how he has abandoned them. Like the pastoral mentor in vv. 17–19, they have hit the rock bottom of despair (3:47): "panic and pitfall have come upon us, devastation and destruction."

The pastoral mentor emerges from his gambit a defeated man. He had carefully crafted the litany of his own travails and vexation with the LORD to mirror theirs in Chapter 2. He traced for them a model of his own slow but fruitful religious reawakening in vv. 19–21. He allowed them to hear the voice of the sapiential creed (vv. 21–39) that does not force conclusions upon the listener but asks the listener to apply their own reason. Finally, he made his overture to them in full empathy, speaking as a member of the community of Zion, all to help coax the community to reconnect with the LORD. Despondent, Bat-Zion has heard none of it.

THE PASTORAL MENTOR RECALIBRATES AND COMPOSES A LAMENT FOR BAT-ZION (VV. 48–66)

In v. 48, we witness two rhetorical changes. The speaker – the pastoral mentor – reverts to speaking in the first-person singular. And he does so no longer speaking as part of the people, but rhetorically distinct from them, referring to the community as Bat-Ami. His goal remains to establish a discourse with her that will allow her to connect with the LORD. Verses 48–51 are his initial reaction to his failure. Here, he will model the response to the destruction that he wishes her to adopt. Picking up with the word destruction (*šeber*) with which Bat-Zion closed her lament in v. 47, the pastoral mentor cries out over that destruction, *šeber* in v. 48. He says that his "eyes flow with rivers of tears." This is far more than an expression of pain. This is the very emotive act of crying to God that he had called her to do in v. 2:18: "Cry aloud to the LORD! O wall of daughter Zion! Let tears stream down like a torrent day and night!" This modeling continues in v. 49, where the pastoral mentor cries, "My eyes will flow without ceasing, without respite" *wəlōʾ tidmeh mēʾên hăpûgôt*, again modeling what he had called upon Bat-Zion to do in 2:18: "Give yourself no rest, your eyes no respite!" *ʾal-tittənî pûgat lāk, ʾal-tiddōm bat-ʿênêk*. In v. 50, he says that he will do so, "until the LORD from heaven looks down and sees." By underscoring that the LORD is far away, in heaven, and must be coaxed to "look down and see," the pastoral mentor offers a nod of legitimation to what Bat-Ami feels: The LORD is far and inaccessible. Note well that in doing so, he abandons the wisdom saying he had cited earlier in vv. 34–36 that when travesties of justice are committed it is obvious that the LORD notices (v. 36): "does the LORD not see it?"[44]

Verse 51 concludes the pastoral mentor's response to Bat-Ami's predicament. All English translations render the verse as does the NRSVue: "My eyes cause me grief at the fate of all the young women in my city." The key here is the conjunction *mem* at the beginning of the second stich, which these translations take as the causative *mem*, "*at the fate of*" or "*because of*" all the young women. However, as Klein notes, the causative *mem* is highly rare in the Hebrew Bible. Moreover, we have seen in Chapters 1 and 2 members of the community that were the foci of the community suffering, particularly the starving children and their mothers, much less so the young women. The young women – indeed, no particular member of the community – are mentioned in the rest of Chapter 3, and thus it seems incongruous at this point for the pastoral mentor to mention these women, without even so much as a detail of their suffering. Rather, we should read following the medieval rabbinic exegete Ibn Ezra that the conjunction *mem* here is the comparative *mem*: "My eye affects my soul with weeping more than all of the daughters of my city where it is the custom of women to weep." Elsewhere, we often find that the phrase "daughters of" a city, land, or ethnic group are those traditionally tasked with reciting laments and elegies.[45] Of particular note in this regard is Jer 9:9–16, which refers to the lamenting women (*məqônnôt*) and to the teaching of the art to their daughters. We may say, following Salters, that in the context of eyes running with water, these "daughters" are the professional mourners.[46] The comparison he establishes, though, needs to be properly construed. Why would the pastoral mentor establish a comparison or competition between himself and the pining daughters of the city? Rather, his emphasis is that his crying is directed to the LORD, and will not cease, as the pastoral mentor says in the previous verse, "until the LORD from heaven looks down and sees." Put

---

[44] Assis, *Lamentations*, 199, is correct to note further that the stich "until the LORD from heaven looks down and sees," *'ad-yašqîp wəyēre' YHWH miššāmāyim* invokes Deut 26:15: "Look down from your holy habitation, from heaven, and bless your people Israel and the ground that you have given us, as you swore to our ancestors – a land flowing with milk and honey."

[45] Klein, *Lamentations*, 201; cf. Jud 11:40; 2 Sam 1:19, 24; Jer 49:3; Ezek 32:16; Pss 48:12; 97:8. See discussion in Salters, *Lamentations*, 261–62.

[46] Salters, *Lamentations*, 262.

differently, the pastoral mentor does not claim here that he pines even more than they do. Rather, he claims that he is the only one who is pining with purpose of appeal and perhaps even protest to the Lord. He had called upon Bat-Zion at the end of Chapter 2 to unceasingly cry to the Lord, but this she did not do, castigating the Lord instead. The pastoral mentor cries his eyes out here to the Lord, because no one else is crying to the Lord. In the previous chapter, we noted the emotional numbing that Viktor Frankl described as a defense mechanism that he witnessed in the inmates of Auschwitz. Verse 51 now emerges in its full force: "My eye causes me grief," that is, I deliberately allow myself to take in and feel the suffering that I see and I shed endless tears before the Lord; "more than all the daughters of the city." These have become numbed and no longer cry.

From here, the text of Lamentations 3 shifts suddenly to what at first blush appears to be an individual lament, spoken in the singular (vv. 52–66). Most scholars assume this to be the voice of the pastoral mentor, and a continuation of his words that had recommenced at v. 48, following the plural voices heard in vv. 40–47.[47] The consensus of scholarship understands that in vv. 52–66, the narrator reverts to speaking of his own woes, this time appealing to the Lord for salvation and relief. Whereas in vv. 1–18, he railed against the Lord's treatment of him, vv. 19–39 offered him a new perspective on suffering, its source, and how to construe the Lord's silence throughout. In vv. 52–66, he is able to dissociate the Lord from his troubles, which are now attributed to his enemies, while the Lord is now construed as his savior. However, this interpretation is challenged when we attend to the differences between the pastoral mentor's opening soliloquy in vv. 1–18 and the closing lament of vv. 52–66.

Presumably, the woes that the pastoral mentor details in vv. 52–66 are those that he bemoaned in vv. 1–18. Yet, note the differences between the travails detailed in each. These go well beyond the question of the perpetrator, which in vv. 1–18 was the Lord, and in vv. 52–66 are the enemies. The suffering itself seems to be of a different form and nature. In vv. 1–18, the pastoral mentor describes prison torture. He was walled in (vv. 5, 7, 9), shackled (7), and physically abused (1, 3, 4, 11–13, 15–16). He was the laughingstock of the entirety of his own people (14). By contrast, the lament of vv. 52–56 details being thrown into a pit (vv. 53–55). In this lament, there is no physical abuse described at all. The mocking he endures is more pronounced

---

[47]   Klein, *Lamentations*, 201; Lee, *The Singers of Lamentations*, 179; Assis, *Lamentations*, 200; Dobbs-Allsopp, *Lamentations*, 125.

in this section – vv. 61–63 – and is carried out by his enemies, who are no longer identified as the entirety of his own people, as per 3:14. In fact, the enemies cannot be *all* of his own countrymen, for in the ultimate verse of the poem, he calls for their utter obliteration from under the heavens (v. 66). Moreover, were this lament to be a "theologically corrected" version of the pastoral mentor's soliloquy of vv. 1–18, we would expect at least some of the terms and expressions found in the soliloquy to be now reused in the lament to the LORD. For example, there are several terms found in vv. 1–18 that could easily have been repurposed to describe the LORD's salvific grace in vv. 52–66: The LORD as a shepherd who "guides" *nāhag* (contra v. 2); who "settles" *hôšîb* (contra v. 6); who hears "prayer" *təfillâ* (contra v. 8); who brings "peace" *šālôm* to one's "soul" *nepeš* (contra v. 17); who offers hope *tôḥelet* (contra v. 18). Yet, none of these are employed.

To set proper prospective on this closing lament and its discontinuities with the opening soliloquy of vv. 1–18, we need to attend to its place within the structure of the chapter. The pastoral mentor began the chapter looking to draw attention to his own person as a model of how to deal with anger at God for suffering. Verses 1–18 drew a parallel between his own experiences and those of Bat-Zion in Chapter 2. The pastoral mentor concluded that he has no hope in the LORD, finding himself abandoned; alone (vv. 19–20). In vv. 21–39, he proceeded to showcase for the community how he reasoned himself out of that posture of anger and abandonment. All of this leads to vv. 40–41 where the pastoral mentor invited the community to join him in a penitential move to restore the relationship with the LORD. At this point, however, the gambit utterly fails. The community utters a half-hearted confession in v. 42a, but overwhelmingly voices its despair over its inability to communicate toward the LORD, and is thus doomed to continue to suffer (vv. 42b–47). He has brought the community no closer to restoring her relationship with the LORD. The community, as we saw, mouths reformulations of the tribulations suffered by Bat-Zion according to Chapter 2.

The pastoral mentor at this point realizes that his tactic has failed; his own experience is of no relevance for the community, whom he now addresses as Bat-Ami (v. 48). She rejects the theology he tried to impress upon her in vv. 21–41. The pastoral mentor responds (vv. 48–51) by engaging in the type of crying to the LORD "in heaven" (v. 50) that he himself had urged her to undertake in 2:18–19. He concluded by stating that he was engaging in heart-wrenching cries to the LORD, "more than all the daughters of the city," who, I claimed were, like Bat-Zion in Chapter 2, not doing that work themselves, having despaired of the efficacy of such appeals.

This is the backdrop to the lament of vv. 52–66. The lament that the pastoral mentor offers has nothing to do with his own travails detailed in vv. 1–18. Rather, this is a lament that he composes as a model for Bat-Ami to say for herself. Unnoted in the modern scholarship is the fact that all medieval rabbinic exegetes construe the speaker of the lament as Bat-Ami, and not as the *geber*. This is not his lament; rather, it is designed for her to say. As we shall see, there are two trends that predominate in this lament, when seen within the context of the larger literary fabric of Lamentations 3. First, within the lament of vv. 52–66, the pastoral mentor repudiates nearly every tenet stated in the sapiential passage of vv. 21–39. Those tenets fell on deaf ears within the Zion community, as we saw in vv. 42–47 and thus the pastoral mentor seeks now to offer a new "script" for Bat-Ami to reengage the LORD. Second, we will see that the travails that he details in this lament are all easily identified as echoes of the tribulations the community describes in vv. 42–47.

I begin by delineating the first trend, the repudiation of the tenets of the sapiential creed. In the ultimate statement of the sapiential creed, the pastoral mentor concluded that if one suffers, then it is surely because of one's sins, and he thus proceeds to appeal to the community to examine its deeds and return to the LORD (v. 40). And yet in the lament of vv. 52–66, the constructed sufferer makes no mention of his own responsibility for his misfortune, of his own sin. In the sapiential passage, the pastoral mentor repeatedly espoused the virtue of silence in the face of suffering (vv. 26, 28–29). The pastoral mentor there asserted that even when great injustices are perpetrated (vv. 34–36), "does the LORD not see it? (*'ădōnāy lō' rā'â*)." The notion that an event could transpire and that the LORD does not see it, is not aware of it, is blasphemous according to these teachings. And yet, this does not stop the petitioner of the concluding lament to cry out – and not remain silent – (3:63), "whether they sit or rise – *see*, I am the object of their taunt songs," which suggests that the petitioner does not have full confidence that the LORD is looking and watching. Many expositors take the perfect verbs in this passage as precative perfects (contrary to the NRSVue). Within these readings, the petitioner further expresses doubt as to whether the LORD is taking note, as he states (3:59–60), "Behold (*rā'îtâ*) the wrong done to me, O LORD; judge my cause. Behold (*rā'îtâ*) all their malice, all their plots against me." In vv. 34–36, the idea that the LORD always acts justly is confidently stated. The very fact that the petitioner here in vv. 59–60 must call upon the LORD to carry out justice shows that he no longer relies on this with certainty. Moreover, we can see how the words of the sapiential voice are echoed and repurposed. The creed spoke of how the LORD surely notices the perversion of justice (*mišpaṭ*) (v. 35)

and the subversion of one's case *lǝ'awwēt ādām bǝrîbô* (v. 36). Yet, here
in vv. 58–59, these words are repurposed to form a demand of the LORD. In
v. 58, the petitioner calls, as per my reading of the precative perfect here,
"take up my case" (*rabtâ rîbê napšî*) and in v. 59, he calls for the LORD to
note "the wrong done to me (*'awwātātî*), O LORD; judge my cause (*šāpǝtâ
mišpāṭî*)." The voice of the sapiential wisdom counseled that it is best when
suffering an injustice, "to give one's cheek to the smiter and be filled with
insults" (*ḥerpâ*) (3:30). However, the petitioner in the concluding lament dis-
regards this counsel when he cries to the LORD (3:61), "Hear their taunts
ḥerpātām, O LORD, all their plots against me."[48]

Moving to the second dominant trend in the concluding lament, we can
see the way in which the pastoral mentor composes a lament that is suited
to the sentiments and imagery that the community – whom he now calls
Bat-Ami – expressed in vv. 42–47. The primary sentiment expressed in this
passage is the inaccessibility of the LORD, as found in vv. 43–44: "You have
wrapped yourself with anger and pursued us, killing without pity; you have
wrapped yourself with a cloud so that no prayer can pass through." The
community concluded by describing the nadir reached: "panic and *pitfall*
have come upon us, devastation and destruction" (v. 47). This well explains
the imagery and thematic push of vv. 52–54: "Those who were my enemies
without cause have hunted me like a bird; they flung me alive into a *pit* and
hurled stones on me; water closed over my head; I said, 'I am lost.'" Like Bat-
Ami in v. 43, the petitioner perceives himself as being hunted, pursued. And
like Bat-Ami, who expresses the feeling of "pitfall" in v. 47, the petitioner
in vv. 53–54 describes being trapped in a pit. Albrektson has noted that the
trope of being hunted like a bird is found at Ps 124:7, where Israel escapes
from the snare of the fowler. For Albrektson, this suggests that the first-
person singular here might well warrant a collective interpretation.[49]

Bat-Ami expresses in v. 44 that she feels that her prayers cannot "pass
through," as though there is a blockage above her. This is metaphorically
expressed by the petitioner in vv. 53–54, where at first stones cover him,
followed by water that rises over his head. Bat-Ami's sense of total despair,
trapped in the proverbial pit and with no access to the LORD in v. 47, is mir-
rored at the close of v. 54, where the petitioner concludes, from under stones
and water in the pit, "I said, 'I am lost.'"

[48]   This, contra to the NRSVue which translates the opening verb as a simple perfect "You
       have heard…"
[49]   Albrektson, *Studies in the Text*, 162.

The constructed lament of the petitioner moves on to begin to redress this hopelessness in vv. 55–56: "I called on your name, O LORD, from the depths of the *pit*; you heard my plea, 'Do not close your ear to my cry for help, but give me relief!'" Note how the pit imagery is explicitly continued, and that the plea that the LORD would not close his ear to his cry well expresses Bat-Ami's concern that the LORD has wrapped himself with a cloud so that no prayer can pass through (v. 44). Bat-Ami concluded that she lives in "*panic and pitfall.*" It is in response to this panic (*paḥad*) that the lament states comfortingly in v. 57, "You came near when I called on you; you said, '*Do not fear!*'" Of course, this is feigned speech, or hoped-for speech, but it creates a palpable reality for the community of what it would be like for the LORD to come out, as it were, from behind his cloud of anger, and to speak comfortingly to the community, "do not fear!"

We earlier saw how the verbs of vv. 58–59 when read as precative perfects constitute a rejection of the sapiential teachings of vv. 34–36. This takes us to vv. 60–66. And here we can see, once again, how the lament is crafted to address the mood and concerns of Bat-Ami in vv. 42–47. Her experience of suffering focuses upon the taunts of the other nations (3:45–46): "You have made us filth and rubbish among the peoples. All our enemies have opened their mouths against us." This is precisely the focus of vv. 61–63, which call for the LORD to note, not the physical mistreatment of the petitioner but the malicious speech of the enemies. Verses 64–66 call for divine revenge, with v. 66 as its carefully crafted denouement. In v. 43, Bat-Ami averred that the LORD wrapped himself in anger (*'ap*), and pursued her (*wattirdəpēnû*). The LORD, for Bat-Ami, is a distant god, he resides in heaven, and to appeal to him, there is a need to spread hands high "to God in Heaven" (3:41). In v. 66, these tropes are now repurposed: "Pursue them in anger (*tirdōp bə'ap*) and destroy them from under the LORD's heavens (*šəmê YHWH*)." The lament underscores that the LORD will one day visit upon the enemies what she herself now experiences. The LORD that dwells in the heavens and is so far that he cannot hear her prayer shall ensure that the enemies are obliterated from all that is under those very same heavens, which is to say from everywhere.

Much discussion about this lament has focused upon the grammatical question of the perfect verbs found throughout. If all are taken as simple perfect verbs referring to a static finished event in the past that includes stress and salvation, problems arise from the evident pleas for a future salvation in vv. 56, 59, 63 and 64–66. Some have proposed parsing out the section such that the pleas for salvation now refer to a current distress, but are predicated on a prior episode of distress that itself was followed by an act of divine salvation. The difficulty here is that the lines of demarcation of the respective incidents – past and present – are not clear. Moreover, this reading is forced to concede that the contours of the purported prior distress and salvation are not fleshed out, and only alluded to. Surely, if a prior act of deliverance was the basis for the current appeal for same, we would expect the prior deliverance to have more detail, rather than mere allusion.[50]

Other scholars have sought to make sense of these verbs with resort to poetic license in the grammar employed, particularly on exceptional uses of the perfect form of the verb. One favored and popular version of this maintains that precative perfects that express a wish abound here. Thus, as opposed to the NRSVue rendering of v. 56, "you *heard* my plea," or v. 57, "you *came* near when I *called* on you," these scholars read "Hear my plea!" and "Come near when I call you." This opinion has become the consensus in recent scholarship.[51] However, other scholars have interpreted these verbs somewhat differently. For them, there is a durative aspect to some of these verbs, thus they read v. 55 as "I have called and continue to call on your name, O Lord, from the depths of the pit," and v. 60 as "You have seen and continue to see all their malice, all their plots against me." Another option put forth is that we have here examples of the "prophetic perfect, which expresses facts which are undoubtedly imminent, and, therefore, in the imagination of the devout speaker, already accomplished."[52] This form expresses the vacillation the petitioner experiences between trust and mere hope. The attempts to firmly define these perfect verbs in one fashion or another have yet to yield a conclusive position and I would aver that this is a deliberate aspect of the poetry. Employing verbal forms that are open to multiple interpretation is a deliberate component of the lament. Some will recite it with its promise that these divine acts "are as good as done." Others will take comfort in the knowledge that they obliquely refer to past episodes of divine salvation, and that when the petitioner calls on the Lord now, it follows previous instances in which he had likewise called on the Lord and had received deliverance. And there will be still others for whom there is less certainty that the Lord is listening, and who will embrace the poem as a lengthy plea to the Lord to be heard and to be delivered.

---

[50] The positions are well surveyed in Thomas, *Poetry and Theology*, 198–203.
[51] Following Iain W. Provan, "Past, Present and Future in Lamentations III 52–66: The Case for a Precative Perfect Re-Examined," *VT* 41 (1991): 164–75.
[52] Provan, "Past, Present and Future," 173. On prophetic perfect, see GKC §106.3.b.

CONCLUSION

If the pastoral mentor has indeed composed a prayer for the community to recite, we might have expected that it would take the form of a communal lament; that is, that it would be expressed using plural forms and accord with the expressions of the community in vv. 42–47. However, the lament contained in vv. 52–66 has all the look and feel of an individual lament, not a communal one. Toward what end has the pastoral mentor composed an individual lament for the sake of a community in trauma?

The author may have in mind that the constructed lamenter in vv. 52–66 is Bat-Ami (as per v. 48), a corporate character, representing a community of individuals. This rhetoric is found in Ps 129:1–3: "Often have they attacked me from my youth – let Israel now say – often have they attacked me from my youth, yet they have not prevailed against me. The plowers plowed on my back; they made their furrows long." The lamenter is a corporate figure, an individual who is Israel as a whole. However, it should be noted that this example of corporate expression is exceptional. Moreover, it is unclear what the pastoral mentor would achieve by putting forward such a composition. After all, in response to his earlier call to turn to the LORD (vv. 40–41), the people demurred, insisting that such efforts were futile, as the LORD has rejected the community and blocks its prayers (vv. 43–44). Having rebuffed his earlier call to turn to the LORD, there is no reason to believe that they would now embrace his implicit call to recite his lament penned for the community through the literary construct of the individual "Bat-Ami" (v. 48).

However, another way to construe the lamenter in vv. 52–66 is that the pastoral mentor composes a lament to be recited by each and every member of the community of Zion as each struggles with his or her own misery. We may draw inspiration for what he has in mind with reference to the spiritual reflections of a concentration camp survivor, as documented by Reeve Robert Brenner:

> I know what kept me from going altogether mad while in Sobibor. What kept me from going under was my powerful and continuous faith in the nearness of God … It was my belief in God and the fact that there was a belief in God held by others that helped me retain my equilibrium and my sanity and some common sense as well. My faith also kept my physical being from falling apart and, in fact, kept me from killing myself at once.[53]

---

[53]   Brenner, *Faith and Doubt*, 102.

What is striking about this statement is what it says about the place of individual faith during a time of communal trauma. No doubt, this former camp prisoner had been acutely aware that he was being persecuted not as an individual, but as part of a people. And, he no doubt had fervently sought from the Almighty the end of the persecution of his people as a whole and their collective rescue from the Nazi regime. But the fact that he was caught up in a collective trauma did nothing to mitigate the fact that even amid collective trauma the struggle for faith takes place one tortured soul at a time. He could – nay, needed to – relate to the Almighty as an individual. This is what gave him fortification. We may understand that when the pastoral mentor composes an individual lament for recitation, he does so because he seeks an avenue of connectedness with the LORD that they may yet embrace. If they were certain that the LORD had rejected them as a community and would not hear their collective cries for salvation, perhaps yet, he could help the members of the community retain their individual connection with the LORD. Perhaps, they, like the inmate from Sobibor cited by Brenner, could be comforted by the possibility of the LORD's nearness to them as individuals, and comforted by the prospect that others might recite this constructed lament as well.

4 Dispelling Delusions II: Zion and Her Social Structures

¹ How the gold has grown dim;
 how the pure gold is changed!
The sacred stones lie scattered
 at the head of every street.

² The precious children of Zion,
 worth their weight in fine gold—
how they are reckoned as earthen pots,
 the work of a potter's hands!

³ Even the jackals offer the breast
 and nurse their young,
but my people has become cruel,
 like the ostriches in the wilderness.

⁴ The tongue of the infant sticks
 to the roof of its mouth for thirst;
the children beg for food,
 but there is nothing for them.

⁵ Those who feasted on delicacies
 perish in the streets;
those who were brought up in purple
 cling to ash heaps.

⁶ For the chastisement of my people has been greater
 than the punishment of Sodom,
which was overthrown in a moment,
 though no hand was laid on it.*m*

⁷ Her princes were purer than snow,
 whiter than milk;

---

m 4.6 Meaning of Heb uncertain

their bodies were more ruddy than coral,
  their hair form cut like sapphire.[n]

8 Now their visage is blacker than soot;
  they are not recognized in the streets.
  Their skin has shriveled on their bones;
  it has become as dry as wood.

9 Happier were those pierced by the sword
  than those pierced by hunger,
  whose life drains away, deprived
  of the produce of the field.

10 The hands of compassionate women
  have boiled their own children;
  they became their food
  in the destruction of my people.

11 The LORD gave full vent to his wrath;
  he poured out his hot anger
  and kindled a fire in Zion
  that consumed its foundations.

12 The kings of the earth did not believe,
  nor did any of the inhabitants of the world,
  that foe or enemy could enter
  the gates of Jerusalem.

13 It was for the sins of her prophets
  and the iniquities of her priests,
  who shed the blood of the righteous
  in her midst.

14 Blindly they wandered through the streets,
  so defiled with blood
  that no one was able
  to touch their garments.

15 "Away! Unclean!" people shouted at them;
  "Away! Away! Do not touch!"
  So they became fugitives and wanderers;
  it was said among the nations,
  "They shall stay here no longer."

---

[n]   4.7 Or *lapis lazuli*

¹⁶ The LORD himself has scattered them;
   he will regard them no more;
no honor was shown to the priests,
   no favor to the elders.

¹⁷ Our eyes failed, ever watching
   vainly for help;
we were watching eagerly
   for a nation that could not save.

¹⁸ They dogged our steps
   so that we could not walk in our streets;
our end drew near; our days were numbered,
   for our end had come.

¹⁹ Our pursuers were swifter
   than the eagles in the heavens;
they chased us on the mountains;
   they lay in wait for us in the wilderness.

²⁰ The LORD's anointed, the breath of our life,
   was taken in their pits—
the one of whom we said, "Under his shadow
   we shall live among the nations."

²¹ Rejoice and be glad, O daughter Edom,
   you that live in the land of Uz;
but to you also the cup shall pass;
   you shall become drunk and strip yourself bare.

²² The punishment of your iniquity, O daughter Zion, is accomplished;
   he will keep you in exile no longer;
but your iniquity, O daughter Edom, he will punish;
   he will uncover your sins.

INTRODUCTION

In many ways, Chapter 4 returns us to themes and modes of discourse familiar to us already from the previous chapters. As in Chapter 2, the focus across much of the chapter is upon the ravages of starvation during the siege of the city. And, like the three previous chapters, we can distinguish within it two voices: a narrator who speaks of Bat-Zion in the third person (vv. 1–16, 21–22) and a voice speaking on behalf of the community in the first person (vv. 17–21), this time in a plural voice, as we also found in 3:40–47.

However, what sets off Chapter 4 even at a first reading is the starkly upbeat note struck at chapter's end (vv. 21–22), which speaks confidently of the impending revenge against Edom and of a reprieve for Bat-Zion. There is nothing remotely like this anywhere else in Lamentations. Seemingly, such sentiments might have been expected elsewhere. Many prophetic books that include forecasts of doom end with a deliberate note of salvation (e.g., Isa 66:12–24; Hos 14:2–10; Amos 9:13–15), and accordingly, these verses might have fit well at the conclusion of the book in Chapter 5. Alternatively, these verses would have made a highly fitting end to Chapter 1. Recall there that Bat-Zion progressed through a ladder of spiritual rehabilitation. The process culminates with her call to the LORD in vv. 1:21c–22: "Bring on the day you have announced, and let them be as I am. Let all their evil doing come before you, and deal with them as you have dealt with me because of all my transgressions; for my groans are many, and my heart is faint." One can hardly think of a finer way for the narrator to respond to Bat-Zion there than with the promise of the sentiments of vengeance against Edom and reprieve for Zion expressed here in 4:21–22.

Moreover, it is hard to see what warrants these sentiments at the end of Chapter 4. The community seemingly expresses no contrition in its monologue of vv. 17–20. In fact, there is no mention of the LORD at all by the community in Chapter 4. Indeed, in every chapter of Lamentations, Bat-Zion, the community, or the narrator addresses the LORD – with the exception of Chapter 4. Nor do we find in the community's words the utter despair from the LORD that we find, say, in 3:42–47. Nor is the narrator particularly invested emotionally here in Bat-Zion as he was earlier (cf. 1:10; 2:11–13; 3:48–51). Other than referring to the community as "Bat-Ami," rendered by NRSVue as "my people" (4:3, 6), he expresses little emotion toward her at all. Frederick Dobbs-Allsopp is correct in his assessment that relative to the earlier chapters, the narrator seems unengaged and that there is "a fall off in emotional intensity."[1]

We do find in the community's cries of vv. 17–20, however, something unique within the chapters of Lamentations, and that is a reckoning with its political positions on the eve of the Babylonian conquest. The community recalls the hopes they had harbored for salvation by a third-party nation (v. 17) and the unwarranted confidence they had placed in the protective office of the Davidic king (v. 20). The role of these political reflections, I maintain, is the key to understanding this chapter. But to understand these reflections by the community and their place between the words of the

---

[1]   Dobbs-Allsopp, *Lamentations*, 129.

narrator before (vv. 1–16) and after (vv. 21–22), we must adduce a profile of the religious typology that is addressed through this poem.

The religious persona that is the target audience of Lamentations 4 may be identified through reference to the phenomenon social psychologists call *belief persistence* or *belief perseverance*. This refers to people's proclivity to passionately cling to, and advocate for, beliefs or attitudes even when the evidence supporting such beliefs is fully invalidated. It is especially prevalent in politics, such as the propensity to retain belief in a fallen leader or regime. Recently, social psychologists have addressed this issue concerning the persistent denial of climate change.[2] The widespread denial of the safety and efficacy of vaccinations in the fight against COVID-19 is another good illustration of the phenomenon. This propensity to develop, maintain, and unwaveringly cling to one's beliefs in the absence of sufficient evidence is one of the most well-established tendencies in the social-psychological canon.[3]

There are two explanations of the phenomenon. Some scholars see deep-seated beliefs as a source of self-identity. Resistance to belief change is therefore fundamentally ego-defensive.[4] Thus, for example, individuals will deny evidence for climate change if doing so would create a sense of incompetence. Others see the issue primarily in sociological terms. For one scholar, "individuals are psychologically disposed to believe that behavior they (and their peers) find honorable is socially beneficial and behavior they find base [is] socially detrimental."[5] By this account, individuals have a stake in affirming beliefs that will support their social standing and connections.

Chapter 4 addresses the problem of belief persistence concerning the political aspects of Zion theology. As I noted in my introduction to Chapter 2, Zion theology as a theological mindset is a focus of the prophetic discourse of Jeremiah during the final years of the existence of the southern

---

[2] R. Kelly Garrett, "Strategies for Countering False Information and Beliefs about Climate Change," *Oxford Research Encyclopedia of Climate Science* (April 2017): 1–30, https://tinyurl.com/28h322bh.

[3] See Craig A. Anderson, and James J. Lindsay, "The Development, Perseverance, and Change of Naive Theories," *Social Cognition* 16 (Spring 1998): 8–30.

[4] Geoffrey L. Cohen, Joshua Aronson, and Claude M. Steele, "When Beliefs Yield to Evidence: Reducing Biased Evaluation by Affirming the Self," *Personality and Social Psychology Bulletin* 26 (2000): 1151–64. See also Claude M. Steele, "The Psychology of Self-Affirmation: Sustaining the Integrity of the Self," *Advances in Experimental Social Psychology* 21 (1988): 261–302.

[5] Dan M. Kahan, Hank Jenkins-Smith, and Donald. Braman, "Cultural Cognition of Scientific Consensus," *Journal of Risk Research* 14 (2011): 148.

kingdom of Judah.[6] Within this mindset, Jerusalem was the seat of the LORD (Ps 132:7–8; Pss 46; 48; 87; esp. 46:5 and 48:4–9), and thus impregnable (Jer 7:1–14). The Davidic king was the LORD's chosen one (Pss 2; 18; 20; 21; 45; 72; 89; 101; 110; 132; 144) and would be granted dominion over his enemies (e.g., Pss 2:9; 48:4–6). The palace and the temple were thought to be practically one royal complex (Ezek 43:7–8).

Critically, Jeremiah notes that the people's commitment to this assumptive world was so great that they were incapable of hearing rational arguments to its contrary. Thus, the prophet excoriates (Jer 21:13): "See, I am against you, O inhabitant of the valley, O rock of the plain, says the LORD; you who say, 'Who can come down against us, or who can enter our places of refuge?'" Indeed, the prophet decries in explicit terms the dogmatic commitment that the people display no matter what claims are brought before them (Jer 18:11–12):

> Now, therefore, say to the people of Judah and the inhabitants of Jerusalem: Thus says the LORD: Look, I am a potter shaping evil against you and devising a plan against you. Turn now, all of you, from your evil way, and amend your ways and your doings. But they say, "It is no use! We will follow our own plans, and each of us will act according to the stubbornness of our evil will."

Belief persistence is registered as well in Jer 2:25: "Keep your feet from going bare and your throat from thirst. But you said, 'It is no use, for I have loved strangers, and after them I will go.'" Even after the exile of Jeconiah, there was an audience ready to hear that restoration of the Davidic king was just around the corner because the LORD is with him and with Judah, as witnessed in the words of Hananiah in Jer 28:1–4.

The sixth-century persistence of belief in Zion theology is not merely a conception about the salvific promise of the Davidic king. Rather, Zion theology inheres a reification of the entire social order that emanates from Davidic kingship. Prophets serve in the service of kings (Jer 20:1–6; 28:1–17). Priests and prophets who offer sacral sanction to royal propaganda are targeted for censure as a pair by Jeremiah (23:11–12). Priests, prophets, and officials in the service of the king come in for censure in Jer 4:9. Those whose status was a function of their proximity to the Davidic king, however, extended beyond priests, prophets, and officers. Further afield, we see mention of those associated with royalty in the royal Psalms (Ps 45:10 [ET9]): "daughters of kings are among your ladies of honor." The Psalmist

---

[6] Broadly, see discussion in Wilhelm J. Wessels, "Zion, Beautiful City of God: Zion Theology in the Book of Jeremiah," *Verbum et Ecclesia*, 27 (2006): 729–48.

writes of the princess with her virgins and companions, "With joy and gladness they are led along as they enter the palace of the king." (v. 16 [ET15]). This gives a sense of a Jerusalem elite tightly constructed around its proximity to the crown. These are all individuals whose worth and standing are deeply invested in Zion theology.

The staying power of the social construct built around Zion theology is evident in the events detailed in Jeremiah 41:1–3, where Nethaniah son of Elishama leads an insurrection against the Babylonian-installed governor, Gedaliah. Scripture identifies Nethaniah as a descendent of royal seed (Jer 41:1), and also as an officer of the king, or perhaps that officers of the king were accomplices in his mission. Either way, the motivation of this group is clear. Formerly, their status stemmed from their proximity to the crown. Their aim was not to restore Zedekiah to the crown – by this point the king had been exiled to Babylon. Rather, their aim was to ensure that power and status within the survivor community would continue to be structured as it had been in the *ancien régime*.

In Lamentations 4, the author addresses members of the surviving community whose identity continues to be nourished by the place they held in this sacred social order; those who cannot conceive of a Judean order construed or constructed any other way. His poem is a critique of this order and is cast as a dialogue between the pastoral mentor and the community. The chapter may be summarized as follows: In vv. 1–16, only the pastoral mentor speaks. He draws attention to the ways in which the expectations of the social and political benefits of Zion theology have not only been unmet, but inverted entirely. In vv. 17–20, the community responds with a collective mea culpa: They reflect upon the futility of the stock they had invested in key aspects of Zion theology. The compositional logic here matches what we saw concerning Bat-Zion's address in Chapter 1. The words the author pens as Bat-Zion's speech are the sentiments that the author wishes his own community to enounce; this is the culture script he wishes to disseminate. Once the community reconsiders and recognizes the futility of its earlier positions, the pastoral mentor offers words of solace in vv. 21–22.

A CRITIQUE OF THE ZION THEOLOGY SOCIAL ORDER (VV. 1–16)

That the pastoral mentor's soliloquy is more critique than lament is evident from the opening image of Chapter 4. It is enigmatic and stands alone within the book of Lamentations in that it communicates solely in metaphoric language, without any explicit signal to its referent or target: "How the gold has grown dim; how the pure gold is changed!" (v. 1). In reality, gold does not oxidize, and some explain that the gold here is covered by dirt. But the impossibility of gold rusting is precisely the point of the metaphor. For many in Jerusalem, the city, the temple, and the king were all thought to be safeguarded under the LORD's protective watch. Defeat and devastation were unthinkable because they were impossible. There is a sardonic rebuff in this opening metaphor. Through his declaration, "How the gold has grown dim; how the pure gold is changed!" the narrator chides the people's misplaced trust in Zion theology. He issues a call to recognize that indeed, "gold can rust," that Zion can fall and with it, the reified social order it undergirds. The phrase functions as a thematic title that will be explored in detail as the poem progresses.

The takedown of Zion theology continues in v. 1b: "How ... the sacred stones lie scattered at the head of every street." The phrase "sacred stones" (*'abnê-qōdeš*) appears nowhere else in Scripture. Some maintain that it refers to the stones of the high priest's breastplate, though these are hardly numerous enough to be "scattered at the head of every street." Others maintain that these are the stones of the temple and of the palaces that in 1 Kings are referred to as "precious stones" (*'ăbānîm yəqārôt*) (1 Kgs 5:31; 7:9–11).[7] The use of the construct *qōdeš* parallels a use witnessed in Isa 43:28 (NCV): "So I will make your holy rulers (*śārê-qōdeš*) unholy." Some say, following 1 Chr 24:5 that these refer to priests, which would support understanding *'abnê-qōdeš* as the stones of the temple. The medieval rabbinic commentators Ibn Caspi and Abarbanel understood the term *śārê-qōdeš* in Isa 43:28 as officers of the king, and by this reading, *'abnê-qōdeš* could mean the stones of the palaces. Either way, these stones that now lay scattered are stones that symbolized the inviolability of Zion, as portrayed by the psalmist (Ps 48:12–14): "Walk about Zion; go all around it; count its towers; consider well its ramparts; go through its citadels, that you may tell the next generation that this is God, our God forever and ever. He will be our guide forever." The narrator draws attention to the shattered stones, themselves a potent symbol of a shattered theological paradigm.

The chiding of Zion theology continues in v. 2: "The precious children of Zion, *worth their weight in fine gold* – how they are reckoned as earthen pots, the work of a potter's hands!" Here we learn that the corroded gold of v.1 in

---

7   Dobbs-Allsopp, *Lamentations*, 130.

primary fashion represents the precious children of Zion. The term "children of Zion" is unusual and invokes the "children of Zion" who rejoice in their heavenly king who guarantees their victory over their enemies (Ps 149:2). Yet, here, these triumphal "children of Zion" are reduced to pottery shards, or, in the language of the metaphor of v.1, scattered like stones at the head of every street. Telling here is the image of "earthen pots, the work of a potter's hands." In the prophetic literature, the metaphor of the LORD as a potter (Isa 64:7[ET 8]; Jer 18:6) highlights his capacity to reshape the destiny of his people whenever he chooses and the earthen pot cannot question how the potter has styled it (Isa 45:9).[8] By comparing the once-triumphant "children of Zion" to earthen pots, the narrator reminds the community that Zion theology in no way limits how the LORD can arrange the affairs of Israel.

Structural analyses of the chapter often note that the victims of suffering are featured progressively, beginning with children in vv. 3–4 and possibly 5. However, more than these concentrate on the suffering of the young, they focus more squarely on the inability of mothers to feed their young. The image of the jackals who "offer the breast" in v. 3 is particularly telling. While jackals, of course, are mammals, they are incapable of the human act of "offering the breast." The image underscores the point that even wild animals are now more "humane" than humans themselves, as "the tongue of the infant sticks to the roof of its mouth for thirst" (2:4). The NRSVue translation of *bat-ʿammî lǝʾakzār* as "my people has become cruel," rightly expresses the inability of parents to care for their children, borne out further by v. 4b, "the children beg for food, but there is nothing for them."

The inability of parents to provide for their children represents a repudiation of Zion theology. The royal psalm of Psalm 144 contains a prayer the Davidic king utters in which he beseeches the LORD (Ps 144:12): "May our sons in their youth be like plants full grown, our daughters like corner pillars, cut for the building of a palace." The most elementary desire of the king, expressing the desire of every parent, is for an environment in which children can be nourished to full maturity. Lamentations 4 opens its critique of the social world in which Zion theology flourished by bringing attention to the utter inability of parents to provide for their children.

In v. 5, the narrator turns his critical eye to the aristocracy. Delicacies (*maʿădannîm*) are the foods of royalty in Gen 49:20. *Tôlāʿ*, the *coccus ilicis* worm, produces the dye used to make crimson, which is also associated with royalty (2 Sam 1:24): "O daughters of Israel, weep over Saul, who clothed

---

8   Berlin, *Lamentations*, 105.

you with crimson, in luxury." Status, which was of such importance prior to the destruction, is of no importance now.[9] Those donned in crimson cling to the garbage heaps, which may be their refuge for warmth, or a way of expressing that their corpses are discarded like dung. The deprivation of those formerly endowed with status is on display for all to see in the most public of spheres – "in the streets" and at the dung heaps.

Verses 1–16 catalog the suffering of Zion with a focus on starvation, as the pastoral mentor creates a mélange of snapshots of individuals in their suffering. However, this collage is punctuated by interruptions. In vv. 6, 11, and 16, the pastoral mentor depicts no new images of suffering, but instead engages in theological reflection, and then returns to his depictions of suffering. This poetic strategy is seen nowhere else in Lamentations. We may read that the pastoral mentor seeks to lead Bat-Zion to reflection, in light of her persistent belief in Zion theology. Verse by verse he paints pictures that highlight the bankrupt nature of this belief. Scholars of belief persistence note that to challenge a flawed but persistent belief system, "the alternative explanation provided by the correction must be plausible, account for the important causal qualities in the initial report, and, ideally, explain why the misinformation was thought to be correct in the first place."[10] This the pastoral mentor achieves in v. 6. Most translations understand the *wayyiqtōl* verb *wayyigdāl* as a perfect: The sin of Bat-Ami is greater than the iniquity of Sodom. But the Geneva Bible more accurately captures the sense of the verse: "For the iniquity of the daughter of my people *is become greater* than the sin of Sodom, that was destroyed as in a moment."[11] This has been a process that reaches its climax. The LORD extended Zion a line of credit. For a long time, her behavior went unpunished and thus it seemed that Zion theology was vindicated: The LORD protects his chosen people, king, city, and temple. This is why "the misinformation was thought to be correct in

---

9   Some understand that this verse also refers specifically to children, following vv. 2–4, and understand the word *'ĕmunîm* not merely as "accustomed to" but as "brought up" in scarlet. See a review of positions in Salters, *Lamentations*, 294.

10 Stephan Lewandowsky, et al., "Misinformation and Its Correction: Continued Influence and Successful Debiasing," *Psychological Science in the Public Interest* 13 (2012): 116–17.

11 Many scholars understand the word *āwôn* here as punishment, because, after all, it is Zion's punishment here that he is describing, an understanding already rendered by the medieval exegete Ibn Ezra. However, *āwôn* here must mean iniquity or sin, as it stands in parallel to the sin (*ḥaṭṭā't*) of Sodom. Indeed, several of the prophets compared Israel's iniquity to that of Sodom (Isa 1:9; Jer 23:14; Amos 4:11; Ezek 16:46–56). This follows the rendering by all the ancient translations. See Salters, *Lamentations*, 296–97, for general discussion.

the first place." Now the pastoral mentor provides the correction by noting that Bat-Ami's sin *has become* greater than that of Sodom, and hence the severity of the divine response. He provides her an alternative lens through which to interpret events. The pastoral mentor refers to her as Bat-Ami (as he had in v. 3), literally, "daughter of my people" and not as Bat-Zion. By this juncture, she no longer finds favor in the LORD's eye; she is not "choice" or "worthy," possible meanings for "Zion." At the same time, the pastoral mentor extends to her his support by referring to her as Bat-Ami; almost as if to say, "she is no longer Bat-Zion, but even in her iniquity, she remains Bat-Ami – daughter of *my* people."

In v. 7, the pastoral mentor returns to his critique of the social order engendered by Zion theology and focuses on the nobles. They are referred to here as *nəzîrêhā*, her nazirs, which likely means elites or princes (cf. Gen 49:26; Deut 33:16; Nah 3:17), and is derived from the word *nēzer*, "crown." The opening stich, "Her princes were purer than snow," may simply be a comment on the light complexion of their skin, and a parallel to the following phrase, "whiter than milk." However, throughout the Hebrew Bible, the term *zāk* bears the connotation not of "bright" nor "light" but of "pure." Likewise, the metaphor of snow is oft-used as a trope for the absence of sin (Isa 1:18; Ps 51:9; Job 9:30). This suggests that the tone of the pastoral mentor's words is one of chiding. All those associated with the king, such as officers, are singled out for condemnation throughout Jeremiah (e.g., Jer 2:26; 4:9; 25:18; 34:21). It would be incongruous for the pastoral mentor to excoriate Bat-Zion because her iniquity is greater than that of Sodom in v. 6, and then declare in v. 7 that her princes were purer than snow. Rather, the pastoral mentor here mirrors or perhaps even parrots what the princes would have said of themselves. The last element of the description, *sappîr gizrātām*, has been interpreted as either "their hair was sapphire" or "their stature was sapphire," and is likewise a sign of the royal standing of those in focus here. Modern commentators point to the statues of Mesopotamian kings, in which hair and beards were designated by inlays of lapis lazuli, and understand our phrase as a borrowing of this image.[12] These, according to v. 8, became unrecognizable at the *ḥûṣôt*. The NRSVue translates this as "in the streets," but it is a term that we have seen twice already. This is the site, where the "sacred stones" are now scattered (v. 1) and where those that would eat royal delicacies now roam with astonishment (v. 5). The debasement of royalty, here too, is laid out on display for all to see.

---

12   Berlin, *Lamentations*, 107.

Verse 9 depicts how those that died of starvation endured a more difficult end than those that were stricken by the sword. But the NRSVue translation, indeed as most translations, doesn't reflect the literal meaning of the words in v. 9b. A literal translation of the verse yields, "More fortunate were the victims of the sword than the victims of starvation; for these oozed, stabbed, from the bounty of the field." The words *tənûbōt śādāy* are normally translated as "produce of the field." However, in the two other references in the Hebrew Bible, the connotation of the term is not merely the produce of the field, but the bounty of the field. This is evident in the King James Version translation to Deut 32:13: "He made him ride on the high places of the earth, that he might eat *the increase of the fields*; and he made him to suck honey out of the rock, and oil out of the flinty rock" (cf. Ezek 36:30). When the author of Lam 4:9 describes the victims of starvation as oozing the bounty of the field, it is a critique that suggests they have squandered the LORD's blessing.

The epitome of this deprivation, this "bleeding" from starvation is laid out in v. 10. The pastoral mentor had noted that Sodom was fortunate relative to Zion because it was "overthrown in a moment, though no hand was laid on it" (v. 6). Here, the pastoral mentor notes a bitter truth. Far worse than any foreign hand that was laid on Zion was the hand that starving mothers in Judah laid on their own children to stave off their own starvation. Grammatically, it is the women that do this, as if, with their own hands. And here, too, the opening metaphor of the chapter is apt: "How the gold has grown dim; how the pure gold is changed!" How is it that the impossible has come to be; how is it that "compassionate women" have come to boil their own children? There is at the same time a note of identification with the community. The pastoral mentor refers to the tragedy that has befallen "Bat-Ami," well translated here in the NRSVue as "my people." Even as they have been rejected as "Bat-Zion," they remain for the pastoral mentor, "Bat-Ami."

Verse 11 is a refrain verse; as in v. 6, the pastoral mentor steps away from his vivid description of the suffering transpiring below on the streets and outskirts of Jerusalem, and takes stock of what has happened above, as it were, in the heavens. The LORD has executed his wrath to full measure. Verse 11 likewise continues the theme of the realization of the impossible: the consumption of the foundations by fire, when, in fact, stone foundations cannot burn.[13] The verse is important, however, particularly in light of the belief persistence of Bat-Zion. These horrible afflictions are not the

---

13   Hillers, *Lamentations*, 148–49.

acts of a human enemy. They are wrought by the very same deity whom the people thought was the guarantor of their safety. The verse comes to dispel the thought that a vicious enemy has done this, and that a merciful god of Israel will notice and bring solace – the LORD has "kindled a fire *in Zion*."

In v. 12, the pastoral mentor chides, and even parodies the people's trust in Zion theology: "The kings of the earth did not believe, nor did any of the inhabitants of the world, that foe or enemy could enter the gates of Jerusalem." As Adele Berlin notes, in reality, other nations would not have been the least surprised that Jerusalem was destroyed by the Babylonian empire. No nation would have harbored the sentiments expressed in this verse on the eve of the destruction. Instead, we should read these musings as those of Judahites who have fallen victim to belief persistence concerning Zion theology, who still hide behind a defense mechanism. They still hear the words of Isaiah stated during the siege of Sennacherib (2 Kgs 19:34): "For I will defend this city to save it, for my own sake and for the sake of my servant David." As noted earlier, the people expressed ultimate belief in the inviolability of the city (Jer 7:9). In invoking the ostensible inner sentiments of the "kings of the earth," it is as if the pastoral mentor parodies the sustained belief by the people in the words of Psalm 48:4–8: "Then the kings assembled; they came on together. As soon as they saw it, they were astounded; they were in panic; they took to flight; trembling took hold of them there … As we have heard, so have we seen in the city of the LORD of hosts in the city of our God, which God establishes forever."

The critique of the social order moves into high gear beginning in v. 13, where the pastoral mentor takes aim at the prophets and priests and lays the blame for the destruction at their feet. By focusing primary aim at the priests and the prophets, the pastoral mentor is able to blunt somewhat his direct accusation of the people, creating a space for them to open up and speak themselves, as they will shortly do. This is a tactic he has used before, as we saw earlier in v. 2:14, where he laid primary blame for the destruction at the feet of the false prophets who had not properly warned Israel about her behavior.

The pastoral mentor charges the priests and prophets with having "shed the blood of the righteous," although nowhere in the Hebrew Bible are either prophets or priests said to engage in actual murder. Adele Berlin maintains that the accusation of shedding blood is a cipher for idolatry as found in Ezek 22:1–5 and Ps 106:37–40, and need not be taken literally.[14] Dilbert Hillers surmises that the priests and prophets overlooked and

---

14 Berlin, *Lamentations*, 110.

thereby provided tacit cover for the murder of the righteous and thus it is as if they did it themselves.[15] Nonetheless, while Jeremiah and Ezekiel condemn the leaders and the people for the killing of innocent people, we find no specific reference to priests and prophets in this regard (Jer 7:6; 19:4; 22:3, 17; Ezek 22:27). Rather, it would seem that the shedding of righteous blood here is a reference to the failed leadership of the priests and prophets, and their responsibility for the destruction of the entire city. Concerning the priests and prophets, Jeremiah says (6:13–15):

> For from the least to the greatest of them, everyone is greedy for unjust gain; and from prophet to priest, everyone deals falsely. They have treated the wound of my people carelessly, saying, "Peace, peace," when there is no peace. They acted shamefully; they committed abomination, yet they were not ashamed; they did not know how to blush. Therefore they shall fall among those who fall; at the time that I punish them, they shall be overthrown, says the LORD.

Verse 14 is an interpretive crux, as it is unclear which group of Judeans is the subject of the verse. Some understand that, as in the previous verse, the subject here is the prophets and the priests, in which case the poet continues his critique of the corrupted spiritual elites.[16] The trope of wandering in blindness here accords with Jer 23:11–12, where the wayward prophets and priests are warned that they will stumble and fall in darkness. Alternatively, I would suggest that the "blindness" is not a dazed stupor due to suffering, but rather a spiritual blindness, a trope oft raised in Second Isaiah (Isa 42:7, 16, 18–19; 43:8; 56:10; 59:10; cf. Zeph 1:17). Isaiah 56:10, particularly, speaks of the blindness of the sentinels – those charged with alarming and warning the people. These failed leaders now meet an ironic fate, and their elect status is inverted: The priests, particularly, are commanded to avoid impurity (Lev. 21:1–15) and to instruct others concerning the distinctions between that which is pure and impure (Lev 10:8–11; 13–14). These priests, who would have been scrupulously observant of the laws of purity and avoid contact with a corpse, are now themselves impure with the blood they have spilt. Others now avoid contact with them, and will not touch their clothing. Alternatively, the difficult clause may be read to say that the priests and prophets themselves stumble around so blindly that their clothes inadvertently rub against the corpses they would normally avoid. This is particularly ironic in light of the statement of Zion theology in Psalm 132, which

---

[15]   Hillers, *Lamentations*, 149.
[16]   See discussion in Salters, *Lamentations*, 315.

states concerning the dress of the priests of Zion (Ps 132:16), "its priests I will clothe with salvation." It is also possible to read that the blood-drenched clothes are their own and stand as a metaphor for their culpability for having brought Israel to doom.

Others maintain that the people as a whole are the subject of the verse.[17] It is they who are blind, and it is they who are so blood-drenched, presumably from the sword, that they are defiled, and others will not touch their clothes. Indeed, if the subject of v. 14 is the people and the blood is literal, this could resonate with imagery further on in vv. 18–19, which suggest that with the breach of the walls, there was an impending sense of doom.

If v. 14 is a crux, v. 15 is even more so. There is little consensus among exegetes across the ages as to the speaker in the first half of the verse, the addressee, or the subject of the verse's second stich, nor to the circumstances described. Some see the verse as the continuation of the inverted status of the priests and prophets. They are so blood-drenched that passersby now call out to others to avoid contact with them. However, most exegetes understand that this verse is speaking of the people. Verse 15b says that this group will no longer be able to reside among the gentiles. This may mean in exile, or it may mean "among the community of the nations" as it does in v. 20b. Both connotations make greater sense when taken as a reference to the people as a whole. Moreover, the term *lōʾ yôsîpû* seems to parallel *lōʾ yôsîp* in v. 16a, which is clearly a reference to the people as a whole. The cry of the passers-by, "Away! Unclean!" in v. 15a is the warning issued to a leper in Lev 13:45 and implies their rejection. Some maintain that these are the words of the gentiles to the Judeans in exile,[18] though the action here seems to occur locally, within Jerusalem and demonstrates the rejection heaped upon the people by their vanquishers or by passers-by while they are yet in their own homeland. The feeling here matches the community's earlier sentiment (3:45), "You have made us filth and rubbish among the peoples." The verse will later be repurposed by Second Isaiah, who implores the returning exiles (Isa 52:11), "Depart, depart, go out from there! Touch no unclean thing; go out from the midst of it; purify yourselves, you who carry the vessels of the LORD." In Isa 52, it is Babylonia, not Judah, who is impure; Judah will distance herself from the impurity of Babylonia as a person distances himself from a leper.[19] If, indeed, v. 15

---

[17]   Hillers, *Lamentations*, 149; Renkema, *Lamentations*, 530; Salters, *Lamentations*, 316.
[18]   Hillers, *Lamentations*, 150, as already found as early as the Targum.
[19]   Berlin, *Lamentations*, 111–12.

focuses on the people and not the priests and prophets as in the previous two verses, the overall critique of the social order rarified by Zion theology is nonetheless maintained. Far from living as the LORD's elected people in his elected land, they have been reduced to ridicule and debasement by foreign conquerors of the land.

Verse 16 is a refrain verse – it details the LORD's activity. The inversion of Zion theology is extended once more in v. 16a. The inhabitants of Jerusalem are scattered – presumably to exile – literally, by "the face of the LORD," a phrase that connotes divine anger (Lev 17:10; Pss 34:17; 80:17). The phrase *lōʾ yōsîp ləhabbîṭām* is rendered by the NRSVue as "he will regard them no more," but more closely bears the connotation found in the New International Version, "he no longer watches over them." This is an inversion of the Zion theology found in Ps 102:18–22:

> [18] Let this be recorded for a generation to come,
>   so that a people yet unborn may praise the LORD:
> [19] that he looked down from his holy height,
>   from heaven the LORD *watched over* (*hibbiṭ*) the earth,
> [20] to hear the groans of the prisoners,
>   to set free those who were doomed to die,
> [21] so that the name of the LORD may be declared in Zion
>   and his praise in Jerusalem,
> [22] when peoples gather together,
>   and kingdoms, to serve the LORD.

The ultimate debasement of the elite classes is registered in v. 16b, "no honor was shown to the priests, no favor to the elders." As the beginning of the verse referred to dispersal, the second half of the verse refers to the absence of deferential treatment that the priests and elders receive from the gentile host nations in exile. The phrase here *lōʾ nāśāʾû zəqênîm lōʾ ḥānānû* is a fulfillment of Deut 28:49–50, "The LORD will bring a nation from far away, from the end of the earth, to swoop down on you like an eagle, a nation whose language you do not understand, a grim-faced nation showing no respect to the old (*lōʾ yiśśāʾ panîm ləzāqēn*) or favor (*yāḥōn*) to the young. Here the curse is applied to the priests and to the elders, who elsewhere are also seen as senior members of a king's court (1 Kgs 12:6; Ps 105:22).

In summary, the soliloquy of the pastoral mentor, in vv. 1–16, highlights the debasement of the elites of royal Zion society: those that eat delicacies (v. 5), the princes (vv. 7–8), the priests, and the prophets (vv. 13–15). He demonstrates how the elect status of Zion has been overthrown as demonstrated

by the degradation of its edifices (v. 1) and in the lost status Zion now has in
the eyes of the nations (vv. 12, 15–16). The reversal of Zion's social structure is
so total that mothers are dehumanized relative to jackals (v. 3) and by bringing their own hands to destroy their precious young (v. 10). At intervals of
refrain – vv. 6, 11 and 16 – he ensures that the community understands that
it is the LORD of Zion who himself has wrought all of this, and that no trust
should be placed in his unconditional love on account of their chosen status.

THE COMMUNITY RECONSIDERS ITS POLITICAL THEOLOGY (VV. 17–20)

Verse 17 begins a four-verse sequence all said in the plural voice. Here, we
find the remnant community rethinking and reconsidering political positions they had harbored, stemming from Zion theology. These four verses
are the culture script that the author pens; these are the sentiments that he
wishes his audience to digest and adopt. The confession begins with v. 17:
"Our eyes failed, ever watching vainly for help; we were watching eagerly
for a nation that could not save." The "vanity" of this search that the foreign
nation in question "could not save" is a recognition that now dawns on them.
It is not the disposition that they harbored at the time, when they yet held out
hope for foreign assistance. Most understand that this is a reference to the
anticipation the remnant had held for assistance from Egypt (cf. Jer 41–44),
or perhaps for the arrival of the forces of Pharaoh Hophra, which caused the
Babylonians to briefly retreat, arousing false expectations of salvation (Jer
34:21; 37:6–8; 44:30). The reference here, "watching vainly for help," seems,
indeed, to be to Egyptian salvation as the language of this phrase echoes
that of the injunction of the prophet Isaiah to turn to Egypt for assistance
(Isa 30:1–7). The terms here, "help" (*'ezrātēnû*) and "worthless," (*hābel*) are
found in Isaiah's assessment of the value of a treaty with Egypt (Isa 30:7):
"For Egypt's help (*ya'zōrû*) is worthless (*hebel*) and empty." There is a self-
incriminating facetiousness to their expression. Now adopting the language
of Isaiah, ruefully they recall their searching eyes; their futile search for a savior that was never there in the first place. In this chapter, devoted to the vanity of status now lost, the last vestige of mastery, of ownership, is lamented
in v. 18: "They dogged our steps so that we could not walk in *our* streets."[20]

At first blush, vv. 18–19 appear to be a lament about persecution, displace-
ment, and despair. However, these verses perform a higher order task as

---

[20]   Salters, *Lamentations*, 328.

well. They enunciate another mistaken conception that had been harbored by the community on the eve of its decimation: that invasion of the city meant assured annihilation. Key here are the linguistic and thematic links between these verses and a passage in Jeremiah 4. There the prophet details the imminent arrival of the enemy and the people's anticipated response to it (Jer 4:13): "Look! He comes up like clouds, his chariots like the whirlwind; his horses *are swifter than eagles* – woe to us, for we are ruined!" The trope of the enemy being "swifter than eagles" and the exclamation that the end is nigh for Judah are both found in Lam 4:18–19. However, the belief that the end was nigh was a mistaken one. In Jeremiah 4, we read that although the people will be convinced they face obliteration, the LORD says (Jer 4:27), "The whole land shall be a desolation, *yet I will not make a full end*" (cf. Jer 5:10, 18; 30:11; 46:28). Zion theology led the people to believe that if, in fact, the LORD was not there to safeguard his elect people and city, then surely nothing could prevent their utter annihilation. The confession of the community in vv. 17–20 clearly happens after the destruction of the city, not during it. Within the world of the poem, the community reflects on its prior assumption that they would be annihilated. Now it is clear that while they indeed have suffered greatly, they have also survived, as well. The author pens a culture script that mandates the listening/reading audience to consider the sentiments for themselves. They too should now realize that their pessimism – rooted in a misunderstanding of covenantal theology – was unfounded. Utter annihilation was never in the offing. Thus, a second conception of the community at the time of the destruction is dispelled.

This leads us to v. 20, the third, and most cardinal confession of prior theological misconceptions. Some interpret the verse as an affirmation of kingship. The term "The LORD's anointed" is oft-found in the royal psalms (e.g., Pss 2:2; 20:7; 132:10, 17). By this reading, just as the psalmist in Psalm 89 laments the LORD's treatment of his anointed one, so too does the author of Lamentations here. Dilbert Hillers notes that this passage is given prominent place as the climax of the tragic fall of the nation that has been detailed until now.[21] Jewish sources have entertained a range of opinions concerning the identity of this anointed king. The Targum maintains that the capture of the king refers to Josiah at the hands of Pharaoh Neco (2 Kgs 23:29–30), an opinion echoed in the Midrash and by Rashi. Other medieval commentators suggest that it may have been Gedaliah or Jehoiachin.[22] However, most

---

[21] Hillers, *Lamentations*, 152.
[22] See review in Klein, *Lamentations*, 246, and in Assis, *Lamentations*, 240.

medieval voices concur with the broad consensus of modern commentators that the reference is to Zedekiah as he fled the city (2 Kgs 25:5–7; Jer 39:4–7; 52:8–11).[23] The verse, though, is less about Zedekiah personally than it is about the office and status of the anointed king.

Rather than a lament about the fall of the Davidic king, however, this verse is better understood as the climax of the communal confession of vv. 17–20 and a recognition of cognitive folly by the community. The key to this understanding is rooted in its use of two phrases that have distinct connotations within biblical and cognate literature: the king as "the breath of our life" and the notion that under the king's "shadow" they would dwell among the nations. Both are terms that are *de rigueur* in the literature of the ancient Near East as expressions of the king's power and status. Neither is ever used within the Hebrew Bible with reference to the Davidic king. Instead, the two are tropes that are reserved for the LORD alone. By recalling that they had ascribed these epitaphs to the Davidic king, they implicitly recognize that they had overestimated his status and powers, and had viewed him in the semidivine terms with which ancient monarchs were regarded by their subjects.

The phrase *rûaḥ ʾappênû* "breath of our life" is a trope found throughout the ancient Near East as a reference to the sustaining power of the monarch for his people. Thus, already in the twentieth century BCE, we find that the Sumerian monarch Lipit-Ishtar boasts in one of his hymns, "I am he who desires/provides/grants inspiration/life for his city."[24] Ramesses II is referred to as "the breath of our nostrils" in an inscription from Abydos.[25] Conversely, it is said of Seti I, "He causes all rebels to desist from all boasting with their mouths – he has taken away the very breath of their nostrils."[26] The first-century Roman philosopher Seneca wrote of the emperor, "He is the breath of life to all these many thousands."[27]

By contrast, we never find elsewhere in the Hebrew Bible that the king "instills spirit/wind into the nostrils" of his subjects. Rather, it is the

---

[23]   See review in Salters, *Lamentations*, 331.

[24]   *ETCSL* translation: 2.5.5.1, line 69: "A Praise Poem of Lipit-Eštar (Lipit-Eštar A)," etcsl. orinst.ox.ac.uk. The *ETCSL* translation reads, "I am he who desires liveliness for his city." The translation offered here is that of Jacob Klein through private communication.

[25]   Salters, *Lamentations*, 331, following J. de Savignac, "Theologie Pharaonique et Messianisme d'Israel," *VT* 7 (1957): 82.

[26]   "Karnak, Campaign Against the Libyans," *KRI* 1:23, line 1–24, line 4. The translated text is found in *COS* 2.3:31 (trans. by K. A. Kitchens).

[27]   Seneca, *Seneca, De Clementia: Edited with Translation and Commentary by Susanna Braund* (Oxford: Oxford University Press, 2011), 101.

LORD who breathes life into the nostrils of man (Gen 2:7; cf. Exod 15:8; Ps 104:29–30). Thus, when the community wails or sighs, "the breath of our nostrils, The LORD's anointed was taken in their pits," the tone is rueful and wry. It is a recognition that they had overvalued and misconstrued the powers and status of the LORD's anointed one, much as they had overestimated in v. 17 the salvation to be delivered by the foreign ally that never arrived.

That this verse has a confessional aspect to it is even more evident from its use of the trope of the king's protective "shadow," when the community members state that they had ruminated that the Davidic king was "the one of whom we said, 'Under his shadow we shall live among the nations.'" The Akkadian phrase *ina ṣilli ša šarri*, "in the shade/shadow of the king," can be used to refer to a king's aegis, protection, or defense, as well as to the financial support that he provides to those close to him.[28] Thus, we find in one letter:

> Quickly may they (i.e., the princes) go to the palace; the month Abu is favorable and all its days are very advantageous (for audiences). I dance for joy (because) it (i. e. the month) is indeed greatly fitting for visiting the king, my LORD! The king my LORD, is looked upon (in this moment) by all the great gods, (therefore) the 'shadow' of the king, my LORD, is (indeed) exceedingly beneficent (in this time). Thus they may go to the palace and stay (ddlu) in the sweet and fine 'shadow' of the king, my LORD![29]

However, in the Hebrew Bible, the Davidic king never offers his people "shade." That sort of protective shade we find proffered only from the LORD, himself (Ezek 17:22–23; Isa 49:2; Pss 17:8; 91:1; 121:5). The protective "shade" of foreign kings is mocked at Isa 30:2 and at Ezek 31:13.[30] As with the phrase "breath of our life," here, too, the reference to the hoped for "shade" is a mea culpa. When they state now, "The LORD's anointed, the breath of our life, was taken in their pits – *the one of whom we said*, 'Under his shadow we shall live among the nations,'" it is a recognition that they had overvalued and misconstrued the powers and status of the LORD's anointed one.

---

[28] *CAD* 16:191–92. See further, David Janzen, "Gideon's House as the אטד ['āṭād]: A Proposal for Reading Jotham's Fable," *CBQ* 74 (2012): 465–75; A. Leo Oppenheim, "Assyriological Gleanings IV," *BASOR* 107 (1947): 7–11. On the trope of protective shade in the Bible see Ariel Kopilovitz, "From Vassal to Empire: The Metamorphosis of Israel's Leadership and Statehood in Ezekiel 17," *CBQ* 85 (2023), 237–55 at 246–48.

[29] *ABL* 652: 12–rev. 13, translated in Oppenheim, "Assyriological Gleanings IV," 9.

[30] Salters, *Lamentations*, 333; cf. Jud 9:15, where the thorn bush, a metaphor for the evil Abimelech, boasts of his protective shade.

THE PROMISE OF SALVATION IN THE WAKE
OF CONFESSION (VV. 21–22)

The culture script of communal confession sets up the final two verses of the poem. In vv. 21–22, we again hear from the pastoral mentor. As we noted in the introduction to the chapter, we find here notes of comfort and salvation unparalleled elsewhere in Lamentations. However, in light of the reading strategy offered here, these are well understood. The chapter is devoted to a critique of Zion theology, and particularly the social and political structures it engendered. In vv. 1–16, the pastoral mentor called attention to the reversed fortunes of all the elites and to the very breakdown of the society that invested in this theology. In vv. 17–20, the community itself undergoes a reckoning concerning its prior positions. Once the constructed communal voice achieves this new and enlightened perspective, it is only natural that the pastoral mentor responds with words of comfort and encouragement.

The speaker predicts with confidence the future that is in store respectively for Edom and for Zion. Some scholars, apparently convinced that the genre of Lamentations disallows the possibility of prophecy within its composition, maintain that these verses are merely warnings to Edom and words of comfort and encouragement to Israel.[31] Adele Berlin in her textual notes to v. 22 writes, "The verbs are in the perfect tense, as if the poet, like a prophet, sees these actions as already completed."[32] Renkema rejects seeing this as prophecy as there is no evidence that Zion's punishment is at an end.[33]

But these verses read naturally as prophecy. They resonate with no other sections of the Hebrew Bible as they do with the prophecies of Jeremiah. The trope of giving the cup of wrath to the nations is central to Jer 25:15–29, which includes references to the land of Uz and to Edom (vv. 20–21). In his lengthy prophecy against Edom (Jer 49:7–22), Jeremiah warns that Edom will one day be forced to drink the cup of wrath (49:12). These verses, then, are the strongest indication that the pastoral mentor is also at times a prophetic figure, buttressing the claim that the implied identity of the pastoral mentor is that of Jeremiah himself, or that he is a Jeremiah-like figure.[34]

---

[31] Hillers, *Lamentations*, 152, understands these as wishes.
[32] Berlin, *Lamentations*, 102.
[33] Renkema, *Lamentations*, 564–66.
[34] The verses were understood as prophecy by all medieval rabbinic commentators and by many modern English translations. For overview, see Assis, *Eichah*, 235, n. 56 and Salters, *Lamentations*, 336.

BRIDGING THE HORIZONS: LAMENTATIONS IN THE CHRISTIAN TRADITION

Patristic interpretation of the Old Testament, generally speaking, engaged in Christological readings of the text, sought out prophetic messages within it, and mined the text for moral instruction for the life of the Church.[35] Patristic readings of Lamentations were no different. Above all, Lamentations was seen as a prophetic witness to the person of Jesus through interpretation of Lam 4:20, "The LORD's anointed, the breath of our life, was taken in their pits – the one of whom we said, 'Under his shadow we shall live among the nations.'" From the second to the seventh century CE, this verse was interpreted as a witness to the spiritual and divine natures of Christ, a prophecy of Christ's coming, and a prophecy concerning Christ's Lordship and death.

Origen derives instruction for the life of the Church, for example, in his commentary to Lam 1:10, "Enemies have stretched out their hands over all her precious things; she has even seen the nations invade her sanctuary, those whom you forbade to enter your congregation." He suggests that Jerusalem in captivity to Babylon spiritually signifies the soul, or the Church's captivity to demonic power. Demons – allegorically represented by the Babylonians – invade the reason, that is, the "sanctuary" of the believer, where the LORD dwells. This invasion leads to confusion in the heart and life of the believer.[36]

Another example of such interpretation is seen in the interpretation of Gregory the Great to Lam 3:1, "I am one who has seen affliction under the rod of God's wrath." For Gregory, Jeremiah expresses the pain involved in banishing any love of the present life in favor of the riches of the heavenly kingdom. In Gregory's interpretation, Lamentations serves

---

[35] On patristic interpretation to Lamentations, see Heath A. Thomas, "Lamentations in the Patristic Period," *Great Is Thy Faithfulness? Reading Lamentations as Sacred Scripture*, eds. Robin A. Parry and Heath A. Thomas (Eugene, OR: Pickwick Publications, 2011), 113–19.

[36] For an English translation of Origen's reconstructed commentary, see Joseph W. Trigg, *Origen* (London: Routledge, 1998), 73–85. For the critical edition of the reconstructed original, see Origenes, *Origenes Werke: Band [vol.] 3; Jeremiahomilien; Klageliederkommentar; Erklärung Der Samuel-Und Königsbücher*, ed. Erich Klostermann, in Die griechischen christlichen Schriftsteller der ersten [drei] Jahrhunderte, Band [vol.] 6 (Leipzig: J. C. Hinrichs'sche Buchhandlung, 1901), 235–78. The comments here are found in Trigg, *Origen*, 80–82.

as a vehicle of instruction for the Church's spiritual formation. It models for the Church how to let go of this world and await God's coming heavenly kingdom.[37] In a similar vein, Cassian cites Lam 2:18, "Cry aloud to the LORD! O wall of daughter Zion! Let tears stream down like a torrent day and night! Give yourself no rest, your eyes no respite!," as a call for penitence and weeping over sin.[38] Eusebius, in his *Ecclesiastical History*, bemoans infighting within the leadership of the Church and highlights the great chasm between its strife-riven reality and its lofty calling with reference to Lam 2:1–2:

> How the LORD in his anger has humiliated daughter Zion! He has thrown down from heaven to earth the splendor of Israel; he has not remembered his footstool in the day of his anger. The LORD has destroyed without mercy all the dwellings of Jacob; in his wrath he has broken down the strongholds of daughter Judah; he has brought down to the ground in dishonor the kingdom and its rulers.[39]

The Fathers also read Lamentations as a prophetic text concerning the suffering of Jesus. In this context, Irenaeus cites Lam 3:30: "to give one's cheek to the smiter, and be filled with insults."[40] In his fourth century "Commentary on the Apostles' Creed," Rufinus sees the foretelling of Jesus' death and burial alluded to in Lam 3:53, "they flung me alive into a pit and hurled stones on me."[41]

The most significant liturgical use of Lamentations has been in the traditional service known as "Tenebrae," which was the Holy Week service of Matins and Lauds that was celebrated on Maundy Thursday,

---

[37] See Gregory the Great, *Expositio in Librum Job, sive Moralium libri xxv*, 3 vols., trans. by Members of the English Church, eds. Edward Bouverie Pusey, John Keble, and John Newman, in A Library of Fathers of the Holy Catholic Church, Anterior to the Division of the East and West 31 (Oxford: John Henry Parker; London: F&J Rivington, 1850), 3.2:622.

[38] Cassian, "John Cassian," in *Sulpitius Severus, Vincent of Lerins, John Cassian* (Repr., New York: The Christian Literature Company; Oxford: Parker & Company, 1894, trans., prolegomena, prefaces, and notes by Edgar C. S. Gibson, *NPNF* 2/11:397).

[39] Eusebius, *Historia ecclesiastica* 8.1.8 (Repr., New York: The Christian Literature Company; Oxford: Parker & Company, 1890, trans., prolegomena and notes by Arthur Cushman McGiffert, *NPNF* 2/1:324).

[40] Irenaeus, *Epideixis tou apostolikou kērygmatos*, paragraph 68 (Repr., London: SPCK, 1920, trans., introduction and notes by J. Armitage Robinson, 129–30).

[41] Rufinus, *Symbolum apostolorum*, paragraph 27 (Repr., New York: The Christian Literature Company; Oxford: Parker & Company, 1892, trans., prolegomena and notes by Canon W. H. Fremantle, *NPNF* 2/3:553).

Good Friday, and Holy Saturday, a tradition stretching back at least to the eighth-century Carolingian church.[42] As part of the service, selections from Lamentations were read as candles inside the church were slowly and systematically snuffed out until, by the end of the service, the church was in total darkness (apart from a single candle that remained lit for the reader). The proclamation of the Lamentations took place during the first Nocturn on each of the three days. It was common that members of the choir would sing in a particular order, beginning with the youngest voice. The great composers of the late Middle Ages and the Renaissance created significant settings of these Lamentations texts, and also of the responsories between each.

On Maundy Thursday, portions of Lam 1:1–14 were read. These verses speak of the affliction that has come to the city as a result of the crimes of the people, ending with an appeal to Jerusalem to return to the LORD. Interspersed between the reading of the verses, the responsory speaks of Christ on the Mount of Olives, overlooking the city, the betrayal by Judas and finally words of the Suffering Servant from Isa 53, demonstrating that both Isaiah and Jeremiah speak prophetically of the sufferings of Christ.

On Good Friday, Lam 2:8–10 and 3:1–9 were read. The former passage speaks of the misery that has come upon the people of the city, with particular attention paid to the plight of women. After Lam 2:8–11, the responsory speaks of the abandonment suffered by the LORD, treated as a common criminal, and given vinegar to drink. The latter portion, Lam 3:1–9, moves to the suffering one, afflicted, broken, and enclosed by stone (Lam 3:53) – words that would be particularly resonant on the day of the commemoration of Christ's Passion and death.

On Holy Saturday, the Lamentations recital began with Lam 3:22–30, which underscores the importance of patient hope and trust, even in the face of peril and destruction. After Lam 3:22–30, the responsory speaks of the suffering Servant, the Lamb who does not speak but who brings life to the people. The second reading is Lam 4:1–6, a lament over the destruction of Jerusalem, following which, the responsory beckons Jerusalem to wear sackcloth in grief over the killing of its Savior. The responsory after Lam 5:1–11, also known as Jeremiah's Prayer, is a longer, pained lamentation at the death of the Savior, calling forth crying and howling.

---

[42]   See Andrew Cameron-Mowat, SJ, "Lamentations and Christian Worship," in *Great Is Thy Faithfulness?*, 139–41.

The service grew less popular when it was moved to mornings in the 1955 reform of Holy Week, and it fell out of use in most places after the renewal of the liturgy after the Second Vatican Council.

Some Protestant scholars note that Lamentations has not played a central role in theology. The text is not greatly referenced in the New Testament. Moreover, the genre of lament to the LORD may seem less in place as the Christian conception of suffering inheres notions in which God shares in the actual suffering and is less of an antagonist.[43]

These scholars see within the genre of lament, generally, and Lamentations, in particular, a vital resource. As Robin Parry notes, when believers are inducted through communal worship exclusively through the modes of thanksgiving, praise, and adoration, believers are denied a language for dealing with the dark periods of life. Lament is sometimes intentionally silenced as somehow inappropriate, irreverent, and unfaithful in spite of the fact that according to Matthew 27 Jesus himself exclaimed words of lament from Psalm 22 while on the cross. In this way, Parry writes, disciples fail to receive the training needed to walk with God through the valley of the shadow of death. Lament can allow the Christian community to acknowledge and affirm the legitimacy of articulating honestly both the awkward and the uncomfortable realities of a broken world.[44]

Alone among Israel's foes, Edom is singled out for reference here. Although Edom's pursuit of the survivors of the destruction is well attested (Ezek 36:1–6; Ob 12–13), Babylon had led the assault on Jerusalem and is only obliquely mentioned throughout Lamentations as "the enemy." The proposition to see "Edom" as a catchphrase for all the enemies of Judah is unfounded, as we find this usage nowhere else.[45] Why then Edom?

Alone among the neighbors of Israel, Edom had historically assumed a position of ambivalence for Israel as both brother and enemy

---

[43]   See Westermann, *Lamentations: Issues and Interpretation*, 89–91. idem, *Praise and Lament in the Psalms*, trans. Keith R. Crim and Richard N. Soulen (Atlanta: John Knox, 1981), 206–13, 259–80; Walter Brueggemann, "The Costly Loss of Lament," *JSOT* 11:36 (1986): 57–71; Mark J. Boda, "The Priceless Gain of Penitence: From Communal Lament to Penitential Prayer in the 'Exilic' Liturgy of Israel," *HBT* 25 (2003): 51–75.

[44]   Robin A. Parry, "Wrestling with Lamentations in Christian Worship," in *Great Is Thy Faithfulness?*, 175–94 at 192.

[45]   Salters, *Lamentations*, 334.

(cf. Gen 25:19–34; 32:4–33; Num 20:14–21; Deut 2:8), with whom even marriage is permitted (Deut 23:8–9). It is only following the destruction of Jerusalem that we find a consistent disposition of animosity toward Edom (Isa 63:1–6; Ezek 25:12–14; 35:3–15; Joel 4:19; Obadiah; Mal 1:2–5). As Elie Assis has argued, this anxiety reflects concern that Edom would emerge as the LORD's chosen nation, replacing the rejected Israel.[46] We can well understand why the pastoral mentor would single out Edom for mention here. Lamentations 4 addresses a segment of the people deeply invested in Zion theology – the election of Israel. The pastoral mentor, in what I have termed the refrain verses of his opening soliloquy (vv. 6, 11, and 16), spelled out in the clearest of terms that Judah had been rejected by the LORD. It is only natural that faced with their own rejection by the LORD, they would naturally consider whom else the LORD might elect in their place; the pastoral mentor cum prophet assures them here in v. 21 that it will not be their arch-nemesis, their brother Edom.

Verse 22, the poem's ultimate verse, revolves around the perplexing word *'ăwôn*. Some understand that the statement to Bat-Zion is that her *punishment* is completed (cf. Gen 4:13). By this reading, the narrator informs her that the LORD will no longer continue to exile her, and that this is said in a Judean context, after the last of the great forced exiles, in 581 (Jer 52:28–30).[47] However, the word *'ăwôn* appears twice in this verse, and in reference to Edom in the second stich, the words *pāqad 'ăwônēk* can only be translated as does the NRSVue: "but your iniquity (*'ăwônēk*) he will punish (*pāqad*)." In this stich, it is clear that *'ăwôn* can only mean iniquity or sin, and thus it must be that this is the meaning of the term in the first stich; what has ceased is not Bat-Zion's *punishment*, but her *sin*, indeed as understood by all the ancient versions.

But on what basis can the pastoral mentor make that claim? Is this prophecy that Israel will sin no more? Rather, we should understand that when the pastoral mentor addresses Bat-Zion in the first stich; he is not speaking about the future. Instead, his words are an evaluation of the progress and growth she has made. The communal statement in vv. 17–20 reflects a maturing of its understanding of events. It expresses a repudiation of

---

[46]   Elie [Eliyahu] Assis, *Identity in Conflict: The Struggle between Esau and Jacob, Edom and Israel*, in SLTHS 19 (Winona Lake, IN: Eisenbrauns, 2016), esp. 7–19 and 74–90.

[47]   Salters, *Lamentations*, 336. NRSVue here reads, "he will keep you in exile no longer." But the verb is in the *hiphil* form and suggests active banishing, as read by the KJV, "he will no more carry thee away into captivity."

previous folly and the community's capacity to break free of the persistence of false beliefs. In v. 17, the community reflects upon its vain reliance on foreign powers to deliver salvation. In verse 18, the community realizes that its earlier certainty that all was lost was, as well, misplaced, and that, in fact, the community has survived even the greatest catastrophe it had ever known, essentially affirming Jeremiah's promise that the LORD would not enact "a full end" (Jer 4:27; 5:10, 18; 30:11; 46:28). Finally, in v. 20, the community articulates its misplaced reliance on the choseness of the Davidic king, and the salvation implicit in that status. This is what enables the pastoral prophet to say to Bat-Zion, "your iniquity has ceased," for indeed, the misapprehensions of yore have all now been repudiated. Three times during his opening soliloquy, the pastoral mentor had referred to the people as Bat-Ami; their sinful ways had denied them their earlier identity in better days of "children of Zion" (cf. v. 2 mentioned earlier and Ps 149:2). But now, in this expression of comfort and salvation, he is able to address her again as Bat-Zion. She has now, once again, earned the LORD's protective favor. The phrase of punishment in v. 16, *lōʾ yōsîp ləhabbîṭām*, "he will regard them no more," is replaced by a parallel phrase of grace, *lōʾ yōsîp ləhaglôtēk*, "He will no longer send you into captivity" (New King James Version.). This accounts for why a note of optimism appears only here in the entire book.

CONCLUSION: THE KING'S PRAYER OF PSALM 144 AS BACKDROP TO LAMENTATIONS 4

Nowhere are the social concerns of the Davidic king on display more than in Psalm 144:9–14, where we find a prayer of the king for the welfare of his kingdom. The images and tropes invoked in the critique of Zion theology in Lamentations 4 bear a remarkable resemblance to those raised in that prayer and suggest that the dystopian portrait of Jerusalem in Lamentations 4 is an inversion of the ideal kingdom as per that psalm, further buttressing the reading of Lamentations 4 as a critique of the social structures engendered by Zion theology. Seven motival elements are shared between the two compositions, in addition to shared particular language. The prayer reads as follows (Ps 144:9–14):

> ⁹ I will sing a new song to you, O God;
>   upon a ten-stringed harp I will play to you,
> ¹⁰ the one who gives victory to kings,
>   who rescues his servant David.

¹¹ Rescue me from the cruel sword,
     and deliver me from the hand of aliens,
   whose mouths speak lies,
     and whose right hands are false.
¹² May our sons in their youth
     be like plants full grown,
   our daughters like corner pillars,
     cut for the building of a palace.
¹³ May our barns be filled,
     with produce of every kind;
   may our sheep increase by thousands,
     by tens of thousands in our fields,
¹⁴ and may our cattle be heavy with young.
   May there be no breach in the walls, no exile,
     and no cry of distress in our streets.

First, the king's opening plea, in vv. 10–11, is that he be delivered from the hands of aliens. In Lam 4:20, this is precisely the fate of the Davidic king, who was captured in the snares of the invading enemy. Second, the verse continues with a plea "deliver me from the hand of aliens, whose mouths speak lies, and whose right hands are false," and in terms of royal diplomacy, this refers to treaty partners who renege on their word. This is decried by the community in Lam 4:17: "Our eyes failed, ever watching vainly for help; we were watching eagerly for a nation that could not save." Their wistful reckoning suggests that an agreement had been reached with a foreign nation – perhaps Egypt – to offer assistance in the face of Babylonian aggression.

The third element picked up in Lamentations 4 is the image in v. 12a of the king's prayer, "May our sons in their youth be like plants full grown," which points to the desire of parents to see their young grow and mature. This is what the author of Lamentations 4 describes in dystopian fashion in v. 4, where mothers vainly struggle to feed their starving children, an image amplified in v. 10, where once compassionate women now boil the flesh of their own children for food. Fourth, in verse 12b, the prayer expresses a wish to see daughters who resemble finely cut stones for the corner of a palace, or a temple. This expresses something about aspirations for daughters, but also expresses the strong impression made by these "corner pillars, cut for the building of a palace," within the visual and symbolic economy of royal thought. This is inverted in Lam 4:1, "The sacred stones lie scattered at the head of every street," which we noted earlier is taken to refer the stones of the temple complex generally.

Fifth, we note that the *ḥûṣôt*, the "outside," is the site of bounty in Ps 144:13. It is the site where sheep multiply by the thousands and the tens of thousands. In Lamentations 4, however, the *ḥûṣôt* are the sites where the ravages of starvation are evident to all. It is in the *ḥûṣôt* that "those who feasted on delicacies perish" (v. 5), and it is in the *ḥûṣôt* that the princes ravaged by hunger are no longer recognizable because their visage is blacker than soot (v. 8).

Sixth, the king's prayer states (Ps 144:13): "May our barns be filled, with produce of every kind." In Lam 4:9, however, those that were felled by the sword are considered more fortunate than those "pierced" by hunger for, literally, they bleed the bounty of the field. Earlier images of starvation spoke simply of the lack of food basics such as in 2:12 (grain and wine) and earlier in v. 4:4 (bread). Here, it seems as though the pastoral mentor is invoking images of the longed-for "good old days" when the *ḥûṣôt* were the site not only of food but of bounty.

Finally, the king's prayer concludes, "May there be no breach in the walls, no exile, and no cry of distress in our streets (*birḥōbōtênû*)." These are all inverted in the account of the destruction in Lamentations 4. Here, the community members describe "our streets, *rəḥōbōtênû*" (Lam 4:18–19): "They dogged our steps so that we could not walk in our streets ... Our pursuers were swifter than the eagles in the heavens; they chased us on the mountains; they lay in wait for us in the wilderness."

While Lamentations 4 does share two lexical features with the king's prayer of Psalm 144 (*rəḥōbōtênû* – our street; *ḥûṣôt* – outside), it is unclear whether the author composed this poem with that prayer specifically in mind. More conservatively, we may say that the king's prayer of Psalms144 reflects the concerns and touchstones of the social world of Zion theology. The shared motifs and images between that psalm and Lamentations 4 serves as an affirmation that the theme of this chapter is a critique of the social structures and political dispositions of royal theology. The snapshots of suffering the author provides throughout Lamentations 4 are unified as a reversal of the reality promised by Zion theology.

A CLOSER LOOK: ACROSTIC STRUCTURE AND THE BOOK OF LAMENTATIONS

The most striking element of the composition of Lamentations is the acrostic structure seen in four out of its five poems. Chapters 1 and 2 feature verses of three stanzas where the first stanza of each verse follows an acrostic pattern. In Chapter 3, the verses have two stanzas each, and here the acrostic is trebled: Each letter is accorded three consecutive verses, for a total of sixty-six verses. Chapter 4 also features verses of two stanzas, where the opening stanza of each verse follows the acrostic form. By contrast, Chapter 5 has twenty-two verses – the number of verses of the alphabet – but does not form an acrostic structure. Some have noted that acrostics are oft found in wisdom literature such as the wisdom psalms, Pss 34; 37; 111 and 112; Prov 31:10–31 and Nah 1:2–8. But it is far from true that most wisdom literature is set in acrostic structure, nor is true that most acrostic compositions in the Hebrew Bible are of the genre of wisdom literature (cf. Pss 9; 10; 25 and 145). Why is the feature so prominent in Lamentations?

Some expositors point to the fact that an acrostic structure easily serves as a mnemonic device. However, that is true only when a composition stands alone. If, indeed, the poems of Lamentations were composed in isolation from one another, we could well entertain the position that their respective authors wished to make it easy for their audiences to commit the poem to memory, especially if we assume that the poems were written for a liturgical purpose, to be chanted by a broad audience. And, if, indeed, the poems of Lamentations were written in isolation one from another, there would be no expectation for the fifth poem, Chapter 5, to conform to the structure of the other four.

However, many scholars understand the poems as emanating from a single circle, if not necessarily from a single hand, and see in the poems of Lamentations a larger unity. But if this understanding is accurate, then the proliferation of poems each boasting an acrostic structure would actually mitigate against ease of memorization. When a stand-alone composition employs acrostic structuring, each verse uniquely invokes a single letter of the alphabet. However, when four poems do so – leaving aside that Chapter 3 is a triple acrostic – the repeated use of the device threatens to introduce interference into the memorization process.[48]

Many expositors have sought not only utility in the employ of the acrostic structure but meaning as well. One approach is to see the *aleph* to *tav* ordering as reflective of a notion of totality, as if, to borrow a modern English idiom, "from A to Z."[49] For the rabbis of the

---

[48] Klein, *Lamentations*, 26.
[49] See, for example, Gottwald, *Studies in the Book*, 28–32; Daniel Grossberg, *Centripetal and Centrifugal Structures in Biblical Poetry*, SBLMS 29 (Atlanta: Scholars Press, 1989), 84.

Midrash, the structure of Lamentations – a work of rebuke – high-lights the fact that Israel sinned in every way imaginable. For modern expositors, the acrostic structure reflects the totality of the devastation, or the totality of the agony and the anguish. However, these positions are not entirely consistent with the textual data. It is true, indeed, that many passages in Lamentations indict Israel for her sins. But the acrostic encompasses verses of comfort as well, such as 4:21–22. And it is true that much of Lamentations expresses anguish. However, passages like 3:21–39 express hope for a better future. And neither of these approaches explains why Chapter 5 – which highlights both Israel's sins and her agony – fails to employ the device.

Others see the acrostic structure of the poems as a reminder that there is hidden order amid what is visibly chaos. In a world of collective trauma that implicitly raises the question, "is there a plan here?," the acrostic structure signals that indeed there is a divine plan, that there is order in the chaos. Here, too, it is unclear why Chapter 5 is devoid of the device.

Alternatively, the acrostic may signal not only order, but process and sequence. Seen in this light, the interpretation of Lamentations offered in this volume can well make sense of the presence of acrostic structure in the first four poems, but not in the fifth. In each of the first four poems, the pastoral mentor engages Bat-Zion in a process of reflection and reha-bilitation. Each poem stands on its own in this regard as former and mistaken postulates about the LORD, election, and Zion are aired and dis-sected. Each chapter carries Bat-Zion from one theological and emotional place at the beginning of the chapter to a more mature one at its close. The acrostic structure that governs these four chapters cues the reader to seek out the process and sequence of steps that Bat-Zion undergoes in her maturation. In the fifth poem, however, the poet abandons the dialectic model that governed the first four poems. There is no interlocutor and the pastoral mentor offers his own prayer. As the chapter details no process or sequence, the poet feels no need to direct his audience to look for these, through the poetic of acrostic structure.

5 Purging Prayer of Zion Theology

¹ Remember, O LORD, what has befallen us;
    look, and see our disgrace!
² Our inheritance has been turned over to strangers,
    our homes to aliens.
³ We have become orphans, fatherless;
    our mothers are like widows.
⁴ We must pay for the water we drink;
    the wood we get must be bought.
⁵ With a yoke*ᵒ* on our necks we are hard driven;
    we are weary; we are given no rest.
⁶ We have made a pact with*ᵖ* Egypt and Assyria
    to get enough bread.
⁷ Our ancestors sinned; they are no more,
    and we bear their iniquities.
⁸ Slaves rule over us;
    there is no one to deliver us from their hand.
⁹ We get our bread at the peril of our lives,
    because of the sword in the wilderness.
¹⁰ Our skin is black as an oven
    from the scorching heat of famine.
¹¹ Women are raped in Zion,
    young women in the towns of Judah.
¹² Princes are hung up by their hands;
    no respect is shown to the elders.
¹³ Young men are compelled to grind,
    and boys stagger under loads of wood.

ᵒ   5.5 Symmachus: Heb lacks *With a yoke*
ᵖ   5.6 Heb *have given the hand to*

¹⁴ The old men have left the city gate,
     the young men their music.
¹⁵ The joy of our hearts has ceased;
     our dancing has been turned to mourning.
¹⁶ The crown has fallen from our head;
     woe to us, for we have sinned!
¹⁷ Because of this our hearts are sick;
     because of these things our eyes have grown dim:
¹⁸ because of Mount Zion, which lies desolate;
     jackals prowl over it.
¹⁹ But you, O LORD, reign forever;
     your throne endures to all generations.
²⁰ Why have you forgotten us completely?
     Why have you forsaken us these many days?
²¹ Restore us to yourself, O LORD, that we may be restored;
     renew our days as of old—
²² unless you have utterly rejected us
     and are angry with us beyond measure.

INTRODUCTION

In several ways Chapter 5 differs from the other four chapters of
Lamentations. On purely poetic grounds, the chapter is the only one that is
not an acrostic. Its stichs are shorter and balanced. If the previous chapters
reflect the searing pain of the immediate aftermath of the fall of Jerusalem,
this chapter seems to depict a time a generation later, although still prior
to the rescript of Cyrus in 538 BCE that allowed the Judeans to return to
Jerusalem to rebuild the temple. This is most evident in v. 7, "Our ancestors
sinned; they are no more, and we bear their iniquities," and v. 20b, "Why
have you forsaken us *these many days*?" implying that even long after the
destruction, the misery continues. Evidence that here we are at a time somewhat removed from the sacking of the city may be adduced from v. 4 as well:
"We must pay for the water we drink; the wood we get must be bought."
This implies that some form of administration of Babylonian occupation
is now in place through which Judeans acquire goods that formerly were
freely acquired.

But of greatest significance for understanding Lamentations 5 is the recognition that this is the only chapter of the book that does not feature multiple speakers. A single agent speaks throughout the chapter's twenty-two
verses utilizing first-person plural forms. Some have taken the first-person

plural forms as a sign that here the entire community speaks.[1] Others, how-
ever, understand the voice as that of the narrator speaking on behalf of the
community.[2] This was apparently the understanding of some Greek and
Latin manuscripts, which bear the superscription "A prayer," "A prayer of
Jeremiah," as also found in the Syriac, or "A prayer of Jeremiah the prophet."
The entire chapter is framed as a prayer, opening with a direct address of the
LORD (5:1), "Remember, O LORD, what has befallen us; look, and see our
disgrace!," and concluding with direct address of the LORD in its final four
verses, vv. 19–22.

Lamentations 5 resembles the communal laments in the book of Psalms,
particularly Pss 74 and 79. Like Lamentations 5, these psalms are written
in the aftermath of the fall of Jerusalem, and decry the desecration of the
Temple (Pss 74:3–4, 7; 79:1; cf. Lam 5:18) and the lowly state of the people
(Pss 74:19, 21; 79:2–4, 11; cf. Lam 5:3–5, 8–16). In all three, the petitioner
appeals to the LORD to end his abandonment of Israel, using the words
nēṣaḥ, "enduring" (Pss 74:1, 10; 79:5; cf. Lam 5:20) and *lāmâ*, "why?" (Pss
74:1; 79:10; cf. Lam 5:20). All three speak of the land (*naḥălâ*) (Pss 74:2; 79:1;
cf. Lam 5:2) and of the shame (*ḥerpâ*) engendered by the conquest of the city
(Pss 74:18; 79:4; cf. Lam 5:1). All three offer assertions of the LORD's strength
(Pss 74:12–17; 79:11; cf. Lam 5:21), and all request some form of delivery for
the people (Pss 74:3, 18–19, 22; 79:6–9, 11–12; cf. Lam 5:21). I draw attention
to these many parallels, not only – or even primarily – to demonstrate a
generic relationship between them. Rather, their similarity highlights just
how distinct Lamentations 5 stands from the two psalms. Writing under
circumstances highly similar to that faced by the poets of Pss 74 and 79,
the poet of Lamentations 5 in multiple ways adopts the road not taken by
his contemporaries writing in the book of Psalms. Reading Lamentations
5 against the control of Pss 74 and 79 reveals the agenda of the poem and
highlights its theological imperatives.

In formulating their petitions in the wake of the destruction, the poets
of Pss 74 and 79 routinely invoke covenantal appellations of endearment
with reference to Israel. Thus, we find in Psalm 74 Israel referred to as "the
sheep of your pasture" (Ps 74:1); "your congregation, which you acquired
long ago, which you redeemed to be the tribe of your heritage" (Ps 74:2);
and "your dove" (Ps 74:19). In like fashion, the poet of Ps 79 refers to Israel

---

[1] Klein, *Lamentations*, 257.
[2] Salters, *Lamentations*, 341.

as "your servants" (Ps 79:2, 10); "your faithful" (Ps 79:2); "Jacob" (Ps 79:7); "your people" (Ps 79:13); and "the flock of your pasture" (Ps 79:13). By contrast, Lamentations 5 uses no appellations whatsoever to refer to Israel, employing instead the spartan, "us/our" some 45 times. The poets of Pss 74 and 79 are quick to point out that the conquest of the city and the destruction of the temple represent a desecration of the LORD's name and fame (Pss 74: 4, 7, 10, 18, 22–23; 79: 1, 6, 9, 10). The author of Lamentations 5 never does pick up this trope. The poets of Pss 74 and 79 offer detailed charge sheets against the heathen invaders, and particularly with regard to their desecration of the temple (Pss 74:3–8, 10, 18; 79:1–3, 7, 10). While the author of Lamentations 5 chronicles in detail the suffering of the people, he carefully avoids fronting the enemy as the explicit subject of the sentence. This rhetorical move implicitly de-emphasizes the aggression and iniquity of the enemy. In fact, the poet of Lamentations 5 rarely refers to the enemy directly. Instead, the people's suffering is portrayed through a passive voice, for example, "We have become orphans" (v. 3); "we are hard driven" (v. 5). The poets of Pss 74 and 79 call for vengeance upon the perpetrators of the destruction (Pss 74:3, 11, 23; 79:6, 12). The author of Lamentations 5, however, issues no such call, even though this is a recurring theme elsewhere in the book (Lam 1:21–22; 3:65–66; 4:21–22). Why does the author of Lamentations 5 eschew so many of the elements that his compatriots writing in similar circumstances found of good service in Pss 74 and 79?

Across four chapters, the protagonist of the book, the pastoral mentor, has engaged various religious typologies found among the survivors of the destruction. Working with each, he has attempted to dispel misnomers and misconceptions, and to help each group take its next step toward spiritual repair. In this concluding chapter, we see the pastoral mentor's own interpretation of events, now in full view, in his own voice. What we will see is that he seeks to drive home for his audience that indeed, the covenant with the LORD is still intact. But it was their misunderstanding of covenant that had led to their downfall in the first place. Zion theology celebrated all of the upsides of covenant – a special, loving disposition toward Israel – but entirely turned a blind eye to the other side of the covenantal coin – its demands, and its promise of calumny and calamity should Israel continually breach its terms.[3] Precisely because the people had so badly misconstrued the nature of the covenantal relationship, the pastoral mentor seeks here to restore that understanding to its proper balance. To do this, he will underscore that Israel

---

[3]   See introductions to Chapters 1 (pp. 28–32) and 2 (pp. 53–58).

is currently in a state of punishment and accursedness, in conformity, particularly with the curse lists of Leviticus 26 and Deuteronomy 28. Of the two, however, only the remonstration of Leviticus 26 speaks of a destroyed and desecrated sanctuary (Lev 26:31). And in such a circumstance according to Leviticus 26, it is the responsibility of the people to confess their sins and the sins of their ancestors. This is the formula offered by Leviticus 26 for rising out of a period of calumny and calamity (Lev 26:39–42):

> And those of you who survive shall languish in the land of your enemies because of their iniquities; they shall also languish because of the iniquities of their ancestors. "*But if they confess their iniquity and the iniquity of their ancestors--their treachery against me* and also their continued hostility to me, so that I in turn was hostile to them and brought them into the land of their enemies--if, then, their uncircumcised heart is humbled and they make amends for their iniquity, then will I remember my covenant with Jacob; I will remember also my covenant with Isaac and also my covenant with Abraham, and I will remember the land."

In his closing prayer, therefore, the pastoral mentor seeks to keep Israel focused entirely on her sins and on her punishment – the aspects of covenant theology that the people had conveniently chosen to overlook – as he confesses their sins (v. 16) and the sins of their fathers (v. 7). He will steadfastly avoid any and all of the trappings of covenantal terminology that had become corrupted through the prism of Zion theology. He will not, therefore, invoke any of the appellations of endearment for Israel. For the pastoral mentor's purposes here, Israel's redemption will come not because Israel is special, or beloved. Her redemption will come solely through hard work, confession, and penance. He will not chronicle the wrongdoings of the enemies because those are entirely beside the point. Israel must focus on her own misdeeds. He will not appeal to the Lord that his name has been desecrated by the enemies, because that only serves to remove the onus from Israel, at a time, when she must learn to accept and rise up to that burden. He will not call for revenge against those enemies, because that, too, is beside the point, and draws attention to the misdeeds of the enemy, perforce at the expense of focusing on the misdeeds of their own.

Verse 1 functions as a thematic title for the entire poem. While the opening word of v. 1, *zəkōr*, is literally translated "remember," as rendered by the NRSVue, more accurately it has the connotation of a plea to "consider."[4]

---

4 Berlin, *Lamentations*, 117.

This is of paramount significance because it is a harbinger of the tone of the entire poem. Lamentations 5 is not, in primary fashion, a call for mercy. In fact, no term for mercy appears anywhere in the composition. Rather, the prayer of the pastoral mentor is a plea to the LORD to, indeed, "consider" the state of the people, to weigh what has befallen them, with an eye toward making the case that their rightful punishment has now been meted out in full measure, and that according to the terms of the covenant itself it is now possible to consider a new stage in the relationship between the LORD and the people of Israel. This opening stich of the poem, calling upon the LORD to "remember" serves as a frame together with v. 20, "Why have you *forgotten* us completely?," where, here, too, the literal translation of tiškāḥēnû, "you have forgotten us," really implies "are ignoring us," and the suffering we have already endured.[5] The translation of the opening stich, "Remember, O LORD, what *has befallen* us," aptly expresses the durative feeling of the verse. This prayer is not said in the immediate aftermath of the destruction. As noted and as we shall see further, the travails depicted are those of Judah under occupation, at some temporal remove from the events of the summer of 586 BCE. This duration adds to the pressing nature of the prayer. The LORD had foretold of the coming destruction; but that has now arrived and passed, and still Judah continues to suffer. It is this continued suffering that the pastoral mentor wishes the LORD to consider.

Many other biblical passages consider the affronts of the heathen enemies as bringing shame *ḥerpâ* to the LORD, as we find in the Wycliffe Bible translation to Ps 74:22, where the poet under similar circumstances following the destruction of the temple says, "God, rise up, deem thou thy cause; be thou mindful of thy *shames* (*ḥerpātəkā*)." Similarly, we find in Ps 79:12 that following the destruction of the temple, the poet writes, "And yield thou to our neighbours sevenfold in(to) the bosom of them; the shame of them *ḥerpātām* (the same rebuke), which they did shamefully to thee (*ḥērəpûkā*), thou LORD" (Wycliffe Bible). In this light, we could have well expected the pastoral mentor to call upon the LORD, "see *your* shame." Instead, he calls upon the LORD to take note of "*our* shame." To appeal to the LORD to intervene on account of the desecration of his name or status would draw away from the pastoral mentor's determination to focus his audience on their own onus and the need to accept guilt and confess their sins. They cannot count on any special divine dispensation.

---

5   Berlin, *Lamentations*, 117.

BRIDGING THE HORIZONS: LAMENTATIONS IN THE JEWISH TRADITION

For the rabbinic tradition, the texts of sacred scripture cannot be left to speak solely about the past; they must be mined to speak about the concerns of the present. The text of Lamentations poses a particular challenge in this regard: It addresses the people of Israel at their very darkest hour; at the moment of greatest divine wrath. The rabbis of the Talmud and Midrash appropriated the verses of Lamentations to speak to later generations of Jews who were also living in exile, but not in the abject conditions described in Lamentations. Midrash *Eichah Rabba*, composed in the sixth to seventh centuries, is the major compendium of rabbinic writings about Lamentations. One of the dominant traits of the work is to highlight divine grace even in a period of darkness. Thus, this midrash teaches that the LORD had indeed brought destruction upon the city. But in the heavens, he wept as he did so out of love for the children he had just punished. The text of Lam 1:1 states that Bat-Zion was "as a widow," the plain meaning of which suggests divine abandonment of Israel. But the midrash states here, "She was as a woman whose husband has left on a distant journey – but whose intentions are to eventually return to her. Thus the text reads that she was '*as* a widow,' but not fully a widow." The LORD may be distant from Israel, but he will surely return to her. Elsewhere in this work, the rabbis point out that within Isaiah there is a tendency to take phrases from Lamentations and to appropriate them and invert their meaning. Thus, the midrash states, it is true that Lam 1:2 says of Bat-Zion, "She weeps bitterly in the night (*bākô tibkeh*)." But in Isaiah it says (Isa 30:19), "you shall weep no more (*bākô lō' tibkeh*). He will surely be gracious to you at the sound of your cry; when he hears it, he will answer you."

On the Jewish calendar, the ninth day of Ab commemorates the destruction of the First and Second Temples. Although rabbinic tradition records the date of the destruction of the Second Temple in seventy CE as the ninth of Ab, scripture identifies the date of the destruction of the First Temple as either the seventh of Ab or the tenth of the month (2 Kgs 25:8–11; Jer 52:12–14). By identifying the ninth of Ab as the anniversary of the destruction of both temples, the rabbis created a liturgical date, not an historical one; a date in which Jews would mark the element of national tragedy in their covenantal relationship with the LORD.

It is the custom for Jews to sit on the floor of the synagogue in mourning on the night of the ninth of Ab and to chant Lamentations although the origins of this practice are unclear. Zechariah already makes reference to "the fast day of the fifth," that is, the fifth month – the month of Ab (Zech 7:1–7; 8:18–19). And some scholars surmise that the poems of Lamentations were originally penned for a liturgical context. But the Talmudic sources pertaining to liturgical readings of scripture in the synagogue make no mention of the practice of reading Lamentations on the ninth of Ab, and the first mention of it is in a rabbinic compendium thought to originate from the eighth century, although the practice itself may be older.[6]

IN THE ABSENCE OF FATHERS (VV. 2–7)

Verses 2–16 detail the phrases from v. 1, "what has befallen us," and "our disgrace," through a montage of deprivations, most a stich in length. The passage is delineated by two statements of confession that accord with the dual dictate of Lev 26:40. The first is at v. 7, where the pastoral mentor confesses the iniquities of the previous generations, and at the close of v. 16, where he confesses the sins of his own generation. The first unit, vv. 2–7, is united by a theme of the absence of fathers. Verses 2–5 details economic impoverishment on the personal level, as it affected individuals and their families. Patrimonies of inherited land were lost to outsiders (v. 2), and families were left vulnerable (v. 3) and without support; the basic commodities of potable water and firewood – once cheap and readily available – became expensive (v. 4), and to eke out even bare sustenance was an exhausting endeavor (v. 5). As Adele Berlin aptly writes, "In ancient Israel, great pains were taken to ensure that land was not alienated from its original owner, family, or tribe (cf. Lev 25:25–28; Num 27; 36; 1 Kgs 21:3). Thus, being deprived of one's 'ancestral land' is more than a financial loss; it is a deeply felt religious or cultural loss as well, and it signifies the breakdown of society."[7]

Just as the shame referred to in v. 1 is the shame of the people, so too, the inheritance in v. 2, is the people's, and not the LORD's. Elsewhere, the land of Israel (*naḥălâ*) is oft identified as the LORD's inheritance (Mic 7:18; Pss 78:62; 94:14; 106:40), or as "your inheritance" referring to the LORD (Exod 15:17; Isa 63:17; Joel 2:17; Mic 7:14; Pss 28:9; 68:10; 74:2; 79:1; 94:5; 106:5). But, here,

---

6   Klein, *Lamentations*, 78–79.
7   Berlin, *Lamentations*, 117.

again, the pastoral mentor wishes to de-emphasize that this is the LORD's land, implying that he should intervene for it his behalf. Instead, the pastoral mentor wishes to build the case that Israel's punishment has reached its full measure, and so he focuses on what Israel has lost and its attendant indignity. What has been lost is, of course, property. But this property is patrimony, and its loss cuts Israel off from continued residence on the lands of their forefathers.

We should also note how the poet depicts what has happened in passive terms: "Our inheritance *has been turned* over to strangers." Compare the discourse here to that employed concerning inheritance in Ps 79:1–3:

> O God, the *nations have come* into your inheritance;
> > *they have defiled* your holy temple;
> > *they have laid* Jerusalem in ruins.
> ² *They have given* the bodies of your servants
> > to the birds of the air for food,
> > the flesh of your faithful to the wild animals of the earth.
> ³ *They have poured* out their blood like water
> > all around Jerusalem.

The poet of Psalm 79 emphasizes the wicked acts of the enemies by fronting the enemy in the syntax of the charge sheet; "they have defiled your holy temple," not "your holy temple has been defiled"; "they have laid Jerusalem in ruins," and not "Jerusalem is laid in ruins." But in Lamentations 5, the aim of the pastoral mentor is not to chronicle the wickedness of the enemy and to call for his destruction. The pastoral mentor does not want to distract the listening audience from the singular, crucial point at hand: Israel must confront her own sins. The loss of her territory, therefore, is cast in the passive voice, rendering the enemy practically invisible while drawing the spotlight on Israel's own state of misfortune.

Various interpretations have been offered for the state of "orphanage" referred to in v. 3. For some, the term is meant literally. By this reading, there is progression within vv. 2–3. Not only have landholdings been lost, but family members – indeed, heads of households – as well. There are no patrimonies (v. 2) and indeed, no fathers (v. 3).[8] By this reading, the *kaph* prior to "widows" is asseverative. However, there are no biblical sources about the fall of Jerusalem that suggest that in wholesale fashion the men

---

[8]   Berlin, *Lamentations*, 118.

were singled out for death or for exile. Moreover, the fact that the word "father" is rendered in the verse in the singular – contra to "fathers" in v. 7 – has led others to suggest that the orphanage here is a spiritual one: Israel is bereft of her true father, the LORD.[9] Support for this reading is found in the resonance between vv. 2–3 here and Jer 3:19–20:

> [19] I thought
>> how I would set you among my children,
> and give you a pleasant land,
>> the most beautiful heritage of all the nations.
> And I thought you would call me, "My Father,"
>> and would not turn from following me.
> [20] Instead, as a faithless wife leaves her husband,
>> so you have been faithless to me, O house of Israel,
> says the LORD.

For Jeremiah, the inhabitance of a "pleasant land" *naḥălat ṣəbî* is associated with Israel calling the LORD "father," and behaving like a faithful wife. In the dystopian world of Lamentations, the people are dispossessed from their own *naḥălâ* (v. 2) and thus bereft of their natural spiritual father and spouse (v. 3).

The most likely reading of "orphanage" here, however, is that it is used as a biblical trope for vulnerability, an understanding already found in the Targum that translates the phrase "we are likened to orphans." By this reading, the pastoral mentor accentuates the extreme sense of vulnerability created by the loss of land and homes. Although we find no usage of orphanage in this metaphoric sense, elsewhere in the Hebrew Bible, we find evidence of a metaphoric use of widowhood in this fashion from the Elephantine papyri (fifth century BCE) where an elegy in the wake of the destruction of the temple there states: "We are wearing sackcloth and fasting; our wives are made as widow(s)."[10]

Verses 4 and 5 go on to portray the harshness of daily survival. The need to pay for basic commodities of *our* water and *our* firewood in v. 4 suggests that the depiction is of reality at some temporal remove from the event of the destruction; there is now a control structure in place that commands fees. We see here, again, the efforts this poet has taken in order to draw

---

[9] The observation, already found in the medieval rabbinic commentaries, is found in Dobbs-Allsopp, *Lamentations*, 145; Renkema, *Lamentations*, 597–98.

[10] "Request for Letter of Recommendation (First Draft)," *TAD* A4.7 Verso, line 20, in Porten and Yardeni, *TAD* 1 (*Letters: Appendix; Aramaic Letters from the Bible*): 68–69, 71.

focus away from the active cruelty of the enemy, and instead to focalize on the suffering of Israel, by twice expressing the victimization in the passive voice: "With a yoke on our necks *we are hard driven*; we are weary; *we are given* no rest."

Poetically, vv. 2–5 stand as a subunit, depicting various foci of deprivation before v. 6 takes up a new topic. The remonstration of Leviticus 26 repeats as a mantra – four times in all – that the LORD will punish them "sevenfold for your sins" (Lev 26:18, 21, 24, 28) and we can see that the poet has carefully orchestrated the deprivations catalogued here in vv. 2–5, through a list of seven entities that suffer (translated literally, "our inheritance" [v. 2]; "our homes" [v. 2]; "orphans" [v. 3]; "our mothers" [v. 3]; "our water" [v. 4]; "our wood" [v. 4]; "our necks" [v. 5]), through seven verbs ("turned over" [v. 2]; "have become" [v. 3]; "drink" [v. 4]; "comes" [v. 4]; "are driven" [v. 5]; "labored" [v. 5]; "given no rest" [v. 5]).

Verse 6 refers to alliances that were attempted with Egypt and Assyria, though the time frame in question is unspecified. Some scholars understand that the survivors turned to these two powers for sustenance following the destruction. However, to speak of a political entity, "Assyria" in the mid-sixth century would be anachronistic. Earlier prophets, however, had spoken of Egypt and Assyria as powers though which Israel had sought respite (e.g., Jer 2:18, 36; Hos 7:11; 12:2) in previous generations. The verbal clause here, "giving hand to" is expressed in the accusative according to the pointing of the Masoretic Text and suggests that Israel made treaties with these two powers. The past perfect construct of many translations, such as the NRSVue "We have made a pact with Egypt and Assyria," is unwarranted grammatically, and the verse should be rendered as does the International Standard Version, "We made a deal with the Egyptians and the Assyrians." "Giving hand to" is a trope for treaty making and for entering a solemn commitment (Ezek 17:18; Ezra 10:19; cf 1 Chr 29:24; 2 Chr 30:8).

The progression of ideas in these verses is that in verses 4–5, the poet chronicled the difficulty of the current circumstance whereby the people were incapable of acquiring basic needs, like water and firewood for cooking. Verse 6 recalls an earlier, if unspecified, period where Israel likewise lacked nutritional security. Turning to Egypt and Assyria, Israel forsook their reliance on the LORD. This is lamented in v. 7: "Our ancestors sinned; they are no more, and we bear their iniquities."

It is possible to read v. 7 as an accusation against the LORD's execution of justice, namely that the present generation is suffering for sins they did not commit – the sins of their fathers. Only for their own sins should they be punished. By this thinking, they would be in line with the theological traditions found in Jer 31:28–29 and Ezek 18:2–4 that eschew transgenerational culpability. However, later in this chapter, in v. 16, the pastoral mentor acknowledges the sins of his own generation. This has lead expositors medieval and modern to read v. 7 otherwise. The speaker believes in transgenerational punishment when the latter generation continues in sinful ways. Rather than expressing protest, the pastoral mentor is expressing a plea to the LORD that he would consider the fact that this generation suffers not only for their sins, but for the sins of their fathers, and are thus deserving of a reprieve following confession of these transgenerational sins.

Most importantly, in this verse, the pastoral mentor confesses the iniquities of the previous generations, in accordance with the teachings of Lev 26:40. This is a theme repeated many places in Scripture – the need and the appropriateness for each generation to consider itself as part of a chain, a heritage, and thus capable and responsible for confessing and atoning for the sins of earlier generations, and is especially prevalent in Jeremiah. Thus, we find in Jer 14:20, "We acknowledge our wickedness, O LORD, the iniquity of our ancestors, for we have sinned against you" (cf. Jer 2:4–9; 3:25; 11:6–8; 16:1–13; 44:9–10; Ps 106:6; Dan 9:16; Ezra 9:6–15; Neh 9:16–17; 26–33). *Sābal* means to carry a burden (Gen 49:15; Isa 46:7), and the pastoral mentor's point is not only to confess but to underscore that even as the destruction has ended, its aftermath of suffering endures; Israel's punishment has reached its full measure.

To appreciate the full import of the sentiment here, we can fruitfully compare the pastoral mentor's stance with regard to the sins of prior generations to the way in which these are construed in Ps 79. There, too, the poet appeals to the LORD in the wake of the destruction of the temple. But regarding the sins of prior generations, that poet states (Ps 79:8), "Do not remember against us the iniquities of our ancestors; let your compassion come speedily to meet us, for we are brought very low." While the poet acknowledges the misdeeds of prior generations, he hardly takes them upon himself. Indeed, by his calculation, divine compassion should separate between the generations, seemingly judging his own generation on its own merits. And concerning his own generation, that poet says (Ps 79:9): "deliver us and forgive our sins, for your name's sake." The poet's highest concern is to elicit divine compassion, and thus he downplays the necessary work of penance and confession. By contrast, our poet seeks to refocus his audience on their responsibilities. He deliberately eschews the standard covenantal tropes found in Ps 79 – that Israel is beloved; that God has compassion; that his name suffers when Israel does, that Israel will flock to his sanctuary to sing him praise, if only they are rescued. The stance of the pastoral mentor to sin is at an even greater divide from the sentiments of the poet of Psalm 74, who turns to the LORD at a point following the destruction of the temple, and crafts his appeal to the LORD with no reference whatever to the sins that Israel may have committed – either in the present generation or in a previous one.

Verse 7 concludes the pericope that began in v. 2 and whose theme is the absence of fathers. Inheritance *nahălâ* (v. 2) is by definition, "the inheritance of the fathers." But in the aftermath of the destruction, "Our inheritance has been turned over to strangers, our homes to aliens." It is as if Israel has been cut off from its fathers. Verse 3 decries the state of fatherlessness as one of immense vulnerability, detailed in vv. 4–5, where there is no security to procure even the most rudimentary commodities. Verse 7, likewise decries "fatherlessness" – here echoing the same words used in v. 3 *ên* and *āb*.[11] While the fathers have left no secure inheritance, and provide no protection for their widows and orphans, they are absent, cruelly, at the moment that their own debt of sinfulness comes due.

THE EXPERIENCE OF HUMILIATION (VV. 8–16)

Verse 8 opens the second pericope of the chapter, serving as a thematic title for the images displayed in the coming verses. In a poem that portrays some two dozen images of suffering at the hand of the enemy, it is worthy of note that syntactically, that enemy is made the explicit subject in only a single verse, and that is v. 8: "Slaves rule over us; there is no one to deliver us from their hand." The poet breaks from his convention here because what is of paramount importance is the subjugating agent itself – slaves, or, perhaps "subordinates." This might refer to a vassal state such as Edom, or low-level Babylonian officials.[12] Either way, to be ruled by one who is deemed a slave is itself a humiliation, as expressed by the author of Proverbs (Prov 30:21–22): The subsequent verses of Lamentations 5 examine the implications of the grip of "their hand". In v. 9, bread is gotten at peril because of "the sword in the wilderness," which could refer to marauding bandits, or to the intense heat of the desert, which accords thematically with v. 10, which speaks of the scorching heat of famine. However, some scholars understand *midbār*, translated here as "desert," to be

---

[11] Provan, *Lamentations*, 129.
[12] See Salters, *Lamentations*, 352, for survey of opinions.

related to the meaning of *dbr* in cognate languages to mean "subdue, drive, lead." By this reading, the translation of the verse yields, "at the peril of our lives we gain our bread because of the sword of the pursuer."[13]

In vv. 11–14, the poet extends his portrayal of social humiliation through images of violence and disrespect at women, princes, elders, and the youth, which taken together represent the dissolution of civil society.[14] Verse 11 tells of the rape of married and unmarried women, inflicting shame on its direct victims and also indirectly humiliating the husbands and fathers of these women.[15] Verse 12 extends the circle of the humiliated to the elites – the princes and the elders. It is unclear whether the princes are tortured or whether this is, perhaps, a display of bodies.[16] It is likewise unclear whether the victims are suspended somehow by their own hand, or whether this is a reference to "the hand" of those from whom there is no deliverance, as per v. 8. Once again, the passive voice predominates: The princes *were hung*; the elders *were not respected*. Although the precise labors are unclear, v. 13 depicts the subjugation of the young men to demeaning tasks, possibly those usually assigned to animals.[17]

Verse 14 adds depth to the previous two verses as it rounds out comments about two of the figures mentioned there, elders and young men. The elders, who are no longer respected (v. 12) had once congregated in the gate, the site where business was conducted (Prov 31:23; Ruth 4:1–2). The young men who now grind (v. 13) had once engaged in musical celebrations. This retroactive pivot harkening the long-gone good times continues in v. 15. Some understand the "joy of the hearts" here as a reference to temple worship on the basis of the use of the word *maśôś* in Ezek 24:25.[18] However, nearly all uses of the word *maśôś* are non-sacral in character, and we find *šābat* and *maśôś* together in Jer 7:34 and 16:9 as references to a day when the LORD will cause the joy of Judah to cease, and the occurrence here seems to resonate with those verses. Indeed, the pastoral mentor will turn his attention to the temple and its loss in v. 17, but at this stage in the composition, he is approaching the climax of the tribulations that the people have suffered. Here it is *their* joy and *their* dancing that have ceased.

---

[13]   See Thomas F. McDaniel, "Philological Studies in Lamentations I," *Bib* 49:1 (1968): 52.
[14]   Berlin, *Lamentations*, 122.
[15]   Berlin, *Lamentations*, 122.
[16]   See Salters, *Lamentations*, 357, for review of opinions.
[17]   See survey of opinions in Salters, *Lamentations*, 359–60.
[18]   Berlin, *Lamentations*, 124; Dobbs-Allsopp, *Lamentations*, 147; Renkema, *Lamentations*, 615.

The fallen crown in v. 16 could symbolize kingship (cf. 2 Sam 12:30; Ezek 21:31; Ps 21:4). But unlike *keter*, which appears exclusively with regard to kinship, *ăṭārâ* does not. Isaiah 62:3 uses the term to refer to Jerusalem, and perhaps the verse here refers to the fall of the city. Moreover, *ăṭārâ* "crown" and *rōʾš* "head" are never found with specific reference to the king. Rather, *ăṭārâ* is a general term for honor, glory, and pride. This is a summary phrase that refers to all that had been once theirs – hence, the use of first-person plural possessive pronouns in the poem more than 40 times – and is now lost. The section concludes by marshaling the enormity and totality of this loss as the trigger for a great act of confession – "woe to us, for we have sinned!"

LOSS OF CONNECTION, APPEAL FOR CONNECTION (VV. 17–22)

The poet declares in v. 17, "Because of *this* our hearts are sick; because of *these* our eyes have grown dim," yet the antecedents of "this" and "these" are unclear. In most instances, this form refers to what came prior (cf. Isa 57:6; 64:11; Jer 5:9; 31:25; Amos 8:8), in which case it refers to the calamities listed in vv. 2–16. However, there are instances of a proleptic "this" as we find in Lam 3:21 and Ps 32:6. A proleptic understanding of the verse is preferable for several reasons. The preposition *ʿal* opens both vv. 17 and 18, and creates the crescendo conveyed by the following translation of the verses: "Because of this our hearts are sick; because of these things our eyes have grown dim: because of Mount Zion, which lies desolate; jackals prowl over it." A proleptic reading of v. 17 gains support as well from the emotional progression in the verses at hand. In both vv. 15 and 17, the pastoral mentor reflects on events with reference to "hearts." In v. 15, he states, "the joy of our hearts has ceased," while in v. 17 he declares, "because of this our hearts are sick." The emotion in v. 17 is stronger. Verse 15 is clearly a verse that begins to summarize the totality of what has been described thus far. But the reference to joy ceasing from the hearts in v. 15 is rendered superfluous if two verses later the poet writes about these same events that "our hearts" are not only without joy, but are "sick," if indeed the poet is referring to those same events. Instead, we should read v. 17 as a transitional verse that furthers the progression of ideas. The tragedies of economic deprivation and social humiliation (vv. 2–16) climax with the confession of sin that appears in v. 16b. Because of these, their hearts are "without joy," as per v. 15. However, greater still for them than the tragedy of economic ruin and social disgrace is the spiritual tragedy of the loss of connection with the LORD as embodied by his destroyed temple. And therefore, looking proleptically, the pastoral prophet states in v. 17 that whereas all the previous calamities have left us without joy in our hearts (v. 15), it is "Because of *this* our hearts are sick, because of these things our eyes have grown dim: because of Mount Zion, which lies desolate." The desolation of the temple stirs a greater heartfelt sorrow than all of the material and social oppression mentioned in vv. 2–16.

In v. 18, the pastoral mentor bemoans the destruction of the temple, and it is useful again to reference Pss 74 and 79 to highlight the paths not taken here. When mourning the destruction of the temple, the poet of Ps 74 writes (Ps 74:3–7):

> ³ Direct your steps to the perpetual ruins;
>> the enemy has destroyed everything in the sanctuary.
> ⁴ Your foes have roared within your holy place;
>> they set up their emblems there.
> ⁵ At the upper entrance they hacked
>> the wooden trellis with axes.
> ⁶ And then, with hatchets and hammers,
>> they smashed all its carved work.
> ⁷ They set your sanctuary on fire;
>> they desecrated the dwelling place of your name,
>> bringing it to the ground.

For this poet, mourning the destruction of the temple involves implicating the enemy and detailing their destructive acts, and their desecration of the LORD's shrine and name (cf. Ps 79:1). By contrast, the pastoral mentor displays no interest in the role of the enemy in desecrating the temple, though he may well have agreed with those sentiments. But they are not at all his focus. Rather, he focuses on the fact that the Temple Mount, upon which God was believed to dwell (Pss 9:12; 76:2; Isa 8:18; 18:7; Joel 3:17), lies "desolate" (*šāmēm*). The verse resonates with Lam 1:4, "The roads to Zion mourn, for no one comes to the festivals; all her gates are desolate." What the pastoral mentor truly mourns is the inability to commune with the LORD. The people can no longer visit the Temple Mount, and instead have been replaced by prowling jackals. His use of the word "desolate" (*šāmēm*) invokes Lev 26:31: "I will lay your cities waste, will make your sanctuaries desolate, and I will not smell your pleasing odors."

The theme of the loss of connection with the LORD animates vv. 19–22, which constitutes a mini-prayer bearing the standard three elements of the communal lament: praise (v. 19), complaint (v. 20), and request (v. 21).

Here, again, it is instructive to compare to Pss 74 and 79. The praise in Ps 79 is brief (Ps 79:11): "Let the groans of the prisoners come before you; *according to your great power*, preserve those doomed to die." The praise affirms belief in the potency of the Lord's agency, his capacity to bring about change and to exact revenge upon the enemy. This prepares the stage for his request in Ps 79:12: "Return sevenfold into the bosom of our neighbors the taunts with which they taunted you, O Lord!" The same is true in Psalm 74:12–17, where in extended fashion, the poet invokes a range of divine actions from primordial times, designed to show that the redress the poet requests is puny relative to the capacities for which the Lord is known. His request follows straight away (Ps 74:18–19): "Remember this, O Lord, how the enemy scoffs, and an impious people reviles your name. Do not deliver the soul of your dove to the wild animals; do not forget the life of your poor forever." And thus, we find extended praises of the Lord's power in other psalms of communal lament, such as Ps 44:1–2: "We have heard with our ears, O God; our ancestors have told us, what deeds you performed in their days, in the days of old: you with your own hand drove out the nations, but them you planted." And similarly, also, in the communal lament of Ps 80 (Ps 80:8): "You brought a vine out of Egypt; you drove out the nations and planted it." By contrast, in Lamentations 5, the pastoral mentor offers praise that emphasizes a different quality. His contention that the Lord is enthroned forever is less an assertion of the Lord's power than an affirmation of his continued existence. Verse 18 had noted that Mount Zion was desolate. Indeed, the destruction of the temple raised the specter that perhaps the Lord had been dethroned. Many passages in Second Isaiah attest to this latent concern. The people of Zion had felt forgotten and forlorn (Isa 49:14). The Lord insists that although he was available, people did not seek him out (Isa 65:1). The prophet emphasizes that, indeed, the Lord is still capable of delivering salvation (Isa 50:2; 59:1). For Second Isaiah, the Lord still reigns, but he does so from on high (Isa 66:1).[19] This is the import of the pastoral mentor's words here. The absence of the temple does not preclude the Lord's kingship. The verse also may be read such that the verb in v. 19a, *yāšab*, is rendered as "remaining" or "existing" as found in Ps 125:1, "Those who trust in the Lord are like Mount Zion, which cannot be moved but *abides* forever."

At the same time, the verse is not said in jubilation, as it gives way to v. 20. Although the Lord reigns or remains forever, so too, his abandonment

---

[19] Assis, *Lamentations*, 278.

seems to know no limits either. The destruction itself has passed and yet the estrangement persists and Israel remains out of his favor. Here, too, comparison with Psalms 74 and 79 is useful. The form of the question here in v. 20 is highly similar to that found in Ps 74:1b: "O God, why do you cast us off forever?" Yet in that psalm, the supplication is augmented with an appeal to the LORD's relationship to Israel (Ps 74:1c): "Why does your anger smoke against *the sheep of your pasture*?" Compare also to Ps 79:5–7: "How long, O LORD? Will you be angry forever? Will your jealous wrath burn like fire? Pour out your anger on the nations that do not know you and on the kingdoms that do not call on your name. For they have devoured Jacob and laid waste his habitation." This supplication is augmented with appeal to the apostasy of the enemy and the slight suffered by the LORD as a result. In our poem, the pastoral mentor neither denigrates the heathens who desecrated the temple nor appeals to the election of Israel. Instead, he relies on the logic of Lev 26:40 – that when the people of Israel are cursed for breach of the covenant, the way to redemption is by confessing their sins and the sins of their fathers, as the pastoral mentor has done here in vv. 7 and 16.

The pastoral mentor issues his request in v. 21. Multiple opinions have been suggested for understanding the verb here, *šûb*, with the *hiphil* form at the opening, *hăšîbēnû* followed by the community's statement, *wənāšûbâ*. The King James Version translates, "Turn thou us unto thee, O LORD, and we shall be turned." By this reading, the community calls upon the LORD to initiate a spiritual awakening of penance within the people, who will then eagerly engage this process and repent. The Targum understands the verse in this way, as do several modern commentators.[20] However, only human agents and not the LORD can change human action and human perception, and thus it seems more appropriate to render the verse as found in the NRSVue: "Restore us to yourself, O LORD, that we may be restored." The verse is a call to the LORD to reengage his covenantal partner, Israel.[21] It is in this sense that we find the term "return" in Jer 3:7, where the LORD speculates that perhaps unfaithful Israel will return to him as an unfaithful wife to her husband: "And I thought, 'After she has done all this she will return to me.'" It is in this sense that the LORD calls for Israel to restore her relationship

---

[20]   Gordis, *Lamentations*, 196; Hillers, *Lamentations*, 165.
[21]   Salters, *Lamentations*, 372; Assis, *Eichah*, 270; Renkema, *Lamentations*, 628; Klein, *Lamentations*, 283–84.

with him in Zech 1:3: "Therefore say to them: Thus says the LORD of hosts: Return to me, says the LORD of hosts, and I will return to you, says the LORD of hosts" (cf. Joel 2:12–14). "Returning" is the opposite of "abandoning" in v. 20. It is this restored covenantal relationship that the pastoral mentor has in mind in v. 20b when he says, "renew our days as of old."

The pastoral mentor's plea to the LORD should be seen against the backdrop of Lam 3:40, which employs similar language. There the pastoral mentor had urged the community, "Let us test and examine our ways and return to the LORD." The formulation there placed the onus upon the people, indeed as is found elsewhere (Deut 30:2; 1 Kgs 8:33, 48; Jer 3:7; Hos 14). That plea, as we saw, however, fell on deaf ears. The people uttered the opening words of a confession in 3:42, but ultimately faltered. They did not truly believe that the LORD would be receptive to their prayers and saw him as hopelessly distant. For this reason, the pastoral mentor comes now at the end of the book and asks the unconventional request that Israel be relieved of the onus of initiating the restoration of the connection between Israel and her God. Instead, hesitatingly, he calls upon the LORD to initiate the process, "Restore us to yourself, O LORD, that we may be restored; renew our days as of old."[22] The poets of Psalms 74 and 79 called for vengeance against the enemy (Pss 74:3, 11, 23; 79:6, 12), or to spare Israel from oppression (Ps 74:19, 21), or for salvation generally (Ps 79:9). Those appeals are predicated, however, on the prior assumption that the LORD is already engaged with Israel in covenantal terms. This is an assumption the pastoral mentor cannot make, and therefore showcases it as the focus of his plea. For the pastoral mentor, only by righting the relationship with the Almighty above, will Israel be able to successfully negotiate its conduct with the nations of the earth below.

The final verse of the book, v. 22, seems to walk back the hopeful sentiments of v. 21, although the precise implication of the opening prepositional

---

[22] This insight is implicit in the comments to this verse by the sixth-century midrashic work, *Eichah Rabbah*: "Take us back, O LORD, to Yourself, And let us come back (Lam 5:21)": The assembly of Israel said before the Holy One, blessed be He: "Master of the universe, it is up to you, 'take us back'." He said to them: "It is up to you, as it is said: 'Turn back to Me, and I will turn back to you – said the LORD' (Mal 3:7)." They said before him: "Master of the universe, it is up to you, as it is said: 'Turn again, O God, our helper, revoke Your displeasure with us' (Ps 85:5)" and so it is said: "Take us back, O LORD, to Yourself, And let us come back" (My translation here is an adaptation of the Sefaria Community Translation available at "Eichah Rabbah," sefaria.org, https://tinyurl.com/bdeac32a).

phrase *kî 'im* is uncertain. The words have a limiting function. Nearly all of the English translations render the verse as does the NRSVue – "unless you have utterly rejected us and are angry with us beyond measure." This would conclude the book on a supremely pessimistic note. By this reading, the narrator himself is unsure whether his appeal to restore the relationship between the LORD and Israel is even tenable and he ends his prayer at the brink of despair.[23] This reading is apparently behind the Jewish custom on the anniversary of the destruction of the first temple on the ninth of Ab, when the scroll is read publicly in synagogue, to end the reading by repeating v. 21 and its hopeful appeal to the LORD and thereby providing a sense of closure.

The interpretation of Lamentations offered in this volume, however, has been predicated on the belief that the narrator – the pastoral mentor – seeks at all times to help repair the breach between the LORD and his people, and to coax and urge his audience to make their way back to their sovereign king. Indeed, his confessions in vv. 7 and 16 of this chapter implicitly are acts of optimism that, indeed, the LORD does hear and is willing to abide by the dictates of Lev 26:40–45 that if Israel confesses its sins and the sins of its fathers, the LORD will recall his covenantal commitments to the patriarchs and restore the covenant with them. Within this interpretation of Lamentations, a note of near utter despair at book's end is incongruent with the thrust of the book as a whole.

Medieval rabbinic commentators as well as several modern scholars read the verse as an argument: "For should you still despise us – you have already exceedingly turned your wrath against us!" By this reading, v. 22 is part of the supplication of v. 21. The LORD should be prepared to restore the covenant with Israel even if she is undeserving, because she has already received the full measure of her punishment.[24] The weakness with this reading is that the verb in the second stich, *qāṣaptā* ("turned your wrath"), normally has the meaning of expressing emotion rather than action. It implies that the LORD has been exceedingly angry with Israel, rather than implying that he has acted harshly with her. Moreover, the two stichs of the verse stand in parallel, and just as the first expresses emotion

[23]   Some see the ending as one of divine anger, cf. Berlin, *Lamentations*, 116, tragedy as per Dobbs-Allsopp, *Lamentations*, 141–42, or with some doubt, as per Provan, *Lamentations*, 124.

[24]   This understanding already found in medieval commentaries such as that of Rashi is found also in Tod Linafelt, "The Refusal of a Conclusion in the Book of Lamentations," *JBL* 120 (2001): 340–43.

(literally "utterly despised us"), so does the second (lit. "exceedingly angry with us").

A third reading seems the most likely, and reads vv. 21–22 as a continuous expression: "Restore us … *even though* you despise us and are exceedingly angry with us."[25] This pleading provides an apt close to the book. With these two verses, the pastoral mentor is essentially appealing to the logic and dynamics of the covenant. Lev 26:40 had stated that in the throes of extreme punishment, Israel need only to confess her sins and those of her fathers, and the LORD will restore the covenant (Lev 26:40–45). That is the theology that undergirds his prayer. When he calls upon the LORD to restore the covenant "even though you despise *mā'astā* us," he appropriates the language of Lev 26:44–45:

> Yet for all that, when they are in the land of their enemies, I will not spurn them or abhor them (*mə'astim*) so as to destroy them utterly and break my covenant with them, for I am the LORD their God, but I will remember in their favor the covenant with their ancestors whom I brought out of the land of Egypt in the sight of the nations, to be their God: I am the LORD.

The pastoral mentor here also invokes the prophecy of Jeremiah 33:25–26:

> Thus says the LORD: Only if I had not established my covenant with day and night and the ordinances of heaven and earth would I reject (*'em'as*) the offspring of Jacob and of my servant David and not choose any of his descendants as rulers over the offspring of Abraham, Isaac, and Jacob. For I will restore their fortunes and will have mercy upon them.

Verse 22 creates a fitting end for the book in a second way. While v. 21 is an entreaty to the LORD, v. 22 is an argument, a negotiation with the LORD – "restore our relationship, yes, even if you abhor us and are exceedingly angry with us." Throughout four chapters, the pastoral mentor has helped the community/Bat-Zion work through theological stances and misunderstandings. And as we saw, the community/Bat-Zion was free to question the LORD and even level accusations against him (cf. vv. 2:20–22). In this closing note, the pastoral mentor himself engages in a challenging posture, which is at once pleading, but at the same time, unafraid to call upon the LORD to do the opposite of what he seemingly wants to do.

---

[25] Albrektson, *Studies in the Text*, 206; Hillers, *Lamentations*, 160–66; Provan, *Lamentations*, 133–34; Dobbs-Allsopp, *Lamentations*, 147–48; Berlin, *Lamentations*, 125–26.

CONCLUSION

To conclude, it is helpful to note how the author of Lamentations 5 has adopted and adapted several genres of biblical literature to create this prayer. The poem shares much in common with the genre of communal lament. However, with few exceptions, such laments in the psalms rarely invoke the issue of sin (cf. Pss 77; 102; 123; 137).[26] In fact, some communal laments tout Israel's virtue and innocence (cf. Pss 44; 80). In this regard, there is convergence between those poems and the cited voices ubiquitous within Jeremiah, that believe they are worthy of the LORD's salvation and do not consider themselves sinful.[27] Similarly, the author of Lamentations 5 eschews invoking the covenant as a reason for the LORD to bring salvation to Israel as is commonly found in these psalms (cf. Pss 44:18–23; 74:20; 80:19; 89:39, 50). The pastoral mentor's use of covenantal images and language in this poem is highly selective. He uses no terms of endearment for Israel. He references no promises to the people of prosperity or of salvation. He makes no reference to the patriarchs. As we have noted, he wishes to wean his audience from their overreliance on the divine election inherent in Zion theology.

At the same time, the pastoral mentor entirely affirms the notion of covenant. But he wishes to emphasize the responsibilities of covenant and to highlight what Israel must do when in the throes of covenantal punishment. His composition invokes the rebuke and curse traditions found in Lev 26:14–45 and in Deut 28:15–68. However, he uses them in different ways. More of the tribulations listed in Lamentations 5 draw from Deut 28 than from Lev 26.[28] However, the two chapters view the resolution of Israel's predicament in different ways. In Deuteronomy, the restoration of the covenantal bond is contingent on Israel's return to LORD (Deut 30:1–3):

> When all these things have happened to you, the blessings and the curses that I have set before you, if you call them to mind among all the nations where the LORD your God has driven you, and return to the LORD your God, and you

---

[26] Exceptions to this are Ps 106 generally and Pss 79:8; 90:8.

[27] See the discussion of Rom-Shiloni, *Voices from the Ruins*, 80–81, who maintains that the similarities between the poetic sources and the quotations in Jeremiah and Ezekiel suggest that each represents a deliberate and articulated opposition to the positions expressed by the prophetic voices.

[28] Klein, *Lamentations*, 47–49, identifies four parallel phrases between Lamentations 5 and Deut 28 (Lam 5:2–4 // Deut 28:30–33; Lam 5:5 // Deut 28:48; Lam 5:11 // Deut 28:30; Lam 5:12–13 // Deut 28: 49–50) and only a single one with Lev 26 (Lam 5:18 // Lev 26:31).

and your children obey him with all your heart and with all your soul, just as I am commanding you today, then the LORD your God will return you from you captivity and have compassion on you, gathering you again from all the peoples among whom the LORD your God has scattered you.

But the author of Lamentations 5 cannot adopt this text as a source of inspiration. It places an onus on Israel that the author of the poem knows the people cannot bear. They are in no place to return to full obeisance of the LORD "with all your heart and with all your soul." In fact, the author of Lamentations 5 seems to adapt Deut 30:2 to new purpose. If that text called on Israel to "return to the LORD," the pastoral mentor calls on the LORD to "Restore us to yourself, O LORD, that we may be restored" (v. 21), placing the onus on the LORD to initiate the process. His justification for reworking that text is based on Lev 26:40–44, where the restoration of covenantal relations unfolds under more favorable terms. For there, all that is required of Israel is confession (Lev 26:40), which then engenders the restoration of the covenantal bond (Lev 26:44–45): "I will not spurn them or abhor them so as to destroy them utterly and break my covenant with them, for I am the LORD their God, but I will remember in their favor the covenant with their ancestors whom I brought out of the land of Egypt in the sight of the nations, to be their God: I am the LORD."

Index of Scriptural Passages

Genesis
2:7, 141
4:13, 147
11:5, 61
15:1, 62
16:10, 62
18:21, 61
25:19–34, 147
26:4, 62
29:32, 97n18
31:18, 97
31:42, 97n18
32:4–33, 147
49:15, 164
49:20, 130
49:26, 132

Exodus
3:1, 97
3:7, 37n10, 97
3:8, 61
4:31, 97
9:29, 43n16
15:6, 62
15:8, 141
15:12, 62
15:17, 160
20:14, 83
24:15–18, 59
40:34–38, 59

Leviticus
6:2, 101n26
10:8–11, 135
13–14, 135
13:45, 136
17:10, 137

21:1–15, 135
25:25–28, 160
26, 157, 163
26:14–45, 174
26:18, 163
26:21, 163
26:24, 163
26:28, 163
26:31, 157, 168, 174n28
26:39–42, 157
26:40–44, 175
26:40–45, 172–73, 175
26:40, 160, 164, 170, 173, 175

Numbers
20:14–21, 147
27, 160
32:16, 98
36, 160

Deuteronomy
1:10, 62
2:8, 147
7:13, 62
23:8–9, 147
26:15, 113n44
28, 1, 1n2, 157
28:15–68, 174
28:30, 174n28
28:30–33, 174n28
28:48, 174n28
28:49–50, 137, 174n28
30:1–3, 174
30:2, 171, 175
32:1, 44
32:13, 133
33:16, 132

Judges
9:15, 141n30
11:40, 113n45

1 Samuel
1:11, 97n18
1:15–16, 82
17:34–35, 98
23:5, 97
25:11, 85

2 Samuel
1:17–27, 2
1:19, 113n45
1:24, 113n45, 130
12:30, 167
16:2, 68n38
19:44, 103
20:1, 103

1 Kings
2:16, 103
2:28, 83
5:31, 129
7:9–11, 129
8:10–11, 59
8:33, 171
8:48, 171
12:6, 137
21:3, 160

2 Kings
19:34, 134
23:29–30, 139
25:5–7, 140
25:8–11, 159

Isaiah
1, 60n14
1:2, 44
1:9, 131n11
1:18, 132
2:1–4:1, 60n15
8:18, 168
9:18–21, 58
10:5, 97
10:17, 62
11:6, 97
18:7, 168
19, 60n15

30:1–7, 138
30:2, 141
30:7, 138
30:19, 159
41:9, 111
41:10, 62
42:7, 135
42:16, 135
42:18–19, 135
43:8, 135
43:28, 129
45:9, 130
46:7, 164
49:2, 141
49:14, 37, 169
50:2, 169
51:2, 62
51:12, 70
52:11, 136
52:13–53:12, 91
53, 145
54:1–4, 36
55:7, 111
56:5, xiv
56:10, 135
57:6, 167
58:10–11, 99
59:1, 169
59:10, 135
62:3, 167
63:1–6, 147
63:13–14, 97
63:17, 160
64:7[ET 8], 130
64:10, 60
64:11, 167
65:1, 37, 169
66:1, 169
66:5–9, 36
66:10–12, 36
66:12–24, 125

Jeremiah
1:10, 78
2:4–9, 164
2:7–8, 16
2:8, 63
2:18, 16, 163
2:23, 30
2:25, 127

Jeremiah (cont.)

2:26, 132
2:35, 30
2:36, 16, 163
3:3–4, 55
3:7, 170–71
3:19–20, 162
3:25, 164
4:5–31, 60n15
4:9, 127, 132
4:10, 93
4:13, 139
4:19–21, 14
4:27, 148, 139
4:30–31, 14
4:31, 43n16
5:2, 54
5:9, 167
5:10, 139, 148
5:12, 55
5:14, 58
5:18, 139, 148
5:19, 30
5:31, 16
6:10–11, 93
6:13–15, 135
6:18–19, 44
6:25, 16
7:1–14, 127
7:4, 55
7:6, 135
7:9, 134
7:10, 84
7:34, 166
8:8, 54, 63
8:18, 13
8:21–23, 13
9:1, 16
9:9–16, 113
9:18, 16
10:19–20, 13
10:21, 13
10:25, 62
11:6–8, 164
11:18–20, 93
11:21, 55
12:1, 43
12:1–4, 93
13:17, 16

14–15, 16
14:7, 93
14:8–9, 93
14:13, 16, 55
14:17, 16, 93
14:18–22, 93
14:20, 93, 164
15:10, 93
15:10–21, 93
15:15–18, 93
15:17, 93
16:1–13, 164
16:9, 166
16:10, 30, 33
18, 76
18:5–12, 111
18:6, 130
18:11–12, 127
18:15–16, 75, 77
18:16, 70
18:18, 55
19:4, 135
20, 93
20:1–6, 127
20:7, 16, 93–94
21:13, 127
22:3, 135
22:17, 135
23:9, 55
23:9–17, 78
23:11–12, 127, 135
23:11–40, 16
23:14, 131n11
23:17, 55, 73
23:20, 78
25:15–29, 142
25:18, 132
26:1–24, 55
26:8, 93
26:24, 93
27:1–28:17, 16
27:16, 55
28:1–4, 127
28:1–17, 127
28:2–4, 55
30:11, 139, 148
30:14, 16
31:14, 99
31:25, 167

31:28, 78
31:28–29, 164
33:25–26, 173
34:21, 132, 138
37:5–10, 16
37:6–8, 138
37:17, 16
38:4, 55
38:6, 93
39:4–7, 140
41:1, 128
41:1–3, 6, 128
41:3–4, 37
41:4–5, 6
42:1–3, 20
42:7–22, 20
42:10, 78
43:2, 6
44:9–10, 164
44:10, 20
44:15–20, 6
44:30, 138
46:28, 139, 148
48:7, 61n20
49:3, 61n20, 113n45
49:7–22, 142
49:12, 142
49:17, 70
49:19, 73n44
50:2, 61n20
50:13, 70
51:47, 61n20
52:8–11, 140
52:12–14, 159
52:28–30, 147

Ezekiel
5:11, 78
7:4, 78
7:9, 78
8:18, 78
9:5, 78
9:10, 78
12:24–25, 74
13:1–10, 55
16:46–56, 131n11
17:18, 163
17:22–23, 141
18:2–4, 164

20:37, 97
21:31, 167
22:1–5, 134
22:26, 55
22:27, 135
22:28, 55
24:25, 166
25:12–14, 147
30:3, 60n15
31:13, 141
32:16, 113n45
34:4, 98
34:5, 98
34:16, 98
35:3–15, 147
36:1–6, 146
36:30, 133
36:37, 101n26
43:7–8, 127

Hosea
7:4–7, 58
7:11, 163
12:2, 163
14, 171
14:2–10, 125

Joel
2:2, 60n15
2:12–14, 171
2:17, 160
3:17, 168
4:19, 147

Amos
3–5, 60n15
4:11, 131n11
5:19, 98
5:23, 98
8:8, 167
9:11, 98
9:13–15, 125

Obadiah
12–13, 146

Micah
7:14, 97, 160
7:18, 160

Nahum
1:2–8, 151
3:17, 132

Zephaniah
1:3–3:8, 60n15
1:17, 135
1:18, 62n22
2:6, 98

Zechariah
1:3, 171
7:1–7, 160
8:18–19, 160

Malachi
1:2–5, 147
3:7, 171n22

Psalms
2, 74, 127
2:2, 139
2:9, 127
7, 13
7:9–10[ET 8–9], 13
9, 151
9–10, 55n2
9:12, 168
9:13, 97
9:14, 36, 97n18
10, 151
10:1, 42n15
12:7, 78
16:11, 62n22
17:8, 141
18, 127
18:5–7, 98
18:31, 78
18:36, 62n22
20, 127
20:7, 139
21, 127
22, 146
22:6, 98
22:22, 99
23, 98
23:2–3, 97
23:4, 97
23:5, 99
25, 151
27:1, 12

27:9, 12
28:9, 160
30:3–4, 98
31:7, 97
32:5, 111
32:6, 167
34, 151
34:9, 96
34:16, 98
34:17, 137
34:20–21[ET 19–20], 98
36:9, 99
37, 102, 151
37:23, 96
37:34, 102
38:16, 100
39:8, 100
40:5, 96
42:6, 101
42:12, 101
43:5, 101
44, 174
44:1–2, 169
44:3, 62n22
44:10, 99
44:18–23, 174
45, 127
45:10[ET 9], 127
46, 74, 127
46:5, 127
48, 74, 127
48:2–3 [ET 48:1–2], 75
48:4–6, 127
48:4–8, 134
48:4–9, 127
48:12, 113n45
48:12–14, 129
50:2, 75
51:9, 132
55:19[ET 18], 99
60:3, 99
63:9, 62n22
65:5, 99
66:12, 99
68:10, 160
69:8–10, 94
72, 127
74, 4, 23, 55n2, 155–56, 165,
    168–71
74:1, 155, 170
74:2, 155, 160

74:3, 155–56, 171
74:3–4, 155
74:3–7, 168
74:3–8, 156
74:4, 156
74:7, 155–56
74:10, 155–56
74:11, 156, 171
74:12–17, 155, 169
74:18, 155–56
74:18–19, 155, 169
74:19, 155, 171
74:20, 174
74:21, 155, 171
74:22, 155, 158
74:22–23, 156
74:23, 156, 171
76, 74
76:2, 168
77, 55n2
77, 174
78:54, 62n22
78:62, 160
79, 4, 23, 155–56, 161, 164, 168–71
79:1, 155–56, 160, 168
79:1–3, 156, 161
79:2, 156
79:2–4, 155
79:4, 155
79:5, 155
79:5–7, 170
79:6, 156, 171
79:6–9, 155
79:7, 156
79:8, 164, 174n26
79:9, 156, 164, 171
79:10, 155–56
79:11, 155, 169
79:11–12, 155
79:12, 156, 158, 169, 171
79:13, 156
80, 55n2, 174
80:8, 169
80:16, 62n22
80:17, 137
80:19, 174
81:17, 99
85:5, 171n22
87, 127
88:3, 81
89, 55n2, 127, 139

89:1–38, 12
89:13, 62
89:24, 62
89:32, 97
89:39, 174
89:39–53, 12
89:50, 174
91:1, 141
97:8, 113n45
101, 127
102, 55n2, 174
102:18–22, 137
104:29–30, 141
105:19, 78
105:22, 137
106, 174n26
106:5, 160
106:6, 164
106:37–40, 134
106:40, 160
107:9, 99
107:13–14, 98
110, 127
111, 151
112, 151
113:8, 98
118:15, 62n22
119:25, 94
119:105, 99
119:123, 78
119:137, 43
119:153, 36
121:5, 141
123, 55n2, 174
124:7, 117
125:1, 169
129:1–3, 91, 120
132, 55n2, 127, 135, 174
132:7–8, 127
132:10, 139
132:15, 99
132:16, 136
132:17, 62, 139
136:25, 99
138:7, 62n22
142:4, 98
144, 127, 148–51
144:9–14, 148
144:12, 130
144:13, 150
145, 151

Psalms (cont.)
145:19, 98
149:2, 130, 148

Proverbs
30:5, 78
30:21–22, 165
31:10–31, 151
31:23, 166

Job
2:10, 93
3:3, 92
3:23, 92
4:17, 92
5:16–18, 93
5:18, 93
8:3, 93
9:18, 92
9:30, 132
9:34, 97
10:11–12, 98
10:15, 97
10:16, 92
12:4, 94
14:14, 92
16:12–13, 92
21:9, 97
22:2, 92
24:3, 97
30:9, 92
33:29, 92
34:7, 92
34:9, 92

Ruth
4:1–2, 166

Lamentations
1:1, 105, 159
1:1–14, 145
1:2, 11, 16, 159
1:4, 168
1:5, 1, 10, 54, 85
1:6, 67n36
1:8–9, 54, 85
1:9, 3, 96
1:10, 11, 84, 125, 143
1:11, 3

1:12, 68, 73
1:12–15, 5, 58
1:12–19, 8
1:14, 54, 105
1:15, 9
1:16, 16, 71, 80
1:17, 9, 71
1:18, 5, 11, 54
1:19, 16
1:20, 54
1:20–22, 86
1:21, 2
1:21–22, 3, 125, 156
1:22, 54
2:1, 2, 110
2:1–2, 144
2:1–10, 96
2:2, 97
2:3, 110
2:4, 99, 110, 130
2:6, 110
2:7, 99
2:8–10, 145
2:8–11, 145
2:9, 98
2:11, 16
2:11–13, 10–11, 91, 125
2:12, 150
2:12–19, 9
2:14, 1, 16, 109, 134
2:15–16, 99
2:16, 111
2:18, 112, 144
2:18–19, 94, 115
2:19, 43n16, 109
2:20, 96
2:20–21, 11, 100
2:20–22, 3, 5, 16, 100
2:21, 110
2:22, 2, 16, 100
3:1, 4n13, 143, 151
3:1–9, 145
3:14, 16
3:21, 167
3:21–39, 152
3:22–30, 145
3:30, 144
3:40, 171

3:40–47, 21
3:42, 1, 171
3:42–47, 125
3:43, 5
3:45, 136
3:48, 67n36
3:48–49, 16
3:48–51, 125
3:53, 144–45
3:53–56, 16
3:56–66, 3
3:65–66, 156
4:3, 67n36
4:6, 1, 67n36
4:10, 67n36
4:13, 16, 63n27
4:15, 76
4:17, 16
4:21, 2, 9
4:21–22, 36, 156
4:22, 67n36
5:1–11, 145
5:16, 1

Daniel
9:16, 164

Ezra
9, 110
9:5–15, 108
9:6–15, 164
9:15, 43
10:19, 163

Nehemiah
9, 110
9:6–38, 108
9:16–17, 164
9:26–33, 164
9:28, 43

1 Chronicles
24:5, 129
29:24, 163

2 Chronicles
30:8, 163

Printed in Great Britain
by Amazon

25600469R00116